Cooking with Style ™

**A step-by-step guide
to great-tasting recipes
and creative food presentation**

Produced by Meredith Publishing Services,
Locust at 17th, Des Moines, IA 50336.
© Meredith Corporation, 1984.
All Rights Reserved. Printed in the U.S.A.
Cooking with Style is a trademark of
Chicago Cutlery Consumer Products, Inc.
ISBN: 0-914091-44-1

Chicago Cutlery Is Old-Fashioned American Quality.

Our reputation for quality began back in the '30s when we offered butchers in the Chicago area a knife sharpening service. The business prospered and before long grew into a full-scale knife manufacturing operation. In 1969, we expanded into the retail market, offering consumers the very same cutlery we have provided commercial kitchens and packing houses for over 50 years. Over the years, whether servicing the professional or home cooks nationwide, we have remained committed to quality—a Chicago Cutlery tradition.

Along with our dedication to quality, we're interested in educating customers, because we believe an educated consumer can better understand, use and appreciate a quality cutlery product. For years, we have sponsored clinics teaching safe cutlery usage and the art of keeping knives sharp.

Now, we're going one step further, sharing still more professional secrets in *Cooking with Style*, the first cookbook of its kind. Combining smart tips from leading chefs and food educators across the country with more than 350 recipes developed and tested by the Better Homes and Gardens® Test Kitchen, *Cooking with Style* promises that good cooking can be creative, easy, and delicious.

In the *Better Homes and Gardens® Test Kitchen* each and every recipe is tested until it meets the Kitchen's high standards of quality. Pictured here, the Test Kitchen Director and a home economist discuss Chocolate Mousse Torte before it is served to a panel of food editors to evaluate recipe preparation and flavor, color, and texture. To make this picture-perfect dessert yourself, turn to page 136.

This seal assures you that every recipe in *Cooking with Style* has been tested in the Better Homes and Gardens Test Kitchen. This means that each recipe is practical and reliable, and meets our high standards of taste appeal.

Cooking with Style

Sharpen Your Skills

Refer to this cutlery primer to get the most efficient use of your fine knives. Once you master the basics, cooking in the kitchen will be extra easy, extra fast!

Quality Cutlery

CUTLERY BUYMANSHIP

A knife is the single most important utensil in the kitchen. A good knife will do the work of dozens of space-consuming gadgets. Consider blade and handle construction and comfort when you purchase fine cutlery.

SELECT FOR SHARPNESS

Steel. Knives are made from one of three types of steel: *carbon, stainless, or high-carbon stainless steel.*

Carbon steel was the most commonly used knife steel for many years. It is a soft metal that is easy to resharpen, but will stain and rust easily, even if cleaned and dried after each use. When highly polished it is nearly impossible to tell the difference between carbon and stainless steel until put into use.

Stainless steel is widely used in the manufacturing of low-end household cutlery because of the ease of caring for this type of blade, its general durability and good looks. Stainless steel is the hardest and the strongest of the three, making it the most difficult to sharpen. However, stainless steel is virtually stain- and rust-resistant. Generally, resharpening of stainless steel must be performed at the factory.

High-carbon stainless steel is the present manufacturing trend used in making quality knives. This high quality stainless steel has sufficient carbon content so that it readily takes a sharp edge and can be kept sharp at home with a butcher steel, hone or Crock Stick®. One such type of this steel is Chicago Special Steel™ which is specially heat treated and ground by Chicago Cutlery®.

Grind. Knife blades are generally ground one of three ways: *hollow ground, flat ground, or taper ground.*

Hollow-ground knives are made by thinning the blade out in an attempt to reduce "drag." This process tends to thin out the knife just behind the final edge of the blade, often causing a weak spot in the knife blade.

Flat-ground knives are made by thinning the blade uniformly, from the back of the blade to the edge and from the heel of the blade to the point.

Taper-ground knives, such as Chicago Cutlery's, are made by making an additional grind on the blade which eliminates the shoulder, giving the edge an even, more uniform and smooth taper. This minimizes the blade's resistance as it cuts, making it sharper and drastically reducing the amount of time and effort needed to restore the edge. It also gives a hollow-ground appearance without undermining the strength or resilience of the blade.

Back

Point

Edge

CHOOSE FOR COMFORT

Balance. The handle should be properly balanced, mated to the blade and constructed to give the maximum amount of control. If the knife is fairly lightweight, such as Chicago Cutlery, it is easier to control and will be less tiresome. Extreme weight in a knife is only advantageous if the blade is very dull or if cutting through bone.

Handle Shape. Knife handles should be contoured to allow the user to hold the knife naturally. A shoulder or "guard" near the blade is a safety feature to prevent slipping when the blade meets sudden resistance. As you hold different knives, think about how your hand will feel after a long chopping or slicing session.

In addition to the traditional straight-handled knives, Chicago Cutlery has developed two new knife lines with handles scientifically designed to fit the hand. The American Chef™ line has *curved walnut handles* and the BioCurve™ line has *curved molded polypropylene handles.* Both lines are based on the concept of designing the tool to fit the user's hand.

Quality knives generally have a hardwood or simulated wood handle. Natural wood is not only beautiful, but feels good. When wet, it resists slippage better than plastic or plastic-treated woods. Molded polypropylene handles are used commercially because of the sanitation factor, although most butchers and chefs prefer the feel of wood.

Tang

Rivet

Heel

LOOK FOR QUALITY CONSTRUCTION

Full Tang. On a quality knife the tang (end of the blade that extends into the handle) will extend the full length and width of the handle, providing added strength and balance to the knife. (On molded polypropylene handled knives, the blade should extend at least 60% of the way through the handle.)

Three Rivets. On quality cutlery the tang will generally be attached to the handle with three rust-resistant rivets to assure it does not loosen from the blade. Quality knives generally use brass or nickel silver rivets.

CUTLERY CARE

Proper care of fine cutlery will guarantee its timeless beauty and dependable performance in the kitchen. Follow these three easy steps in caring for your cutlery:

Cleaning. Quality cutlery deserves good care. Chicago Cutlery recommends that quality knives be washed separately from the rest of your dishes and utensils and thoroughly dried after each use. Do NOT put quality knives in the dishwasher. They can be dulled by knocking against other items, and natural wood handles will be damaged.

Oiling. Wood handles require a bit of extra care, but their good looks and resistance to slippage make them superior to other handles. Soaking knives in water will remove the natural oils from wooden handles. They will lose their color and may even pull away from the tang. To help restore the color and put some "life" back into the handles, rub or soak the handles with mineral oil, vegetable oil, or a food-grade wood conditioner.

Chicago Cutlery offers a convenient waste-free bottle of Wood Conditioning Oil, especially designed for natural wood knife handles, butcher blocks, knife blocks, and cutting boards. This unique bottle has an applicator which allows the user to apply the oil with no mess or waste. After oiling, you may periodically polish the handles lightly with fine steel wool for a beautiful new handle finish. This treatment is good for all natural wood-handled knives from time to time, as the natural oils wash out even with the best of care.

Storing. Sharp knives should never be stored loose in a drawer because contact with hard objects will dull the blades. Knife holders with a slot for each knife make both an attractive and safe storage area.

CUTLERY SAFETY

For obvious reasons, knife safety is of utmost importance in the home. Not only are injuries unpleasant, but most times they are avoidable. Learn to apply these practical knife safety rules in the kitchen:

● *Keep knives sharp!* A sharp knife is safer than a dull one because it requires less pressure in cutting. The knife will not slip as easily and your hand will not tire as quickly.

● *Use the correct size and type of knife for the job.* Hold the knife firmly in your hand and cut away from the body. Use a wood or polyethylene cutting board. Acrylic, ceramic and similar hard surfaces are tough on a knife edge because they do not "give" with the edge.

● *Don't use a knife to:* lift bottle caps, jar lids or tacks; to cut string or tear packages open; or as a screwdriver or ice pick. Nor is a knife intended to be used for "hacking" or prying apart frozen food.

● *Make sure that knives lying on flat surfaces are never covered with towels, napkins or other materials.* After handling a knife, lay it down in a cleared area, with the blade and point away from the body, and away from the edge of the table or cutting area.

● *Do not reach blindly for a knife; reach deliberately for the handle.* When handing a knife to another person, do so with the handle toward him or her.

● *Never try to catch a falling knife.*

● *Sharp knives should be washed separately, not with other utensils.* Each knife should be dried separately, always keeping the sharp cutting edge away from the hand. Dry knife blades from the back to the cutting edge, NOT from the handle to the tip.

● *Do not store knives loose in a drawer.* Keep knives stored in a rack or holder when not in use. If using a magnetic rack, be sure magnets are strong enough to hold knives securely in place and that knives are clean. A greasy knife will not adhere properly to a magnetic rack. (Chicago Cutlery does not recommend magnetic racks because of potential safety hazards.)

● *Keep knives safely out of reach of children.*

● *Never test the sharpness of a blade by running your finger along the edge.*

Keeping Knives Sharp

Sharp knives in the kitchen are the secret to success in all your cooking ventures. To keep your fine cutlery sharp, it is recommended that the butcher steel or the Crock Stick® be used regularly.

BUTCHER STEEL
Below are some commonly asked questions about using the butcher steel.

Q **How do you keep a knife sharp?**

A Professional butchers and chefs use a "butcher steel" (also called "sharpening steel") to keep their knives sharp. The butcher steel is a metal rod which has a higher hardness factor than the knife blade. Sharpness is maintained by stroking the blade over the rod on a regular basis.

Q **Does a butcher steel re-edge a knife?**

A If you examined a knife under a microscope, you would see that the edge is made up of thousands of small cutting teeth. Through use, these "teeth" are bent out of line and the blade becomes dull. By "steeling," stroking the knife on a butcher steel, you can straighten these teeth and realign the cutting edge. A butcher steel does NOT put a new edge on a knife; it simply renews the existing edge.

Q **What is the best way to use a butcher steel?**

A There are two basic methods of using the butcher steel—the Simplified Method and the Professional Method. Both methods produce the same end result, but the Simplified Method is preferred for home use.

1

2

Simplified Method
Hold the butcher steel in your left hand with the point of the steel firmly placed on a cutting board or similar surface. Hold the knife in your right hand in a natural position for cutting. (Instructions are given for a right-handed person; reverse procedure if left-handed.) Place the heel of the blade against the butcher steel just under the steel handle. Angle the knife approximately 20 degrees.

With medium pressure, bring the knife blade down at this 20 degree angle, pulling the knife handle toward you as you go down the steel. Be sure to stroke the entire blade edge from base to tip. Alternate from left to right sides of the steel 4 or 5 times.

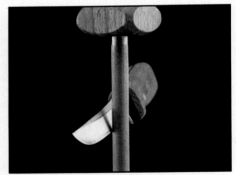

Proper Sharpening Angle
The best angle for sharpening the knife blade can vary from almost flat to 45 degrees, depending on the bevel of the knife. Start at an angle of 20 degrees, as shown. If the blade does not respond at this angle, increase in increments of approximately 5 degrees to a maximum of 45 degrees.

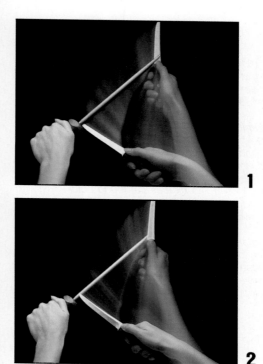

1

2

Professional Method

Hold the butcher steel in your left hand with your thumb tucked behind the hand guard. Hold the knife in your right hand as shown.

Keeping the angle at 20 degrees, draw the blade across the steel. The tip of the blade will be near the steel handle when the stroke is completed. Give a similar stroke to the other side of the blade. Repeat these alternating strokes 4 or 5 times on each side.

What is "back steeling?"

Back steeling is a process used to raise rolled edges. Do this routinely before steeling for best results.

To back steel, put the point of the butcher steel against a firm surface. Pull the blade across the butcher steel, moving in the opposite direction of normal cutting. You will feel resistance if the edge is rolled. Repeat the process on the other side of the knife edge.

How often should a butcher steel be used?

Ideally, every time the knife is used. A butcher carries a steel at his side and uses it every few minutes to keep his knife sharp. It's much easier to keep the knife sharp with regular steeling than to let it get dull and then try to sharpen it. Steel knives before or after each use just as automatically as you wash them.

Will my butcher steel work on all knives?

All butcher steels are not alike. The hardness of the butcher steel must be greater than that of the knife in order to do its job. If you do not have success in steeling your knives, the butcher steel may be at fault.

CROCK STICK

The Crock Stick knife sharpener is very effective in resharpening knives. Follow these simple steps:

Place the base on a solid flat surface at a comfortable height. Put the ceramic rods in the base to form a narrow "V" (15°). Be sure each rod is firmly placed in the base. This angle removes the blade's shoulder build-up as you sharpen.

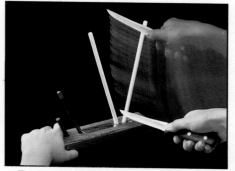

1

To thin the blade, place your hand behind the hand guard for protection, holding the base firmly. Using the other hand, place the heel of the blade at the top of one rod.

With medium pressure, stroke down and across the rod so the tip of the blade ends up at the bottom of the rod. Keep the blade in a vertical position. Alternate from rod to rod to sharpen both sides of the blade.

2

To finish the edge, place the rods in the wide "V" angle (22½°). This angle creates a sharp beveled knife edge. Stroke the knife in the same manner as directed above, using a downward motion. Repeat 8 to 10 times.

Knife Selection

Professional cooking tools make kitchen work easy. Knives are the most important tools in the kitchen. Chicago Cutlery® has been producing quality knives for professional butchers and chefs since 1930. These same rugged tools are now available for home use and will make any cook's job an enjoyable experience.

No single knife can do every job in the kitchen. An assortment of good knives will assure you of having the right tool to meet every cutting need.

Knives should never be used for purposes other than those for which they are intended. Unless specifically designed for cutting through bones, knives should never be used for this purpose. The following knives and sharpening implements are listed with common uses and are suggested as important items for your kitchen.

A. *Grapefruit-Melon knife (3½″ blade)*—Specially designed to loosen grapefruit sections and remove melon from the rind.

B. *Parer (2¼″, 3″, and 3½″ blades)*—Use to clean and peel fruits and vegetables; bone poultry; prepare intricate garnishes.

C. *Steak knives (4″ blade)*—Attractively designed for individual table use.

D. *Boner/Utility, straight-bladed (5″ and 6″ blades)*—Trim meat and fat from bones; good all-around utility knife for slicing cold cuts, cheese, tender vegetables, and cutting up poultry.

E. *Boner/Utility, curved blade (5″ and 6″ blades)*—Has the same uses as straight-bladed boners; preference varies with users.

F. *Fillet (6¾″ and 7½″ blades)*—Flexible blade for efficient filleting of all types of fish; also excellent lightweight slicer for tender foods such as tomatoes.

G. *Slicer (8″ and 10″ blades)*—Use to slice meat and poultry.

H. *Chef knife, also called "cook's knife" (4″, 6″, 8″, and 10″ blades)*—Use to dice, slice, bias-cut and chop fruits, vegetables, and meats.

I. *Bread knife (9″ blade)*—Use to slice bread, delicate fruits, and vegetables. Also excellent for carving roasts. The Break-Through Point™ tip pierces the tough outer crust and the smooth ground edge guarantees a smooth interior slice.

J. *Meat slicer (10″ and 12″ blades)*—Great for slicing beef from beef rounds. An excellent carver. Ideal ham slicer or for carving any large cut of meat. The 10-inch knife is also available with full-length serration for slicing bread.

K. *Chinese chef knife*—Use to dice, chop, and slice fruits, vegetables, meats, and fish; especially good for use in Oriental cooking. (Knife not shown.)

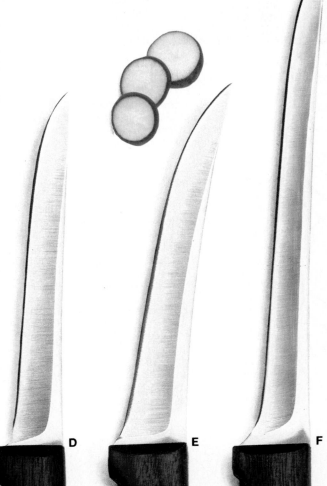

A   B   C   D   E   F

Here's a buyer's guide for cutlery, beginning with the basic starter items that are a must, then advancing to the extras and specialty knives you'll want to eventually own.

The Basics: 3-inch parer, 5-inch boner/utility, 6-inch chef knife, 8-inch slicer, and 10-inch butcher steel.

To Round Out Your Selection: 4-, 8-, and 10-inch chef knives; 6-inch boner/utility; 10-inch meat slicer; an additional paring knife; ceramic hone; professional cleaver; Chinese chef knife; grapefruit-melon knife; fillet knife; and bread knife.

"The chef knife is the most versatile of all knives for food preparation. Available in a variety of sizes, this invaluable knife is designed to make all your slicing and cutting needs easy!"

G   H   I   J

Kitchen Accessories

Professional kitchen accessories generally offer more functional styling and sturdier construction than the same products made specifically for home use. Chicago Cutlery's® line of kitchen accessories is used professionally by chefs, so rugged design is inherent. These quality tools will provide a lifetime of cooking pleasure.

This large collection of spatulas and turners performs a multitude of culinary tasks. Turners have offset blades with the handle set at an angle to permit the tool to reach down into a pan—to flip a pancake or turn a hamburger. Spatulas have handles in line with a flexible blade—with rounded edges to scrape a bowl or frost a cake. Complete your kitchen with any of these handsome, professional cooking accessories:

A. *Superburger turner*—Ideal for flipping pancakes, burgers and steaks. It's great for transferring delicate foods such as layer cakes and omelets, too!

B. *Pie/Cake server*—Perfect for serving slices of pie, cake and quiche.

C. *Deluxe forged carving fork*—Designed for holding large roasts, ham, and turkey for carving.

D. *Kitchen turner*—Every kitchen needs this all-purpose turner for everyday cooking chores.

E. *Frosting spatula*—The 6½-inch blade makes icing cakes and pastries and spreading sandwich fillings easy.

F. *Barbecue set*—Also sold individually, this boxed set contains three essential barbecue utensils—the Barbecue turner, Barbecue knife, and the Barbecue fork.

G. *Kitchen fork*—This 13-inch all-purpose fork is convenient to use in various cooking tasks.

H. *Sandwich spreader*—The flexible blade is perfect for spreading butter, jam and sandwich fillings.

I. *Hamburger turner*—A heavy-duty turner for meat and poultry.

J. *Dough cutter/scraper*—Use to cut and remass dough when shaping; scrape sticky dough from a pastry board.

K. *Kitchen accessory rack*—A specially designed compact oak wall rack with seven slots to hold an assortment of spatulas and turners. (Rack not shown.)

A   B   C   D   E

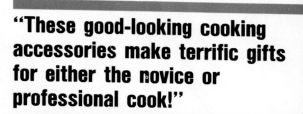

Chicago Cutlery also makes attractive cutting and serving boards. These durable kitchen accessories feature the unique BioCurve™ handle, a handle that conforms to the natural contours of the hand. This handle design makes the Cutting and Serving Board *easy to lift, easy to carry, and easy to control and balance.*

An incredibly versatile board, the American Chef™ Cutting and Serving Board has been created to meet your every need. Handcrafted from hard maple, these boards come in three sizes, perfect for cutting, serving, carrying food, or cooling baked goods.

J

"These good-looking cooking accessories make terrific gifts for either the novice or professional cook!"

13

Team your creative ideas with the food presentation skills shown on these pages. Save money too— use the do-it-yourself guide to custom-cut meat at home.

Beautiful Foods

Rich in color and texture, garnishes are an adventure for the eye and invite even the most discriminating palate. In the art of "garde manger," or edible garnishes, fruits and vegetables are put to creative use. You can make flowers from green peppers or red cabbage, and fruit baskets from grapefruit or watermelon. Or, capitalize on one of the ingredients in a recipe for a final touch. For example, serve fresh fruit balls in a decoratively carved melon, or make carrot flowers to top a creamy vegetable soup.

There's no limit to the ways you can present a meal with style and beauty. It's easy, inexpensive, and fun. All you need is a sharp knife and your choice of fresh fruits and vegetables. We'll show you how. Just follow the step-by-step photographs on these pages and, with a little ingenuity, you'll soon be creating your own colorful garnishes.

Fluted Mushrooms

1

Select large, well-rounded mushrooms. Hold the mushroom by the stem with one hand. With the other hand, use a sharp paring knife to divide the mushroom into 6 to 8 portions. Press the tip of the knife (using flat side) into the *center* of the mushroom to make a star design. Continue pressing tip of knife all around mushroom to create star-like pattern, increasing in number of V-shaped impressions in each divided portion as you work around mushroom.

2

Select large, well-rounded mushrooms. Hold the mushroom by the stem with one hand. With the other hand, hold a sharp paring knife at an angle and cut 4 to 6 inverted V-shaped grooves around the outside surface of the mushroom, as shown. Press tip of knife (using flat side) between grooves to make star-like designs as shown in step 1. (To keep mushrooms looking white, gently wash them in a water-lemon juice solution.)

Onion Flower

Select medium-sized, well-rounded onions. Peel the outer skin; leave the root end intact, but cut off any loose roots. Using a sharp paring knife and starting at the top of the onion, make **deep** cuts downward toward the root end, stopping about ½ inch from the base, as shown.

Continue making deep cuts completely around the onion. Place in bowl of ice water to allow flower to "bloom."

Cabbage Flower

1

Trim root end of green onion and cut to a 1-inch length. With a sharp paring knife make several slashes, starting slightly up from the base to the top to produce a fringe, as shown. Place onion in bowl of ice cold water so ends curl back.

2

Remove three good outer leaves from red or green cabbage. Trim the cabbage leaves to make oval-shaped "petals."

3

Trim the thick midrib portion of the stem (from outside of leaves) to make same thickness as rest of cabbage leaf.

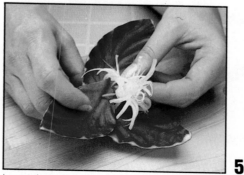

4

Cut a ¼-inch-thick slice from a carrot. Insert wooden pick through the carrot slice. To assemble the cabbage flower, insert cabbage leaves on pick so they curve upward, with carrot slice behind leaves. Fan the cabbage leaves to look like flower "petals."

5

Insert the onion brush, with the slashed end out, so that the cabbage petals circle onion brush.

Beautiful Foods

Fruit Cartwheels

1

Cut long, V-shaped grooves all around oranges, lemons, or limes, as shown, with a sharp paring knife.

2

Slice fruit ⅛ inch thick to make cartwheel shapes.

Green Onion Brush

Slice off root end of green onion and trim most of the top portion. Hold onion steady with fingers. With a sharp paring knife make slashes at both ends to produce a fringe. Place the onion in a bowl of ice cold water so the ends will curl back to resemble brushes.

Radish Accordion

Trim roots and leaves from long, narrow radishes with a sharp paring knife. With each radish, begin at one end and make 6 to 8 narrow, crosswise cuts about ⅛ inch wide to the center. *Slice to, but not through, the base.* Turn radish and continue making 6 to 8 crosswise cuts on other end. Place radish in bowl of ice cold water so slices will fan out.

Carrot Petals

1

Select a large, well-rounded carrot; peel. Cut a 3-inch portion from the carrot. Stand carrot on end. Cut 5 or 6 flat sides all around the carrot with a sharp paring knife. Cut a lengthwise V-shaped groove *inside* each flat edge, about ¼ inch thick, as shown.

2

Cut carrot crosswise into desired thicknesses, as shown, to make petal-shaped carrot slices.

> **"Use room temperature vegetables when making garnishes. They will be more flexible to work with and cutting will be easier."**

Beautiful Foods

Citrus Loops

Slice an orange, lemon, or lime crosswise with a sharp paring knife. Halve each fruit slice. To loosen peel from fruit, cut around slice through the white membrane to within ¼ inch of opposite end. Tuck the loosened peel under to form a loop, as shown.

Radish Mum

1

Select well-rounded radishes. Trim roots and leaves with a sharp paring knife. Start at one side of the radish and make a row of parallel cuts to center. *Slice to, but not through, the stem end.* Turn radish and repeat on other side. Keep the slices straight and close together.

2

After completely slicing the radish in one direction, give it a quarter turn and make a second series of cuts across the first cuts (like a checkerboard). Place in ice cold water so radish will "puff" open like a flower.

"After making a green onion or radish garnish, place in a bowl of ice cold water at least 1 hour so the garnish opens where decorative cuts have been made."

Fruit Twists

1

Slice oranges, lemons, or limes ⅛ inch thick with a sharp paring knife. Cut into center of the slice, as shown.

2

Twist ends in opposite directions, as shown.

Tomato Rose

1

Place tomato stem end down. Begin by cutting a "base" from tomato with sharp paring knife; *do not sever*. Continue cutting one continuous strip (¾ inch wide) in spiral fashion, using sawing motion, and tapering the end into a point to remove.

2

Curl strip, skin side out, onto its base in the shape of an opening rose. Add green onion tops, small lettuce leaves, fresh herb leaves, or parsley to enhance and complete effect.

Fanciful Napkin Folds

Colorful napkins creatively folded are a quick, inexpensive way to embellish a dinner table. Whether you want a formal setting or a freewheeling one, the decorative folds shown here are easy to do—just follow the step-by-step directions.

Napkin know-how

Even though napkins vary in size from Grandma's heirloom 24-inch squares to today's 15-inch dinner squares, all can be folded to enhance an attractive place setting. The larger the size, the more dramatic the fold. Consider the fabric, too. Fabrics with woven-in pattern or color are well-suited to folding. A thin, soft fabric will not hold a crease. For best results, lightly starch cotton and linen napkins when laundering, or use spray starch when pressing. Even permanent press fabrics should get a spray of starch. To have napkins ready for the next party, press them flat and store them unfolded.

The Bow Tie

Use this easy fold for casual dining. Any size cloth napkin will do; don't use a paper napkin because it does not have the strength to withstand knotting.

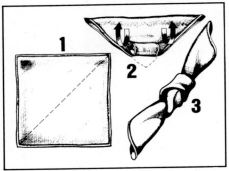

1. Fold the napkin in half diagonally to form a triangle.
2. Place the folded edge at the top, then starting at the bottom point, roll up the napkin.
3. Tie a knot in the center of the completed roll.

The Buffet Fold

Make transportation easier for buffet guests with this easy napkin fold. It features a pocket for holding flatware.

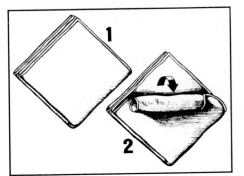

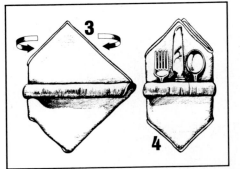

1. Fold the napkin into quarter size with the open edges at top.
2. Take the top corner and roll it to the center of the napkin.
3. Fold under the right and left sides.
4. Use the pocket for flatware.

22

The Bishop's Hat

If you use a starched linen, the folded napkin will stand formally at attention.

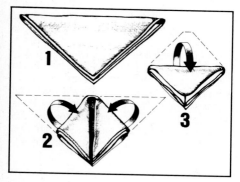

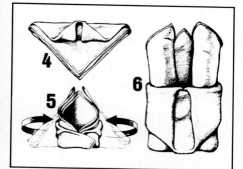

1. Fold the flat napkin into a triangle.
2. Fold the right and left points to the center point.
3. Fold top corner down to within one inch of bottom point.
4. Turn the folded point back to the upper edge.
5. Turn the entire napkin over. Fold the right and left points across the overlap; tuck one inside the other.
6. Stand the napkin up.

The Double Cone

Tuck a pretty flower in the top for a special occasion.

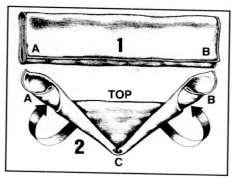

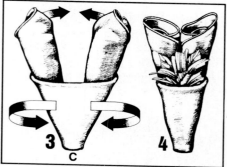

1. Fold the napkin lengthwise into thirds, with fold at top.
2. Tightly roll bottom corners "A" and "B" to top where "cones" meet at point "C."
3. Turn napkin over; point "C" should be at bottom. Continue rolling the two cone shapes so they meet in the center.
4. Position at place setting; insert flower or appetizer fork in top, if desired, as shown on the cover or on page 15.

The Art of Carving

The presentation of any meal, whether it's everyday or special occasion, should be a reflection of the cook's enjoyment of fine food. Not only should food taste good, but garnishes, servingware, and meat carving should contribute to making the meal attractive and enjoyable for both family and guests.

The art of carving can be a great appetite stimulator. Carving meat and poultry with flair and confidence needn't be intimidating. With a few basic rules and carving tips, the specific techniques become an easy procedure anyone can learn.

● To ensure that each serving is hot when eaten, it's always advisable to heat the platter on which the meat or poultry will be carved. Also, when carving vertically, it's wise to protect both the knife blade and porcelain or metal platters by carving on a wooden cutting board or, if possible, use a platter with a wooden insert.

● To carve successfully, keep the knife's cutting edge very sharp. For best results, sharpen knives with a hand-held sharpening steel or the Crock Stick® before each use.

● Essential to a good carving technique is allowing the meat or poultry to stand for at least 10 to 15 minutes after it has been placed on the heated platter. This permits the meat to firm up and thus makes carving much easier. Smooth, uniform cuts can be made with ease, enhancing both the appearance and flavor of the meat.

Beef Chuck Blade Pot Roast

This cut of beef contains part of one rib and a piece of the bladebone. Usually, the pot roast bones can be easily removed immediately after cooking.

1

Place pot roast on a cutting board. Steady meat with a carving fork. Trim away any excess fat. With a bread/utility knife cut between the muscles and around the bones to remove one solid section of roast at a time.

2

Carve the pot roast *across the grain* with a sharp knife, cutting slices about ¼ inch thick.

Rolled Rib Roast

Large boneless roasts like the rolled rib roast are carved horizontally. Smaller roasts, such as sirloin tip roasts and rolled veal roasts, are best carved vertically.

1

For a large roast, place the roast on a platter with the largest surface down. Insert a carving fork into the left side. With a meat slicer proceed to remove slices across the grain from right to left. Remove any strings as you come to them. (Do not cut strings prior to carving or the roast will fall apart.)

2

For smaller roasts, place the roast on the carving board or on a wooden insert in the carving platter. Anchor it firmly with the carving fork and, with meat slicer, simply carve off slices approximately ¼ inch thick.

Standing Rib Roast

Carving the standing rib roast is easier if the chine bone (part of backbone) is removed and the rib bones are cut short by the butcher. If necessary, remove a slice of meat from the large end to form a steady base for the rib roast.

1

Insert carving fork between top two ribs. Starting on fat side of the piece of meat, slice across the meat to rib bone with slicing knife. Slice thin or as thick as ½ inch.

2

Use tip of slicing knife to cut along rib bone to loosen each slice, if whole rib is not served. Keep as close to rib bones as possible, so that no meat is wasted.

3

Slide the knife under the slice, steady it with a fork, and lift the slice to a platter.

Crown Rib Roast

Place the crown on cutting board or platter with a wooden insert. (Crown roasts of lamb or pork are carved in the same manner.) Set aside any garnish that may interfere with carving. If roasted with stuffing, portions of stuffing should be served with each rib slice.

1

Insert carving fork securely between two ribs in the left side of crown. Allowing one rib for each slice, carve vertically between two ribs with slicing knife.

2

Lift each slice of meat onto the knife blade as it is carved, steadying it with a fork, and place on individual serving plates. Continue carving around the crown in the same manner for each serving.

Porterhouse Steak

Place steak on a cutting board. Hold steak steady with a carving fork.

1

Using the tip of a utility knife, start at the top of the T-shaped bone and cut down and around to the bottom of bone. Start at the top of the bone on the other side and cut around to the bottom. Lift out the bone and discard.

2

Slice across the full width of the steak, cutting through both the top loin and the tenderloin muscles. Trim off any fat and discard. (For thick steaks, diagonal slicing rather than cross-wise slicing is recommended.)

Beef Brisket

Place meat on a cutting board or platter with a wooden insert. The fat side should be up and the rounded side should face away from the carver. Remove excess fat.

Insert kitchen fork securely in the left portion of the meat. With a slicing knife carve several thin slices (⅛ to ¼ inch thick) at a slight angle across the grain. Rotate brisket as the direction of the fibers changes, always carving across the grain.

Beef Flank Steak

Place the flank steak on a wooden cutting board, holding the meat steady on the board with a carving fork.

With the narrow end of the steak to carver's right, begin slicing. With the slicing knife blade at an angle almost parallel to board, cut meat in very thin, bias slices all at the same angle. Carving this way cuts with the grain of the flank steak.

Shank Half of Ham

Place ham shank on a cutting board.

1

With shank at the carver's left, turn ham so that the thick cushion side is up. Steady ham with carving fork. Using sharp meat slicer, cut along the top of the leg and the shank bones and under fork to lift off the boneless cushion.

2

Remove the cushion and place it on a cutting board. Cut perpendicular slices, as shown.

3

Turn shank half so that the cut side is down. Remove small cushion of meat in same manner as step 1 and place on cutting board. Cut perpendicular slices in the same manner as the boneless cushion piece shown in step 2.

Pork Loin Roast

When purchasing a pork loin roast, ask the butcher to separate the backbone from the ribs—this will make carving much easier.

1

Place roast on a cutting board. To remove the backbone, anchor a carving fork in top of roast. Insert the tip of sharp slicing knife between backbone and meat, and cut away the backbone, leaving as little meat on the bone as possible.

2

Place the roast on a cutting board, rib side facing carver. Insert carving fork in top of roast. Slice meat by cutting closely along each side of rib bone. One slice will contain a rib. The next slice will be boneless.

Salmon

Place salmon on a cutting board.

1

Pull away any fins that were left on during cooking. Cut along the center of the backbone, from head to tail, with the tip of a sharp fillet knife. Knife tip should just touch the rib cage.

2

Peel off the top skin, pulling toward the stomach cavity (belly).

3

Run a wide kitchen turner along the backbone over ribs and under meat; lift off top half of salmon to platter. Pull away the thick backbone remaining and discard. Turn half of salmon remaining and remove skin. Slice salmon and serve.

Leg of Lamb

Place leg of lamb on a cutting board or on a serving platter with wooden insert. The thick side (or cushion) should be on the left side of the carving surface facing up and the shank bone should be to the right.

1

Insert carving fork securely in cushion; carve two or three slices from thin side facing the carver with a sharp slicing knife. Turn leg to rest on this base.

2

Insert carving fork securely in leg. Starting at the shank (or right) end, carve ¼- to ½-inch vertical slices straight down almost to the leg bone.

3

With carving fork still in place, start at shank end and cut along leg bone to release slices. Tip roast on side to carve the remaining meat.

Leg of Lamb, Chef Style

Place leg of lamb on a cutting board or a serving platter with wooden insert.

Start carving from rounded side of the leg with a slicing knife, as shown. Slice meat thin, always cutting away from carver and keeping knife blade almost parallel to bone.

Next, turn leg and continue carving meat from the flatter muscle on the opposite side of the leg bone.

Roast Turkey

Traditional carving of a roast turkey requires carving the breast meat from a turkey frame that is intact. The method shown here for "filleting" a turkey is a departure from the traditional; the breast is removed from the turkey frame before slicing. To begin, remove stuffing from turkey.

1

To remove drumstick and thigh in one piece, pull leg away from body and slice through joint with a slicing knife. Separate leg and thigh by cutting through the connecting joint. Slice each piece individually, if desired, removing bones.

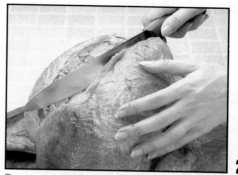

2

To remove the breast, place bird on its back with tail near the carver. Remove left breast first by making a vertical cut along the breastbone approximately 1 inch deep, the entire length of the breast, until you reach the bone. Place fingers in the slit and peel the meat away from the bone with the aid of a very sharp knife.

Turn the bird around so the neck is facing the carver; remove the other breast in the same manner. Set aside. You will have two large breast sections, perfect for slicing.

3

To remove the wings from bird, pull the wings away from the bird and cut through the joint closest to the breast. Separate the wing into sections at the joints for serving.

4

To slice the turkey breast, place the breast sections on a cutting board. Insert a carving fork in breast section to hold steady. Starting at the small end, make thin diagonal slices at about a 30 degree angle. Lift the sliced turkey onto the serving platter, overlapping slices.

If you're searching for a new way to save money on meat, start checking your supermarket for meat-in-a-bag (also called subprimal meat and bulk meat).

Meat-in-a-bag is a boneless 3- to 25-pound section of fresh beef or pork that is trimmed of excess fat, then vacuum-packed in a plastic bag at the packing plant. You'll probably find these sections in your supermarket's refrigerated meat case. If not, you can ask your butcher to get them for you.

It's a simple job to divide these meat sections into roasts, steaks, chops, and cubes because there are no bones to cut around. Just equip yourself with a sharp knife and follow the step-by-step how-to photographs for the most popular cuts.

Meat-in-a-bag basics
You may find these meats cost a bit more than smaller meat cuts with bone. But you can cut the meat into cooking-size portions rather than paying the butcher to do it. And because there's minimal waste with boneless cuts, you get more edible meat. In fact, meat-in-a-bag may yield up to *two servings more per pound* than a comparable bone-in meat cut.

At present, the boneless beef sections that are available include: top round, chuck roll, top loin, tenderloin, rib eye, top sirloin, brisket, and tip. The boneless pork sections available include blade and picnic shoulder roasts, tenderloin, loin, and fresh (leg) smoked ham.

Cutting and storing
After buying meat-in-a-bag, cut it into smaller portions as soon as you get home. Place the meat in a sink and open the plastic bag. Drain off any juices. Transfer the meat to a cutting board and follow our photographs for cutting each section. Although some excess fat is removed at the packing plant, it usually is necessary to trim some fat from the meat.

Meat-in-a-bag is darker in color than meats that are cut and wrapped in the store. When the bag is opened and the meat is exposed to air, the meat acquires the familiar brightness.

After cutting the meat, immediately cover it and store it in the refrigerator. Or, wrap the pieces in moisture-vaporproof material and freeze them. Storage time and cooking methods are the same for meat-in-a-bag as for other fresh meats.

Top Sirloin
The popular top sirloin can be cut into steaks and roasts.

1

With fat side up, use a sharp slicing knife to cut steaks across the grain (lengthwise slices as shown), about 1 to 2 inches thick for broiling; 1 inch or less for panbroiling or panfrying.

2

For roasts or smaller steaks, cut the top sirloin crosswise.

Beef Chuck Roll
Cut meat with slicing knife. Leave the strings intact when cutting this roll, and when cooking the roasts and steaks.

1

Cut 1-inch-thick steaks from the center of the beef chuck roll.

2

Cut cubes from either end for braising. Any large portions can be roasted or braised.

Beef Rib Eye

The rib eye offers a fine selection of tender steaks and roasts.

1

Use the entire subprimal as one roast or cut it into 2 to 4 smaller roasts with slicing knife, as shown.

2

Cut the entire rib eye across the grain into steaks 1 to 1½ inches thick for broiling; less than 1 inch for panbroiling or panfrying.

Beef Tenderloin

The tenderloin is the most tender of the meat cuts.

Beginning at large end, cut tenderloin into steaks to desired thickness. Cut across the grain with slicing knife, as shown. Cut a roast from the center section of the tenderloin. The tapered end of the tenderloin is ideal for beef cubes.

Beef Top Round

The top round is a versatile and economical cut that can be divided into roasts and steaks suitable for preparation by a variety of cooking methods.

1

Cut the meat in half lengthwise with slicing knife. Then cut two or three steaks from each half across the grain (1 to 1¼ inches thick); use for broiling or braising.

2

Cut cubes of meat for braising from the tapered end. Use the large portions as roasts.

Cutting Chicken, Butcher Style

Whole Chicken

Save money by purchasing whole chickens to cut up at home. Follow these easy steps:

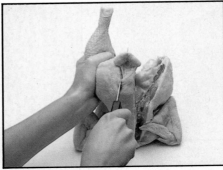

1

Hold chicken upside down, grasping leg firmly with left hand. Place boning knife on right side of tail and cut down right side of backbone. Repeat on left side of backbone, as shown. Remove backbone and save for stock. Remove excess fat from inside of chicken and discard.

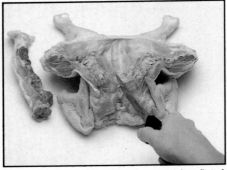

2

Open chicken, skin side down, to lay flat. Make a notch in white piece of cartilage at base of breastbone, as shown.

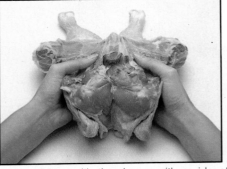

3

Hold chicken with thumbs on either side of rib cage and fingers underneath. Push up with fingers and down with thumbs to release breastbone.

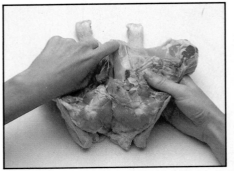

4

Run index finger along each side of breastbone to separate membrane holding bone to breast meat.

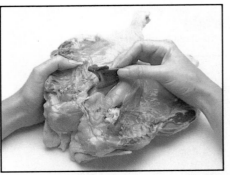

5

Grasp the breast bone firmly and pull to remove bone and cartilage.

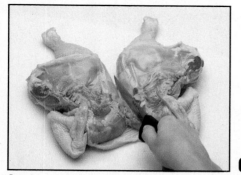

Starting at tip of breast, cut through meat and skin to make equal halves. **6**

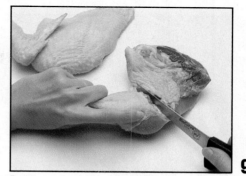

Pull finger back; place knife blade at joint and cut through, being careful to cut *between* bones at joint. **9**

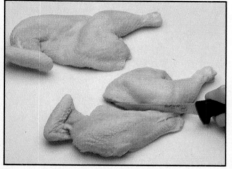

Turn chicken halves skin side up. To quarter chicken, cut along curve between bottom of breast and upper portion of thigh. **7**

To remove wings, place breast skin side up on cutting surface; pull wing firmly to straightened position. Place knife at point where wing joins breast; cut straight down, exposing joint. Turn knife at angle and complete cut through joint. **10**

To separate thigh and drumstick, run index finger up inside of chicken leg to locate knot at joint of thigh and drumstick. **8**

"After cutting up the chicken, rinse the chicken pieces in cold water and pat dry with paper toweling before using in recipe preparation."

34

Now put the basics to work. This chapter offers more than 300 great-tasting recipes and dozens of step-by-step photos guaranteed to make meals more exciting.

Salmon Mousse

1 15½-ounce can salmon
2 envelopes unflavored gelatin
2 cups mayonnaise or salad dressing
½ cup chili sauce
2 tablespoons lemon juice
1 tablespoon Worcestershire sauce
½ teaspoon dried dillweed
1 6½-ounce can tuna, drained and
finely flaked
4 hard-cooked eggs, finely chopped
½ cup pimiento-stuffed olives, finely chopped
¼ cup finely chopped onion
Lettuce
Party rye bread or assorted crackers

Drain salmon, reserving liquid; add water, if necessary, to equal ½ *cup* liquid. Bone and finely flake salmon; set aside. Sprinkle gelatin over reserved salmon liquid. Place over hot water and stir to dissolve.

In mixing bowl gradually blend dissolved gelatin into mayonnaise. Stir in chili sauce, lemon juice, Worcestershire sauce, dillweed, and ¼ teaspoon *pepper*. Fold in flaked salmon, tuna, chopped eggs, olives, and chopped onion. Turn into a 6-cup mold. Cover and chill till firm.

Unmold onto a lettuce-lined platter. Garnish the salmon mousse with additional pimiento-stuffed green olives, tomato roses, or fruit decorations shown on pages 18-21, if desired. Serve with party rye bread or crackers. Makes 6 cups.

Bacon-Mushroom Spread

4 slices bacon
8 ounces fresh mushrooms, chopped (3 cups)
1 onion, finely chopped
1 clove garlic, minced
2 tablespoons all-purpose flour
1 8-ounce package cream cheese, cubed
2 teaspoons Worcestershire sauce
1 teaspoon soy sauce
½ cup dairy sour cream
Party rye bread or crackers

In a skillet cook bacon till crisp. Drain, reserving 2 *tablespoons* of the drippings. Crumble bacon; set aside.

Cook chopped mushrooms, chopped onion, and garlic in the reserved bacon drippings till vegetables are tender and most of liquid evaporates. Stir in flour, ¼ teaspoon *salt*, and ⅛ teaspoon *pepper*. Add cream cheese, Worcestershire sauce, and soy sauce. Cook and stir till cream cheese melts. Stir in sour cream and crumbled bacon. Heat through; do not boil. Sprinkle with snipped chives or parsley, if desired. Serve warm with bread or crackers. Makes 2½ cups.

Quick Chicken Spread

2 cups chopped cooked chicken
½ cup sliced celery
2 tablespoons dry sherry
2 tablespoons mayonnaise or salad dressing
1 teaspoon lemon juice
3 parsley sprigs
¼ teaspoon salt
¼ teaspoon ground nutmeg
½ cup finely chopped almonds, toasted
Assorted crackers or party rye bread

Combine chopped chicken, celery, sherry, mayonnaise or salad dressing, lemon juice, parsley, salt, nutmeg, and dash *pepper*. Process the mixture, half at a time, in a blender container till nearly smooth. (Or process the chicken mixture all at once in food processor bowl.) Shape mixture into a ball. Cover and chill. At serving time, roll the ball in the toasted almonds. Serve with crackers or rye bread. Makes 2 cups.

Pork and Liver Pâté

2 slices bacon, halved
½ cup chopped onion
2 cloves garlic, minced
1 pound ground pork
¼ pound chicken livers
1 cup milk
2 eggs
2 tablespoons fine dry bread crumbs
2 tablespoons anchovy paste
1 tablespoon cornstarch
2 teaspoons prepared mustard
½ teaspoon dried sage, crushed
½ teaspoon dried basil, crushed
¼ teaspoon salt
⅛ teaspoon pepper
Sieved egg yolk, chopped egg white, or snipped parsley for garnish (optional)
Assorted crisp crackers

Cook bacon till crisp. Set bacon aside; reserve 2 *tablespoons* of the drippings. In drippings cook onion and garlic till onion is tender. Add ground pork and chicken livers. Cook and stir over medium-high heat about 5 minutes or till livers are no longer pink. Drain well; cool.

In a blender container place ½ *cup* of the milk, the pork-onion mixture, and cooked bacon. Cover; blend on medium speed till smooth. Add remaining ingredients. Cover; blend thoroughly. Pour into an 8x4x2-inch loaf pan. Set in shallow baking pan; pour hot water around loaf pan to depth of ½ inch. Bake in a 325° oven for 1 hour.

Cool; cover and chill. To serve, unmold on serving platter and garnish with egg yolk, egg white, or parsley, if desired. Slice and spread on crisp crackers. Makes about 4 cups.

Pictured: **Fruit and Prosciutto Appetizers (see recipe, page 40).**

Smoky Cheese Ball

Finely chopped walnuts, peanuts, or toasted almonds make a crunchy coating—

- 2 8-ounce packages cream cheese, softened
- 2 cups shredded smoky cheddar cheese (8 ounces)
- ½ cup butter or margarine, softened
- 2 tablespoons milk
- 2 teaspoons steak sauce
- 1 cup finely chopped nuts
  Assorted crackers

In a mixer bowl or food processor bowl combine softened cream cheese, shredded cheddar cheese, softened butter or margarine, milk, and steak sauce. Beat mixture with electric mixer or process mixture till fluffy. Chill slightly; shape into a ball. Place nuts on waxed paper; gently roll cheese ball in nuts to coat. Serve with crackers. Makes about 3½ cups.

Three-Way Cheese Ball

- 1 8-ounce package cream cheese, softened
- ½ cup dairy sour cream
- ¼ cup butter or margarine, softened
- 2 tablespoons finely chopped pimiento
- 1 tablespoon snipped parsley
- 1 teaspoon grated onion
- ⅓ cup finely chopped nuts
- ⅓ cup snipped parsley

In mixer bowl or food processor bowl combine cream cheese, sour cream, and butter or margarine; beat with electric mixer or process till fluffy. Stir in pimiento, the 1 tablespoon parsley, and the onion. Chill. Shape into a ball. Coat with nuts and ⅓ cup parsley. Makes about 1¾ cups.

Dilled Salmon Dip: Prepare Cheese Ball as above, *except* omit nuts and the ⅓ cup parsley. Combine cheese ball mixture; one 7¾-ounce can *salmon*, drained, flaked, and skin and bones removed; and ¼ teaspoon dried *dillweed*; stir. Cover; chill. Add *milk*, if necessary, to make of dipping consistency. Makes 2½ cups.

Swiss Cheese-Ham Spread: Prepare Cheese Ball as above, *except* omit nuts and the ⅓ cup parsley. Have 1 cup shredded *Swiss cheese* (4 ounces) at room temperature. Combine cheese ball mixture, the shredded Swiss cheese, one 3-ounce can *deviled ham*, and 1 teaspoon *prepared mustard*. Beat till almost smooth. Cover; chill. Makes 3 cups.

Guacamole

- 2 medium avocados, seeded and peeled
- 1 thin slice of small onion
- 1 tablespoon lemon juice
- 1 clove garlic, minced
- ½ teaspoon salt
  Assorted fresh vegetable dippers or tortilla chips

In a blender container combine avocados, onion, lemon juice, garlic, and salt. Blend till smooth, scraping down sides of container as necessary. Place in a serving bowl. Cover and chill before serving. Serve as a dip with fresh vegetables or tortilla chips. Makes about 1 cup.

Tomato-Chili Guacamole: Prepare Guacamole as directed above, *except* stir in 1 small *tomato*, peeled and finely chopped, and 2 tablespoons finely chopped canned *green chili peppers*. Cover; chill before serving. Makes 1⅓ cups.

Artichoke-Chili Dip

To keep this rich dip warm, place it over a low flame—

- 1 14-ounce can artichoke hearts, drained and chopped
- 1 4-ounce can green chili peppers, rinsed, seeded, and chopped
- 1 cup grated Parmesan cheese
- 1 cup mayonnaise or salad dressing
  Tortilla chips
  Breadsticks

Combine the chopped artichoke hearts, chopped chili peppers, cheese, and mayonnaise or salad dressing. Turn mixture into an 8-inch round baking dish. Bake in a 350° oven about 20 minutes or till heated through. Serve warm with tortilla chips and breadsticks. Makes about 2⅔ cups.

Creamy Dill Dip

- 1 cup dairy sour cream
- 1 cup mayonnaise or salad dressing
- 1 tablespoon minced dried onion
- 1 tablespoon dried dillweed
- ½ teaspoon seasoned salt
  Assorted fresh vegetable dippers or crisp crackers

Thoroughly combine sour cream, mayonnaise or salad dressing, minced dried onion, dillweed, and seasoned salt. Cover and chill thoroughly to blend flavors. Serve with fresh vegetable dippers or crackers. Makes 2 cups dip.

Chili con Queso

½ cup finely chopped onion
1 tablespoon butter or margarine
2 medium tomatoes, peeled, seeded, and chopped
1 4-ounce can green chili peppers, rinsed, seeded, and chopped
¼ teaspoon salt
1 cup shredded cheddar cheese (4 ounces)
1 cup shredded Monterey Jack cheese food (4 ounces)
Milk
Tortilla chips or corn chips

In a medium saucepan cook onion in butter or margarine till tender but not brown. Stir in chopped tomatoes, chopped chili peppers, and salt. Simmer, uncovered, for 10 minutes. Add cheeses, a little at a time, stirring just till melted. Stir in a little milk if mixture becomes too thick. Heat through over low heat. Transfer to a small serving bowl; serve warm with tortilla chips or corn chips. Makes 1¾ cups.

Crab Appetizer Puffs

1 pound fresh crab meat, cooked, or 1 pound frozen crab meat
½ cup butter or margarine
1 cup boiling water
1 cup all-purpose flour
¼ teaspoon salt
4 eggs
¼ cup mayonnaise or salad dressing
¼ cup dairy sour cream
¼ cup chili sauce
1 teaspoon prepared horseradish
Few drops bottled hot pepper sauce
¼ cup sliced celery
2 tablespoons thinly sliced green onion

Thaw crab meat, if frozen. Remove any cartilage from crab meat and flake meat; set aside. In saucepan melt butter or margarine in the boiling water. Add flour and salt all at once, stirring vigorously. Cook and stir till mixture forms a ball that does not separate. Remove pan from heat; cool 10 minutes. Add eggs, one at a time, beating after each addition till batter is smooth.

Drop batter by rounded teaspoonfuls 2 inches apart on greased baking sheet. Bake in a 400° oven for 10 to 15 minutes or till golden brown and puffy. Remove from oven; split puffs. Cool completely on a wire rack.

In mixing bowl combine the mayonnaise or salad dressing, sour cream, chili sauce, prepared horseradish, and bottled hot pepper sauce. Stir in crab meat, celery, and green onion. Fill each puff with about *1 tablespoon* of the crab mixture. Makes 30 appetizers.

Dill-Stuffed Mushrooms

24 large fresh mushrooms
2 tablespoons sliced green onion
2 tablespoons butter or margarine
¼ cup fine dry bread crumbs
½ teaspoon dried dillweed
⅛ teaspoon salt
⅛ teaspoon Worcestershire sauce

Remove stems from mushrooms; chop stems. In skillet cook the chopped mushroom stems and green onion in butter or margarine till tender. Remove from heat. Stir in bread crumbs, dillweed, salt, and Worcestershire sauce; fill mushroom crowns with bread crumb mixture. Place in shallow baking pan. Bake in a 425° oven for 6 to 8 minutes. Makes 24.

Cream Cheese and Ham Roll-Ups

1 3-ounce package cream cheese, softened
2 tablespoons minced dried onion
2 tablespoons milk
1 4-ounce package boiled ham, (5 rectangular slices)
15 small, whole sweet or dill pickles, about 2 inches long (one 16-ounce jar)

Stir together cream cheese, onion, and milk. Spread a rounded tablespoon of the cheese mixture on each ham slice. Cut each rectangle of ham crosswise into 6 strips (about 1 inch wide and 4 inches long). Cut pickles in half crosswise; place one pickle piece on each ham strip. Roll up. Secure with wooden pick. Cover and chill. Makes 30 appetizers.

Miniature Sesame Drumsticks

3 pounds chicken wings
¼ cup finely crushed rich round crackers
¼ cup sesame seed, toasted
1 teaspoon paprika
¾ teaspoon salt
¼ cup butter or margarine, melted

Cut chicken wings into two pieces, discarding the bony tips. Combine crushed crackers, sesame seed, paprika, and salt. Brush the meaty chicken pieces with melted butter or margarine. Roll in seasoned cracker mixture. Place in large, shallow baking pan; don't crowd. Bake in a 375° oven for 40 to 45 minutes. Makes 16 to 18 appetizers.

Appetizers

Cocktail Meatball Fondue

For a crowd, double the meatball recipe and offer several dipping sauces, such as mustard sauce or curry sauce—

  1 beaten egg
  2 tablespoons fine dry bread crumbs
  2 tablespoons thinly sliced green onion
  2 tablespoons finely chopped green pepper
  ¼ teaspoon salt
  ¼ teaspoon dried thyme, crushed
     Dash pepper
  ½ pound lean ground beef
     Cooking oil
  1 teaspoon salt
     Tangy Cranberry Sauce

In a mixing bowl combine egg, bread crumbs, green onion, green pepper, the ¼ teaspoon salt, the thyme, and pepper. Add ground beef; mix well. Shape beef mixture into ¾-inch meatballs as shown on page 55. (Allow meatballs to stand at room temperature 30 minutes before cooking.)

Pour cooking oil into metal fondue pot to no more than ½ capacity or to a depth of 2 inches. Heat oil atop range to 350°. Add the 1 teaspoon salt to the hot oil. Transfer to fondue burner. Spear individual meatballs with a fondue fork; cook in hot oil about 1 minute or till browned. Transfer meatballs to a dinner fork; dip into warm Tangy Cranberry Sauce. Makes about 40 meatballs.

Tangy Cranberry Sauce: Combine one 8-ounce can *jellied cranberry sauce*, 3 tablespoons *bottled steak sauce*, 2 teaspoons *brown sugar*, 2 teaspoons *cooking oil*, and 1 teaspoon *prepared mustard*. Beat till smooth with a rotary beater. Heat through. Makes 2 cups.

Hot Pineapple-Bacon Appetizers

  9 slices bacon, halved crosswise
  9 fresh or canned mushrooms, halved
 18 fresh or canned pineapple chunks
  ¼ cup soy sauce
  1 tablespoon sugar
  ⅛ teaspoon ground ginger

Partially cook bacon; drain on paper toweling. Combine halved mushrooms and pineapple chunks with the soy sauce, sugar, and ginger. Marinate about 20 minutes, stirring occasionally; drain.

Wrap *1* mushroom half and *1* pineapple chunk in a *half-slice* of bacon; repeat with remaining. Secure with wooden picks. Place in an 8x8x2-inch baking pan. Bake in a 450° oven for 10 to 12 minutes or till bacon is crisp. Makes 18.

Cheese-Filled Pastries

These savory appetizer bundles use phyllo dough as the wrapper. If you like, make them ahead and serve chilled—

  1 8-ounce package cream cheese, softened
  ½ cup feta cheese
  ¼ cup snipped parsley
  1 tablespoon snipped fresh dill or 1 teaspoon dried dillweed
  1 egg yolk
  8 sheets frozen phyllo dough, thawed (8 ounces)
  ¼ cup butter or margarine, melted

For filling, in a mixing bowl beat cream cheese till creamy. Add feta cheese, parsley, and dill to beaten cream cheese. Add egg yolk; beat just till combined.

Stack *2 sheets* of the phyllo dough. (Cover unused sheets with a damp cloth to prevent drying.) Brush stack of phyllo dough with some of the melted butter or margarine. Cut lengthwise into quarters.

For each piece, spoon about *1½ tablespoons* of filling about 1 inch from end of one of the narrow sides. Fold end over filling at 45-degree angle. Continue folding to form a triangle that encloses the filling, using entire strip of 2 layers. Place on baking sheet; brush with melted butter or margarine. Bake in a 375° oven for 18 minutes. Serve warm or chilled. Makes 16.

Fruit And Prosciutto Appetizers

This easy and elegant appetizer is pictured on page 36—

     Medium honeydew melon or cantaloupe, chilled
     Thinly sliced prosciutto
     Strawberries, halved
     Green grapes
     Sweet red cherries
     Fresh mint leaves (optional)

Cut 1 melon in half; remove seeds. Cut *each* half into quarters. On each salad plate place melon wedge. Arrange in each melon wedge 1 slice prosciutto and some halved strawberries, grapes, and cherries. Garnish with fresh mint leaves, if desired. Makes 8 servings.

Shrimp Tartlets

Pastry for Double-Crust Pie
(see recipe, page 130)
1   3-ounce package cream cheese, softened
¼   cup dairy sour cream
2   tablespoons cocktail sauce
1½ teaspoons snipped fresh dillweed or
      ½ teaspoon dried dillweed
2   4½-ounce cans shrimp
⅓   cup finely chopped celery

Form pastry dough into a ball. Roll to about ⅛-inch thickness; cut into 2-inch squares. Place squares in 1¾-inch-diameter muffin pans, pressing to fit. Prick with fork. Bake in a 400° oven for 8 to 10 minutes or till golden. Cool.

Meanwhile, beat together softened cream cheese, sour cream, cocktail sauce, and dill. Rinse and drain shrimp. Coarsely chop shrimp; stir shrimp and celery into cream cheese mixture. Chill thoroughly. To serve, spoon a *rounded teaspoonful* of shrimp mixture into each tart shell. Garnish with fresh dill, if desired. Makes 4 to 5 dozen appetizers.

Piroshki

½   pound lean ground beef
½   cup finely chopped onion
1   hard-cooked egg, chopped
½   teaspoon salt
½   of an 8-ounce package cream cheese
½   cup butter or margarine
1¾ cups all-purpose flour

In a small skillet cook meat and onion till meat is browned and onion is tender. Add chopped egg, salt, and dash *pepper*. In mixing bowl cut cream cheese and butter into flour till mixture resembles fine crumbs. Press mixture into a ball. Divide in half; roll one half to ⅛-inch thickness. Cut into 2¾-inch rounds. Place about *1 teaspoon* of the meat mixture on each round; moisten edges with a little water and fold over. With tines of fork, press to seal. Repeat cutting and filling with remaining dough and meat mixture. Place on an ungreased baking sheet. Bake in a 400° oven for 12 to 15 minutes or till golden. Serve warm. Makes about 36.

Chinese Mustard

¼   cup water
¼   cup dry mustard
2   teaspoons cooking oil

In small saucepan bring water to boiling. Combine dry mustard, cooking oil, and ½ teaspoon *salt*. Stir boiling water into mustard mixture. Makes about ⅓ cup sauce.

Chicken and Vegetable Egg Rolls

½   cup whole dried mushrooms
2   tablespoons soy sauce
2   teaspoons cornstarch
1   teaspoon grated gingerroot
½   teaspoon sugar
1   whole large chicken breast, skinned, split,
      and boned
1   clove garlic, minced
1   tablespoon cooking oil
1   16-ounce can bean sprouts, drained
2   cups small spinach leaves
½   cup thinly sliced green onion
½   cup thinly sliced bamboo shoots
12 egg roll skins
      Cooking oil for deep-fat frying
      Chinese Mustard (recipe bottom left)
      Sweet and Sour Sauce (recipe below)

Soak mushrooms in warm water for 30 minutes; drain and chop, discarding stems. Blend soy sauce into cornstarch; stir in gingerroot, sugar, and ¼ teaspoon *salt*; set aside.

For filling, chop chicken. Stir-fry chopped chicken and garlic quickly in the 1 tablespoon hot oil about 2 minutes. Add bean sprouts, spinach leaves, green onion, and bamboo shoots; stir-fry about 3 minutes more. Stir soy sauce mixture; stir into chicken mixture. Cook and stir till thickened. Cool.

Place egg roll skin with one point toward you. Spoon ¼ *cup* of the chicken-vegetable filling diagonally across and just below center of skin. Fold bottom point of skin over filling; tuck point under filling. Fold side corners over, forming an envelope shape. Roll up toward remaining corner; moisten point and press firmly to seal. Repeat with remaining egg roll skins and filling. Fry egg rolls, a few at a time, in deep hot oil (365°) for 2 to 3 minutes or till golden brown. Drain on paper toweling. Serve warm with Chinese Mustard and Sweet and Sour Sauce, if desired. Makes 12 egg rolls.

Sweet and Sour Sauce

½   cup packed brown sugar
1   tablespoon cornstarch
⅓   cup red wine vinegar
⅓   cup Homemade Chicken Broth
      (see recipe, page 73)
¼   cup finely chopped green pepper
2   tablespoons chopped pimiento
1   tablespoon soy sauce
¼   teaspoon garlic powder
¼   teaspoon ground ginger

In small saucepan combine brown sugar and cornstarch. Stir in wine vinegar, chicken broth, green pepper, pimiento, soy sauce, garlic powder, and ginger. Cook and stir till thickened and bubbly. Serve warm. Makes 1¼ cups sauce.

Rib Roast Barbecue

This juicy grilled roast is pictured on the cover—

    1   5- to 6-pound boned and rolled beef rib roast
    ½   cup burgundy
    ½   cup vinegar
    ¼   cup cooking oil
    ¼   cup finely chopped onion
    2   tablespoons sugar
    1   tablespoon Worcestershire sauce
    1½ teaspoons salt
    ½   teaspoon dry mustard
    ¼   teaspoon pepper
    ¼   teaspoon chili powder
    ¼   teaspoon dried thyme, crushed
    1   clove garlic, minced
        Several drops bottled hot pepper sauce

Place meat in a plastic bag; set in deep bowl. Combine remaining ingredients. Pour over meat; close bag. Marinate 6 to 8 hours or overnight in refrigerator; turn several times.

Drain meat; reserve marinade. Pat excess moisture from meat with paper toweling. In covered grill, arrange *slow* coals around edge of grill. (Position drip pan in center of coals, directly beneath where meat will be grilled.) Place meat in center of grill; close hood. Roast meat about 2¾ hours or till meat thermometer registers 140° for rare, 160° for medium, and 170° for well-done. Brush frequently with the marinade during the last 30 minutes of roasting. Let stand 15 minutes before slicing. Garnish roast with a tomato rose as shown on page 21, if desired. Carve rib roast as shown on page 24. If desired, heat remaining marinade and pass with slices of meat. Makes 15 to 20 servings.

Marinated Pork Roast and Gravy

    1   3- to 5-pound pork center loin roast
    5   cloves garlic, halved
    ¼   cup cooking oil
    ¼   cup burgundy
    ¼   cup finely chopped onion
    1   tablespoon Worcestershire sauce
    ½   teaspoon dried thyme, crushed
    ½   teaspoon dried oregano, crushed
    ½   teaspoon celery salt
    ¼   teaspoon ground sage
        Several dashes bottled hot pepper sauce
    2   tablepsoons all-purpose flour
    1   teaspoon instant chicken bouillon granules

Trim excess fat from roast. Stud roast with garlic halves by inserting tip of knife into meat and pushing cloves into meat pocket as you remove knife. Makes sure garlic is evenly spaced on meat's surface. For marinade, in bowl combine oil, burgundy, onion, Worcestershire, thyme, oregano, celery salt, sage, pepper sauce, and ¼ teaspoon *pepper*. Place meat in plastic bag; set in shallow baking dish. Pour marinade

over meat; close bag. Marinate in refrigerator 6 to 8 hours or overnight, turning roast occasionally. Drain roast; reserve marinade. Place roast, rib side down, in shallow roasting pan. Insert meat thermometer. Roast, uncovered, in a 325° oven for 2½ to 3 hours or till thermometer registers 170°. Remove roast from oven; place on warm serving platter. Remove garlic clove halves from meat, if possible.

For gravy, pour off fat from roasting pan. Return *2 tablespoons* of the fat to pan. Add flour; stir to combine with the fat and to loosen meat particles. To reserved marinade add the bouillon granules and enough water to make *1 cup* liquid. Add all at once to the mixture in the roasting pan. Cook and stir till mixture is thickened and bubbly. Cook and stir 1 minute more. Carve the pork roast as shown on page 27. Pass gravy with slices of meat. Makes 6 to 8 servings.

Sauerbraten

Marinating the roast for 72 hours gives it a unique flavor—

        Marinade
    1   4-pound boneless beef round rump roast
    2   tablespoons cooking oil
    ½   cup chopped onion
    ½   cup chopped carrot
    ½   cup chopped celery
    1   cup broken gingersnaps
        Spaetzle or hot buttered noodles

Prepare Marinade. Place meat in a plastic bag; set in a shallow pan. Pour Marinade over meat; close bag. Refrigerate 72 hours, turning meat occasionally. Remove meat; pat excess moisture from meat. Strain Marinade; set aside.

In a Dutch oven brown meat on all sides in hot oil. Drain off fat. Add reserved Marinade, chopped onion, carrot, and celery. Cover; simmer about 2 hours or till meat is tender. Meanwhile, prepare Spaetzle.

Transfer meat to a platter; keep warm. Reserve *2 cups* of the cooking liquid and vegetables in Dutch oven. Stir in broken gingersnaps and ⅔ cup *water*. Cook and stir till thickened and bubbly. Slice meat and arrange slices over Spaetzle or noodles; spoon some gravy over meat. Pass remaining gravy. Makes 12 servings.

Marinade: Combine 1½ cups *water*; 1½ cups *red wine vinegar*; 2 medium *onions*, sliced; 1 *lemon*, sliced; 12 whole *cloves*; 6 whole *black peppercorns*, crushed; 4 *bay leaves*, crushed; 1 tablespoon *sugar*; 1 tablespoon *salt*; and ¼ teaspoon *ground ginger*.

Spaetzle: Combine 2 cups *all-purpose flour* and 1 teaspoon *salt*. Mix 2 *eggs* and ¾ cup *milk*; stir into flour mixture. Pour batter into a colander with large holes (at least ³⁄₁₆-inch diameter) or spaetzle maker. Hold colander over kettle of boiling salted water. Press batter through the colander to form the spaetzle. Cook and stir 5 minutes. Drain well. Combine ½ cup fine *dry bread crumbs* and ½ cup *butter*, melted; sprinkle over spaetzle. Makes 4 cups.

Pictured: **Lemon-Marinated Sirloin Steak (see recipe, page 46).**

43

Pot Roast Italiano

    1   3- to 4-pound beef chuck pot roast
        Shortening or cooking oil (optional)
    1   16-ounce can tomatoes, cut up
    1   10½-ounce can condensed beef broth
    1   8-ounce can tomato sauce
    2   cloves garlic, minced
    1   teaspoon sugar
    ¾   teaspoon dried oregano, crushed
    ¾   teaspoon dried basil, crushed
    ½   cup chopped green pepper
    ⅓   cup chopped onion
    ¼   cup cornstarch
        Hot cooked spaghetti or other pasta

Trim excess fat from roast as shown at right. In Dutch oven heat trimmings till *2 tablespoons* fat accumulates (add shortening or cooking oil, if necessary); discard trimmings. Brown meat on all sides in hot fat. Add *undrained* tomatoes, beef broth, tomato sauce, garlic, sugar, oregano, basil, and ⅛ teaspoon *pepper*. Cover and simmer for 1½ hours. Add chopped green pepper and onion. Cover and simmer about 30 minutes more or till meat is tender. Transfer roast to heated platter; keep warm. For sauce, skim excess fat from pan juices. Measure juices. Add water, if necessary, to equal *4 cups*. Stir together cornstarch and ¼ cup *cold water*; stir into pan juices. Cook and stir till sauce is thickened and bubbly. Cook and stir 2 minutes more. Carve roast as shown on page 24. Pass sauce with roast and spaghetti. Makes 8 servings.

Savory Blade Pot Roast

    1   3-pound beef chuck blade pot roast
        Shortening or cooking oil (optional)
    ¼   cup red wine vinegar
    ¼   cup catsup
    2   tablespoons soy sauce
    2   tablespoons Worcestershire sauce
    1   teaspoon dried rosemary, crushed
    ½   teaspoon garlic powder
    ½   teaspoon dry mustard

Trim excess fat from pot roast as shown at right. In Dutch oven heat trimmings till *1 tablespoon* fat accumulates (add shortening or cooking oil, if necessary). Brown meat slowly on both sides in the hot fat; remove from heat.

Combine wine vinegar, catsup, soy sauce, Worcestershire sauce, rosemary, garlic powder, dry mustard, and ¼ cup *water*; pour over roast. Return to heat. Cover tightly; simmer 1½ to 1¾ hours or till meat is tender. Transfer meat to serving platter. Carve roast as shown on page 24. Skim fat from pan juices; spoon over slices of meat. Serves 6 to 8.

To Trim Fat from Pot Roast

To trim excess fat from a pot roast, place roast on cutting board. Use a sharp utility knife to cut away the excess fat, as shown. (Reserve the trimmings to use when browning the roast as many recipes direct.)

Golden Beef Pot Roast

    1   3- to 3½-pound beef chuck pot roast
    3   tablespoons all-purpose flour
    2   tablespoons cooking oil
    ¼   teaspoon celery seed
    ¼   teaspoon dried oregano, crushed
    ¼   cup frozen orange juice concentrate, thawed
    1½ pounds sweet potatoes, peeled and halved
            (4 medium potatoes)
    2   medium onions, quartered
    2   tablespoons all-purpose flour

Trim excess fat from meat as shown above. Combine the 3 tablespoons flour, 1 teaspoon *salt*, and ¼ teaspoon *pepper*; coat meat with flour mixture. In Dutch oven brown meat slowly on all sides in hot oil; drain excess fat. Add ¼ cup *water*, the celery seed, and oregano. Cover tightly; simmer 1½ hours.

Combine ½ cup *water* and orange juice concentrate; pour over meat. Add potatoes and onions, pushing vegetables down into liquid. Cover; simmer about 1 hour more or till meat and vegetables are tender.

Transfer meat and vegetables to platter; keep warm. Pour pan juices into measuring cup; skim off fat. Add enough water to juices to equal *1¼ cups*. Stir ¼ cup *cold water* into 2 tablespoons flour; stir into juices. Cook and stir till thickened and bubbly. Cook and stir 1 minute more. Season to taste with *salt* and *pepper*.

To serve, carve roast as shown on page 24. Spoon a little gravy over meat and vegetables. Garnish platter with parsley sprigs, if desired. Pass remaining gravy. Serves 6 to 8.

Roast Beef with Horseradish Sauce

- 1 4- to 6-pound boneless beef round rump roast
  Salt and pepper
- ¼ cup dairy sour cream
- 2 tablespoons grated fresh or prepared horseradish
- ¼ teaspoon sugar
- ¼ teaspoon salt
  Dash ground nutmeg
- ½ cup whipping cream

Sprinkle meat with some salt and pepper. Place meat, fat side up, on rack in roasting pan; insert meat thermometer. Roast in 325° oven for 2 to 2½ hours or till thermometer registers 150° to 170°. Let stand 15 minutes before carving.

Meanwhile, combine sour cream, horseradish, sugar, salt, and nutmeg. Let mixture stand at room temperature while meat cooks. To serve, beat whipping cream to soft peaks; fold into horseradish mixture. Serves 10 to 12.

Sausage-Stuffed Lamb Roast

- 1 6-pound leg of lamb
- ½ pound bulk pork sausage
- 1 medium onion, chopped
- 1 clove garlic, minced
- ½ cup slivered almonds or pine nuts
- ½ cup rice
- ½ cup dry white wine
- ¼ cup raisins
- 1 teaspoon instant chicken bouillon granules
- ¼ teaspoon ground nutmeg

Bone and butterfly lamb as shown at right. Pound lamb on the inner meat surface to ¾-inch thickness. In skillet cook sausage, onion, and garlic till sausage is done; drain. Add nuts and rice to skillet; cook and stir 2 minutes. Stir in wine, raisins, bouillon granules, nutmeg, and ½ cup *water*. Bring to boiling; reduce heat. Cover and cook 12 to 15 minutes or till liquid is absorbed. Spread sausage mixture over lamb. Roll up, jelly-roll style, starting from longest side. Tie with string. Place on rack in shallow roasting pan. Insert meat thermometer into thickest part of meat. Roast in a 325° oven about 2 hours or till thermometer registers 170°. Makes 12 servings.

Note: If you don't have the time to bone a leg of lamb for your dinner party, order it boned and butterflied from your butcher. Or simply serve a bone-in lamb roast with the sausage stuffing served alongside. Bake, covered, in a 1½-quart casserole in a 375° oven for 20 to 25 minutes.

To roast a bone-in leg of lamb, sprinkle the roast with salt and pepper. Insert a meat thermometer into center of roast, making sure the bulb does not touch bone. Place, fat side up, on a rack in a shallow roasting pan. Roast in a 325° oven for 2½ to 3 hours or till meat thermometer registers 160° for medium doneness. Let stand 15 minutes before carving.

To Bone and Butterfly Leg of Lamb

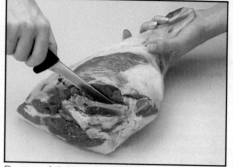

1

Remove fell (thin membrane) from leg, pulling from large end to shank. Turn leg, bone side up, and run sharp boning knife around the aitch bone. Work knife around bone to loosen it, keeping the blade close to the bone. (You should feel the blade against the bone as you cut.) Remove aitch bone.

2

Start cutting at the ball joint of leg bone (from which the aitch bone was removed). Make a straight cut to center of leg *to* and *along* the bone until the blade reaches the next joint, known as the stifle joint. Run the point of the blade around the stifle joint close to the bone all the way to the end of the shank.

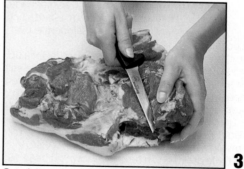

3

Carefully work the point of the knife blade all around the leg bone, stifle joint, and shank bone, until all are completely exposed and loosened. Remove the leg bone and the shank bone. Cut along the natural seam that separates the two largest muscles and open to lay flat. Trim away excess fat.

Roast Pork with Fennel

    1 3- to 4-pound pork loin blade roast
    ½ teaspoon fennel seed
    2 tablespoons sugar
    1 teaspoon ground sage
    1 teaspoon dried marjoram, crushed
    ¼ teaspoon celery seed
    ¼ teaspoon dry mustard
    1 tablespoon snipped parsley

Stud roast with fennel seed by inserting tip of knife into meat and pushing 4 or 5 seeds into a meat pocket as you remove knife. Cut about 15 evenly spaced pockets on meat surface.

In a small bowl combine sugar, sage, marjoram, celery seed, mustard, 1 teaspoon *salt*, and ⅛ teaspoon *pepper*. Thoroughly rub the roast with sugar-herb mixture. Cover roast; let stand 4 hours in the refrigerator.

Remove roast from refrigerator. Place meat on rack in shallow roasting pan. Insert meat thermometer. Roast, uncovered, in a 325° oven for 2¼ to 2¾ hours or till meat thermometer registers 170°. Remove from oven; place roast on serving platter. Sprinkle roast with parsley. Carve pork roast as shown on page 27. Makes 8 to 10 servings.

Teriyaki Roast Beef

    1 6- to 7-pound boneless beef rib roast
    1 cup soy sauce
    ½ cup cooking oil
    ¼ cup light molasses
    1 tablespoon ground ginger
    1 tablespoon dry mustard
    4 cloves garlic, minced
       Salt and pepper

Place meat in plastic bag; set in deep bowl. For marinade, combine soy sauce, oil, molasses, ginger, mustard, and minced garlic; pour over meat. Close bag. Refrigerate overnight, turning occasionally.

Remove meat, reserving marinade. Place meat, fat side up, on rack in shallow roasting pan. Sprinkle roast with a little salt and pepper. Insert a meat thermometer. Roast in a 325° oven for 3 to 3¾ hours for rare or till thermometer registers 140°; 3½ to 4¼ hours for medium (160°); or 4 to 4¾ hours for well-done (170°). During roasting, baste several times with reserved marinade. Remove roast from oven; cover with foil. Let stand 15 minutes before serving.

Garnish roast with green onion brushes shown on page 18, if desired. Carve boneless rib roast (same as rolled rib roast shown on page 24). Makes 14 servings.

Lemon-Marinated Sirloin Steak

Pictured on page 42—

    1 2-pound sirloin steak, cut 2 to 2½ inches thick
    1 teaspoon finely shredded lemon peel
    ½ cup lemon juice
    ⅓ cup cooking oil
    2 tablespoons sliced green onion
    4 teaspoons sugar
   1½ teaspoons salt
    1 teaspoon Worcestershire sauce
    1 teaspoon prepared mustard
    ⅛ teaspoon pepper

Score fat edges of steak, being careful not to cut into meat, as shown on page 47. Place meat in a shallow baking dish. Combine lemon peel and juice, cooking oil, green onion, sugar, salt, Worcestershire sauce, mustard, and pepper. Pour over steak. Cover; let stand 4 hours in the refrigerator or overnight, turning steak several times.

Remove steak from marinade, reserving marinade. Pat excess moisture from steak with paper toweling.

Grill steak over *medium-hot* coals 17 to 20 minutes. Turn; cook 15 to 17 minutes more for rare to medium-rare. Heat reserved marinade on grill.

Remove steak to serving platter. Carve steak across the grain; spoon marinade over slices. Garnish with lemon cartwheels as shown on page 18, if desired. Makes 6 servings.

Steak with Almonds and Mushrooms

   1¾ pounds beef sirloin, porterhouse, or T-bone steak, cut 1½ inches thick
    1 cup sliced fresh mushrooms
    2 tablespoons snipped chives
    2 tablespoons toasted slivered almonds
    2 tablespoons butter or margarine
    ⅓ cup dry white wine
    ¼ teaspoon salt
    ⅛ teaspoon dried fines herbes, crushed

Place steak on unheated rack of broiler pan. Broil 4 inches from heat 8 minutes; turn and broil 7 to 10 minutes more for rare or to desired doneness.

Meanwhile, in a small skillet cook the sliced mushrooms, snipped chives, and toasted slivered almonds in the butter or margarine till mushrooms and chives are tender.

Stir in the dry white wine, salt, and fines herbes. Heat through; do not boil. Serve over steak. Carve steak as shown on page 26. Makes 2 servings.

Individual Mushroom-Stuffed Steaks

    4 beef top loin steaks, cut 1 inch thick
    2 sliced fresh mushrooms
    ¼ cup chopped onion
    ¼ cup chopped celery
    2 tablespoons butter or margarine
    ⅛ teaspoon salt
    ⅛ teaspoon pepper
    ⅛ teaspoon dried thyme, crushed
       Dash Worcestershire sauce

Cut a 2-inch-wide slit horizontally in fat side of each steak. Insert knife in slit; make pocket by "fanning" knife (same as pork chops shown on page 52).

In a saucepan cook mushrooms, onion, and celery in butter or margarine about 5 minutes; stir occasionally. Stir in salt, pepper, thyme, and Worcestershire sauce. Fill each steak pocket with about ¼ cup of the mushroom mixture. Place steaks on unheated rack of broiler pan. Broil 4 inches from heat till desired doneness; turn once (allow 16 to 18 minutes total time for medium-rare). Makes 4 servings.

Onion-Stuffed Steak

    2 beef porterhouse steaks, cut 1½ inches thick
       (about 1½ pounds each), or beef sirloin steak,
       cut 1½ inches thick (about 2 to 2½ pounds)
    ½ cup sliced green onion
    1 large clove garlic, minced
    3 tablespoons butter or margarine
       Dash celery salt
       Dash pepper
    ¼ cup dry red wine
    2 tablespoons soy sauce
    1 cup sliced fresh mushrooms

Slash fat edges of steaks at 1-inch intervals as shown at right. Slice pockets in each side of meat, cutting almost to bone (same as for pork chops shown on page 52).

In a skillet cook onion and garlic in *1 tablespoon* of the butter or margarine. Add celery salt and pepper. Stuff pockets with onion mixture; skewer closed. Mix wine and soy sauce; brush on meat. Grill over *medium-hot* coals for 8 to 10 minutes; brush often with soy mixture. Turn; grill 8 to 10 minutes more for rare. Brush steak often with the soy mixture.

In a small skillet cook mushrooms in the remaining 2 tablespoons butter or margarine till tender. Carve steaks across the grain as shown on page 26. Pass mushrooms to spoon atop slices of steak. Makes 6 servings.

To Slash Edges of Steaks for Cooking

To prevent meat from curling during broiling or grilling, slash the fatty edges with a sharp boner/utility knife. Place steak on a cutting board. Without cutting into meat, carefully slash the fat edge at 1-inch intervals.

Saucy Orange Pork Steaks

    4 pork blade or arm steaks, cut ½ inch thick
       (2 pounds)
    2 tablespoons cooking oil or shortening
       Salt and pepper
    4 medium sweet potatoes, peeled and cut
       lengthwise into ½-inch-thick slices
    1 medium orange, peeled and thinly sliced
    ⅓ cup packed brown sugar
    ⅓ cup orange juice
    ⅛ teaspoon ground cinnamon
    ⅛ teaspoon ground nutmeg
       Dash salt

Cut each pork steak into 2 serving-size pieces. In skillet slowly brown meat on both sides in hot oil or shortening. Sprinkle with some salt and pepper. In 12x7½x2-inch baking dish arrange sweet potatoes. Place orange slices atop potatoes; cover with pork steaks.

For sauce, combine brown sugar, orange juice, cinnamon, nutmeg, and salt; pour over steaks. Cover; bake in 350° oven for 45 minutes. Uncover; continue baking about 30 minutes more or till meat and sweet potatoes are tender. Transfer to platter; spoon sauce over. Garnish with green onion brushes or fruit decorations shown on pages 18-21, if desired. Makes 8 servings.

Meats & Main Dishes

London Broil

1 1- to 1¼-pound beef flank steak
⅓ cup cooking oil
1 teaspoon vinegar
1 small clove garlic, minced
   Salt
   Freshly ground pepper

Score steak on both sides. Place meat in a plastic bag; set in a deep bowl. Combine oil, vinegar, and garlic; pour over meat. Close bag. Let stand at room temperature 2 to 3 hours; turning several times.

Remove meat from marinade; place on an unheated rack in a broiler pan. Broil 3 inches from heat 4 to 5 minutes. Sprinkle with salt and pepper. Turn; broil 4 to 5 minutes more for medium rare. Sprinkle with salt and pepper. Carve flank steak as shown on page 26. Makes 4 or 5 servings.

Beef Stroganoff

1 pound beef tenderloin, sirloin,
   or round steak
1 tablespoon all-purpose flour
½ teaspoon salt
2 tablespoons butter or margarine
1½ cups sliced fresh mushrooms
½ cup chopped onion
1 clove garlic, minced
2 tablespoons butter or margarine
3 tablespoons all-purpose flour
1 tablespoon tomato paste
1 teaspoon instant beef bouillon granules
¼ teaspoon salt
1 cup dairy sour cream
2 tablespoons dry white wine
   Hot cooked noodles

Partially freeze meat; thinly slice across the grain as shown on page 49. Combine the 1 tablespoon flour and the ½ teaspoon salt; coat meat with flour mixture. In a skillet heat 2 tablespoons butter. Add meat; brown quickly on both sides. Add mushrooms, onion, and garlic; cook 3 to 4 minutes or till onion is crisp-tender. Remove meat and mushroom mixture from pan. Add 2 tablespoons butter or margarine to pan drippings; stir in 2 tablespoons of the flour. Add tomato paste, beef bouillon granules, and the ¼ teaspoon salt. Stir in 1¼ cups *water*. Cook and stir over medium-high heat till bubbly. Cook and stir 1 to 2 minutes longer. Combine sour cream and remaining 1 tablespoon flour. Return meat and mushrooms to skillet. Stir in sour cream mixture and wine. Heat through; do not boil. Serve over noodles. Makes 4 servings.

Sweet-Sour Pork

1 beaten egg
¼ cup chicken broth
¼ cup cornstarch
¼ cup all-purpose flour
1 pound boneless pork
   Cooking oil for deep fat frying
1 large green pepper, chopped
½ cup chopped carrot
1 clove garlic
2 tablespoons cooking oil
1¼ cups chicken broth
½ cup sugar
⅓ cup red wine vinegar
2 teaspoons soy sauce
2 tablespoons cornstarch

Cut meat into 1-inch cubes as shown with beef on page 49. Combine egg, the ¼ cup broth, cornstarch, flour, and ½ teaspoon *salt*. Beat till smooth. Dip pork cubes into batter. Fry in deep hot cooking oil (365°) for 5 to 6 minutes or till golden. Drain; keep warm. In a skillet cook green pepper, carrot, and garlic in hot oil till vegetables are tender but not brown. Stir in the 1¼ cups broth, sugar, wine vinegar, and soy. Bring to boiling; boil rapidly 1·minute. Blend ¼ cup *cold water* into cornstarch. Stir into vegetable mixture. Cook and stir till thickened and bubbly. Cook and stir 2 minutes more. Stir in pork cubes. Serve with hot cooked rice, if desired. Serves 4 to 6.

Shish Kabobs

1½ pounds boneless beef or lamb
¾ cup chopped onion
⅓ cup lemon juice
3 tablespoons olive oil
¾ teaspoon dried thyme, crushed
12 large fresh mushrooms
2 medium green peppers, cut into 1½-inch pieces
3 medium tomatoes, quartered

Cut meat into 1-inch cubes as shown with beef on page 49. For marinade, in a bowl combine onion, lemon juice, olive oil, thyme, 1 teaspoon *salt*, and ¼ teaspoon *pepper*. Add meat. Cover and refrigerate several hours or overnight. Drain meat, reserving marinade. Pour some boiling water over mushrooms and green peppers in a bowl. Let vegetables stand 1 to 2 minutes; drain. Thread meat on skewers alternately with tomatoes, green pepper, and mushrooms. Grill over *medium* coals about 25 minutes, brushing with marinade and turning skewers often. (For firm-cooked tomatoes, grill on separate skewers 8 to 10 minutes.) Makes 6 servings.

Swiss Steak

1½ pounds beef round steak, cut ¾ inch thick
3 tablespoons all-purpose flour
2 tablespoons shortening
1 16-ounce can tomatoes, cut up
1 small onion, sliced
1 stalk celery, sliced
1 medium carrot, thinly sliced
½ teaspoon Worcestershire sauce
Hot cooked rice or noodles

Cut meat into 6 serving-size pieces. Combine flour and 1 teaspoon *salt*; pound *2 tablespoons* of flour mixture into meat as shown with veal steak at right. In a 10-inch skillet brown meat on both sides in hot shortening. Drain off excess fat. Add *undrained* tomatoes, onion, celery, carrot, and Worcestershire sauce. Cover and cook over low heat about 1¼ hours or till meat is tender. Remove meat to serving platter; keep warm. Skim excess fat from tomato mixture. Combine ¼ cup *cold water* and remaining flour mixture; stir into tomato mixture. Cook and stir till thickened. Cook and stir 1 minute more. Serve meat and sauce with rice or noodles. Serves 6.

Oven Swiss Steak: Prepare Swiss Steak as above, *except* after browning meat in hot shortening, transfer meat to a 12x7½x2-inch baking dish. Stir remaining flour mixture into pan drippings in skillet. Stir in *undrained* tomatoes, onion, celery, carrot, and Worcestershire sauce. Cook and stir till thickened and bubbly. Pour over meat in baking dish. Bake, uncovered, in a 350° oven for 1 hour 20 minutes or till meat is tender. Serve with hot cooked rice or noodles.

Crockery Cooker Directions: Prepare Swiss Steak as above, *except* cut meat to fit an electric slow crockery cooker. After browning meat in hot shortening, transfer meat to crockery cooker. Stir the remaining flour mixture into pan drippings in skillet. Stir in *undrained* tomatoes, onion, celery, carrot, and Worcestershire sauce. Cook and stir till thickened and bubbly; pour over meat in crockery cooker. Cover and cook on low-heat setting for 8 to 10 hours. Season to taste with *salt* and *pepper*. Serve with hot cooked rice or noodles.

Peppery Lamb with Green Onions

¾ pound boneless lamb
2 tablespoons soy sauce
1 tablespoon dry sherry
2 tablespoons cooking oil
2 cloves garlic, minced
8 green onions, bias sliced into 1½-inch lengths

Partially freeze lamb; slice thinly into bite-size strips as shown with beef at right. In a small bowl combine the soy sauce, dry sherry, and ½ teaspoon *pepper*. Set aside. Preheat a wok or large skillet over high heat; add cooking oil. Stir-fry garlic in hot oil 30 seconds. Add meat; stir-fry 1½ minutes. Add green onions and soy mixture; stir-fry about 1½ minutes or till green onion is crisp-tender. Serve at once. Makes 3 or 4 servings.

To Pound Meat to Tenderize

Place meat between two pieces of clear plastic wrap. Using the fine-toothed side of a meat mallet, pound each piece to a ⅛-inch thickness, working from the center to edges.

To Cut Meat into Cubes

To cut a roast or round steak into 1-inch cubes, trim excess fat with sharp utility knife. Cut meat into 1-inch slices, as shown with round steak. (If using a roast, cut each slice in half lengthwise.) Then cut the slices into 1-inch pieces.

To Slice Meat for Stir-Frying

To thinly slice meat, partially freeze it (or partially thaw frozen meat) first. Allow 45 to 60 minutes to partially freeze a 1-inch-thick piece of meat. Use one hand to firmly hold the meat. Hold a sharp chef's knife in the other hand and cut meat, across the grain, into very thin strips, as shown.

Stir-Fried Pork with Mandarin Oranges

    1 pound boneless pork
    2 tablespoons soy sauce
    2 teaspoons cornstarch
    1 teaspoon shredded orange peel
    ½ cup orange juice
    2 tablespoons cooking oil
    1 teaspoon grated gingerroot
    2 cups fresh pea pods or one 16-ounce package
        frozen pea pods, thawed
    1 11-ounce can mandarin orange sections, drained

Partially freeze pork; slice thinly into bite-size strips as shown on page 49. Blend soy sauce into cornstarch; stir in orange peel and juice. Set mixture aside. Preheat a wok or large skillet over high heat; add cooking oil. Stir-fry gingerroot in hot oil 30 seconds. Add pea pods; stir-fry 2 minutes for fresh pea pods or 1 minute for thawed frozen pea pods. Remove pea pods. (Add more oil, if necessary.) Add *half* of the pork to *hot* wok or skillet; stir-fry 2 to 3 minutes. Remove meat from wok. Stir-fry remaining pork 2 to 3 minutes. Return all pork to wok or skillet. Stir soy sauce mixture; stir into pork. Cook and stir till thickened and bubbly. Stir in pea pods; cover and cook 1 minute more. Remove from heat; stir in mandarin oranges. Serve at once. Garnish with additional pea pods and a green onion brush as shown on page 18, if desired. Serves 4.

Home-Style Stew

    1½ pounds stew meat, cut into 1-inch cubes
        (choose from beef, pork, lamb, or veal)
    2 tablespoons cooking oil
    1 clove garlic, minced
    1 bay leaf
    1 teaspoon prepared mustard or horseradish
    ¾ teaspoon dried herb, crushed (choose from basil,
        oregano, marjoram, or thyme)
    1 10½-ounce can condensed beef broth
    5 cups fresh vegetables cut into 1-inch pieces
        (any combination of peeled potatoes, carrots,
        celery, rutabagas, turnips, onions, or parsnips)
    2 tablespoons all-purpose flour

In a large saucepan brown meat, half at a time, in hot oil. Return all meat to pan. Stir in garlic, bay leaf, mustard or horseradish, choice of herb, 1 teaspon *salt*, and ¼ teaspoon *pepper*. Add beef broth. Bring to boiling. Reduce heat; cover and simmer till meat is nearly tender (about 30 minutes for pork, lamb, or veal; about 1¼ hours for beef). Add choice of vegetables. Cover and simmer about 30 minutes or till meat and vegetables are tender. Blend ¼ cup *cold water* and flour; stir into stew. Cook and stir till thickened and bubbly. Cook and stir 1 minute more. Remove bay leaf; discard. Serves 6.

Pictured: **Stir-Fried Pork with Mandarin Oranges.**

Chimichangas

    2 pounds beef stew meat
    2 cloves garlic, minced
    2 tablespoons chili powder
    1 tablespoon vinegar
    2 teaspoons dried oregano, crushed
    1 teaspoon ground cumin
    12 10-inch flour tortillas
        Cooking oil for frying
    2 cups shredded lettuce
    2 cups Guacamole (see recipe, page 38)

In saucepan combine meat, garlic, chili powder, vinegar, oregano, cumin, 1½ cups *water*, 1 teaspoon *salt*, and ⅛ teaspoon *pepper*. Bring to boiling. Cover; reduce heat. Simmer 2 hours or till meat is very tender. Uncover; boil rapidly 15 minutes or until water has almost evaporated. Watch closely and stir near end of cooking time so meat doesn't stick. Remove from heat. Using 2 forks, shred meat very fine.

Meanwhile, wrap tortillas in foil; heat in 350° oven 15 minutes. Spoon about ¼ cup meat mixture onto each tortilla, near one edge. Fold edge nearest filling up and over filling just till mixture is covered. Fold in the two sides envelope fashion; roll up. Fasten tortilla with wooden pick, if needed. In skillet or saucepan fry meat-filled tortillas in ½ inch hot oil 1 minute on each side or till golden brown. Drain on paper toweling. Keep warm in 300° oven while frying remaining. Serve with lettuce and Guacamole, if desired. Makes 12.

Spicy Roasted Pork Chops

    1 cup chopped onion
    1 clove garlic, minced
    2 tablespoons cooking oil
    ¾ cup catsup
    ¼ cup lemon juice
    3 tablespoons sugar
    2 tablespoons Worcestershire sauce
    1 tablespoon prepared mustard
    1 teaspoon salt
    ¼ teaspoon bottled hot pepper sauce
    6 pork loin chops or rib chops, cut
        1¼ to 1½ inches thick

For sauce, cook the onion and garlic in hot cooking oil till tender. Stir in catsup, lemon juice, sugar, Worcestershire sauce, mustard, salt, and hot pepper sauce. Simmer, uncovered, for 5 minutes, stirring once or twice.

Place pork chops in a wire grill basket. Grill chops over *medium* coals about 25 minutes. Turn meat and grill about 20 minutes more or till done, brushing the chops with sauce occasionally. Makes 6 servings.

Wild Rice-Stuffed Chops

¼ cup wild rice
¾ cup water
3 tablespoons dry sherry
¾ cup chopped fresh mushrooms
3 tablespoons chopped onion
½ teaspoon salt
¼ teaspoon pepper
¼ teaspoon ground sage
2 tablespoons butter or margarine
¼ cup chopped almonds
6 pork loin rib chops, cut 1½ inches thick (4 pounds)
¼ cup sliced fresh mushrooms
2 tablespoons chopped onion
2 tablespoons butter or margarine
2 teaspoons cornstarch
⅛ teaspoon salt
⅛ teaspoon dry mustard
Dash pepper
1 cup beef broth

Run cold water over wild rice in a strainer for 1 to 2 minutes, lifting rice with fingers. In saucepan combine wild rice, ¾ cup water, and sherry. Bring to boiling; reduce heat. Cover and simmer about 40 minutes or till rice is tender. Drain rice, if necessary.

Meanwhile, in a skillet cook the ¾ cup chopped mushrooms, the 3 tablespoons onion, the ½ teaspoon salt, the ¼ teaspoon pepper, and the sage in 2 tablespoons butter or margarine till onion is tender but not brown. Remove from heat. Stir in wild rice and almonds.

Make a pocket in each chop by cutting from fat side almost to bone edge as shown at right. Lightly spoon ¼ *cup* of the wild rice mixture into each chop. Close the opening with wooden picks. Place stuffed chops on unheated rack of broiler pan. Broil chops 5 inches from heat about 18 minutes. Sprinkle chops lightly with salt and pepper. Turn chops and broil 18 minutes more or till chops are done.

Meanwhile, prepare sauce. In saucepan cook ¼ cup sliced mushrooms and 2 tablespoons chopped onion in 2 tablespoons butter till tender. Stir in cornstarch, the ⅛ teaspoon salt, the dry mustard, and the dash pepper. Add beef broth all at once. Cook and stir till thickened and bubbly. Cook 2 minutes more. Remove from heat. To serve, remove wooden picks from chops. Spoon sauce over. Makes 6 servings.

To Make Pockets in Pork Chops

1

To make a pocket in the chop, first cut a 1½- to 2-inch-long slit in fatty side of chop, as shown, with a sharp steak knife.

Insert the knife into slit, drawing from side to side to form a larger pocket inside the chop. Try not to make the initial slit much larger (so it will be easier to close).

2

After filling each chop with stuffing mixture as directed in recipe, securely close the pocket opening with 1 or 2 wooden picks inserted diagonally, as shown. This is done to help ensure that the stuffing stays inside the pocket during baking.

Ham Slice with Orange-Rum Sauce

- ¼ cup frozen orange juice concentrate, thawed
- ¼ cup rum
- 2 tablespoons brown sugar
- 2 tablespoons honey
- ¼ teaspoon ground ginger
- ¼ teaspoon ground cinnamon
- 1 1½- to 2-pound fully cooked ham center slice, cut 1 inch thick

For sauce, combine thawed concentrate, rum, brown sugar, honey, ginger, and cinnamon. Simmer, uncovered, about 5 minutes, stirring once or twice.

Slash fat edge of ham to prevent curling (same as for steaks shown on page 47). Grill over *medium* coals 10 to 15 minutes; brush occasionally with sauce. Turn; grill 10 to 15 minutes more, basting occasionally. Heat remaining sauce on edge of grill. Cut ham into slices and pour sauce over. Makes 6 to 8 servings.

Ham with Plum Sauce

- 1 5- to 7-pound fully cooked ham shank portion
- ⅓ cup honey
- 2 tablespoons soy sauce
- 2 tablespoons lemon juice
  Plum Sauce

Place ham on rack in shallow baking pan. Insert meat thermometer. Bake, uncovered, in a 325° oven for 1½ to 1¾ hours or till meat thermometer registers 130°. Stir together honey, soy sauce, and lemon juice; baste ham with honey mixture. Continue baking and basting occasionally till thermometer registers 140°. Carve ham shank as shown on page 27. Serve with Plum Sauce. Makes 12 to 16 servings.

Plum Sauce: In liquid measure drain one 16-ounce can whole, unpitted *purple plums*, reserving *¼ cup* of the syrup. Remove pits and force plums through sieve. In a saucepan combine sieved plums, reserved syrup, ¼ teaspoon finely shredded *orange peel*, 3 tablespoons *orange juice*, 2 tablespoons *sugar*, ½ teaspoon *Worcestershire sauce*, and ¼ teaspoon *ground cinnamon*. Bring mixture to boiling; reduce heat. Cover and simmer 10 minutes.

Ham with Spiced Cider Sauce

A brown sugar and ground clove mixture is patted on the ham to create a delicious crust—

- 1 5- to 7-pound fully cooked ham, rump half
- 4 cups apple cider or apple juice
- 2 medium onions, quartered
- 2 tablespoons lemon juice
- 1 beaten egg
- ⅓ cup packed brown sugar
- 1 teaspoon ground cloves
- ½ cup raisins
- ⅔ cup orange marmalade
- 2 tablespoons cornstarch
- 1 tablespoon lemon juice
- ¼ teaspoon ground allspice

Place ham, fat side up, on rack in shallow roasting pan. Score in diamonds as shown below on ham shank. Combine cider, onions, and the 2 tablespoons lemon juice. Add to roasting pan. Bake in 325° oven for 1¾ hours. Brush the fat surface of ham with beaten egg. Combine brown sugar and cloves; pat onto the fat surface of ham. Insert meat thermometer, making sure tip does not rest on bone or fat. Return ham to oven. Continue baking for 30 minutes or till thermometer registers 140°, basting ham occasionally with cider mixture. Remove from oven. Transfer ham to serving platter; keep warm.

Strain cider mixture; skim fat. Reserve *1 cup* of strained liquid. Combine the reserved cider mixture, raisins, marmalade, and 1 cup *water*. Combine cornstarch, the 1 tablespoon lemon juice, and allspice; stir into raisin mixture. Cook and stir till bubbly. Cook and stir 2 minutes more; keep sauce warm.

To carve ham, place cut side down on cutting board. Cut along bone from top to board to remove a large boneless piece. Place this boneless piece of ham cut side down on the cutting board and slice meat across the grain. To carve meat remaining on the bone, make horizontal slices. Serve the warm fruit sauce with slices of ham. Makes 12 servings.

To Score Ham

Remove the skin from the meaty portion of ham with a sharp utility knife, being careful not to cut away fat.

To score ham fat, use a sharp knife to make diagonal ¼-inch-deep cuts across ham in a diamond pattern. A flexible strip makes a handy cutting guide, as shown.

Brisket Carbonnade

- 1 3- to 4-pound fresh beef brisket
- 1 12-ounce can (1½ cups) beer
- 1 tablespoon brown sugar
- 2 teaspoons instant beef bouillon granules
- 4 whole black peppercorns or ⅛ teaspoon cracked pepper
- 1 clove garlic, minced
- 1 bay leaf
- ¼ teaspoon dried thyme, crushed
- 3 medium onions, sliced
- ¼ cup all-purpose flour

Trim excess fat from brisket. Place in a 13x9x2-inch baking pan. Reserve ⅓ *cup* of the beer. Combine remaining beer, brown sugar, bouillon granules, peppercorns, garlic, bay leaf, and thyme; pour over meat. Cover brisket with onion slices; sprinkle lightly with some *salt*. Cover with foil. Bake in a 350° oven for 3 to 3½ hours or till meat is tender. Remove meat to a platter; keep warm. Skim off excess fat from pan juices; remove bay leaf and discard. In a saucepan cook juices down to *2 cups*. Combine reserved beer and flour; stir into pan juices. Cook and stir till thickened and bubbly. Cook and stir 1 minute more. Slice meat across grain as shown on page 26. Pass gravy with slices of meat. Makes 10 servings.

Mustard-Glazed Country Ribs

Country-style ribs are the meatiest of all pork ribs. They're cut from the shoulder end of the back ribs, then split open—

- 4 pounds pork country-style ribs
- ½ cup sugar
- ½ cup vinegar
- ⅓ cup prepared mustard
- ¼ cup chopped onion
- 2 cloves garlic, minced
- 2 teaspoons celery seed
- 1 teaspoon ground turmeric
- 1 medium onion, thinly sliced

In large saucepan or Dutch oven pour enough *water* over ribs to cover. Bring to boiling; reduce heat. Cover; simmer for 45 minutes. Drain well.

Meanwhile, in small saucepan combine sugar, vinegar, mustard, chopped onion, garlic, celery seed, turmeric, and 1 teaspoon *salt*. Bring to boiling, stirring till sugar dissolves. Place ribs, meaty side up, in shallow roasting pan. Brush some of the mustard mixture over ribs. Roast, uncovered, in 350° oven about 15 minutes. Top with sliced onion and some additional sauce. Roast 15 minutes more, brushing occasionally with mustard sauce. Transfer ribs to warm platter. Reheat remaining sauce and pass with ribs. Makes 4 to 6 servings.

Short Rib-Vegetable Stew

- 2 pounds beef short ribs, cut into serving-size pieces
- 1 tablespoon cooking oil
- 2½ cups water
- 1 16-ounce can tomatoes, cut up
- 1 medium onion, chopped (½ cup)
- 1 clove garlic, minced
- 1½ teaspoons instant vegetable or beef bouillon granules
- 1 teaspoon salt
- ½ teaspoon dried basil, crushed
  Dash pepper
- 1 pound tiny new potatoes (10 to 12)
- 3 carrots, cut into ½-inch pieces
- 1 8½-ounce can peas, drained
- 1 8½-ounce can lima beans, drained
- 2 tablespoons snipped parsley

Trim excess fat from ribs. In Dutch oven slowly brown ribs in hot oil on all sides; drain off fat. Add water, *undrained* tomatoes, onion, garlic, bouillon granules, salt, basil, and pepper; bring to boiling. Reduce heat; cover and simmer for 2 hours or till meat is nearly tender.

Skim off fat. Peel strip around center of each potato, if desired. Add potatoes, carrots, peas, lima beans, and parsley to Dutch oven. Cover and simmer about 30 minutes more or till vegetables are tender. Makes 6 servings.

Swedish Burgers

- 1 beaten egg
- 1 cup dairy sour cream
- 1 cup soft bread crumbs
- ½ cup finely chopped onion
- ½ teaspoon dry mustard
- ½ teaspoon ground mace
- 1 pound ground beef
- ½ pound ground pork
- 8 kaiser rolls, split and toasted
  Lettuce leaves

In a bowl combine egg and ½ *cup* of the sour cream; stir in bread crumbs, onion, mustard, mace, and 1 teaspoon *salt*. Add ground meats; mix well. Shape into eight ½-inch-thick patties. In large skillet brown slowly on both sides. Cover; continue cooking over low heat for 15 minutes. To serve, place patties on roll halves; spread with remaining sour cream. Top with lettuce; cover with tops of rolls. Serves 8.

Italian Meatball Sandwiches

2 beaten eggs
3 tablespoons milk
½ cup fine dry bread crumbs
½ teaspoon salt
⅛ teaspoon pepper
1 pound ground beef
1 tablespoon cooking oil
½ pound bulk Italian sausage
½ cup chopped onion
½ cup chopped green pepper
1 cup water
1 8-ounce can tomato sauce
1 6-ounce can tomato paste
2 teaspoons sugar
1 teaspoon garlic salt
½ teaspoon dried oregano, crushed
¼ teaspoon dried parsley flakes
8 French-style rolls
   Grated Parmesan cheese

In bowl combine eggs and milk. Stir in bread crumbs, salt, and pepper. Add ground beef; mix well. Shape meat mixture into 1-inch meatballs as shown at right (should make 24 meatballs). In a large skillet brown meatballs in cooking oil; remove meatballs.

In same skillet cook sausage, onion, and green pepper till sausage is browned. Drain off fat. Stir in water, tomato sauce, tomato paste, sugar, garlic salt, oregano, and parsley flakes. Return meatballs to skillet. Cover; simmer about 15 minutes, stirring occasionally. Cut a thin slice from tops of rolls (reserve for another use). Hollow out bottoms, leaving a ¼-inch wall. Fill each roll with *3 meatballs* and some of the tomato mixture. Sprinkle with Parmesan cheese, if desired. Makes 8 servings.

Basic Oven Meatballs

To save time, make these ahead and freeze for later use—

1 beaten egg
¼ cup milk
1 cup soft bread crumbs (about 1½ slices)
2 tablespoons chopped onion
¾ teaspoon salt
1 pound ground beef

In bowl combine egg and milk. Stir in bread crumbs, onion, and salt. Add ground beef; mix well. Shape into 1-inch meatballs as shown at right. Place in shallow baking pan. Bake in 375° oven for 25 to 30 minutes. Makes 24 meatballs.

Note: When freezing meatballs, arrange cooked and cooled meatballs in a single layer on a baking sheet or in a shallow pan so that the edges do not touch. Place the baking sheet or pan in the freezer. As soon as the meatballs are frozen firm, transfer them to moisture-vaporproof freezer bags or containers and seal. Return to freezer.

Quick Meatball Minestrone

24 Basic Oven Meatballs (recipe at left)
1 15-ounce can great northern beans
1 tablespoon instant beef bouillon granules
1 tablespoon minced dried onion
1 teaspoon dried basil, crushed
1 large bay leaf
½ of a 7-ounce package spaghetti, broken into
   2-inch lengths
1 10-ounce package frozen mixed vegetables
1 16-ounce can tomatoes, cut up
1 teaspoon sugar
   Grated Parmesan cheese

In 4-quart Dutch oven combine meatballs, *undrained* beans, bouillon granules, onion, basil, bay leaf, and 4 cups *water*. Bring to boiling. Add spaghetti and vegetables. Cover; simmer 20 minutes or till spaghetti is tender. Stir in *undrained* tomatoes and sugar. Heat through. Remove bay leaf; discard. Sprinkle individual servings with Parmesan cheese. Serves 8.

To Shape Meatballs

1

Shaping 1-inch meatballs of uniform size is easily done by gently patting the meat mixture into a 1-inch-thick rectangle on waxed paper. Cut the rectangle into 1-inch cubes, as shown, with a sharp utility knife. Roll each cube into a ball.

2

Or, shape meat mixture into a roll, as shown. The diameter of the roll should be the same size as the diameter you want for the meatballs. Slice the roll into equal lengths and roll into meatballs. (Wet hands with cold water before shaping meatballs to help prevent meat from sticking to your hands.)

Pita Burgers

     2 cups shredded lettuce
     1 medium cucumber, seeded and finely chopped
     1 8-ounce carton plain yogurt
     1 tablespoon sesame seed, toasted
    ½ cup chopped onion
     1 clove garlic, minced
     1 teaspoon salt
     1 teaspoon dried oregano, crushed
    ½ teaspoon dried basil, crushed
    ¼ teaspoon dried rosemary, crushed
    1½ pounds ground beef or ground lamb
     6 pita bread rounds

Combine lettuce, cucumber, yogurt, and sesame seed; set aside. Combine onion, garlic, salt, oregano, basil, and rosemary. Add ground beef or ground lamb; mix well. Shape into 6 thin patties, each 5 inches in diameter.

Grill over *medium* coals till desired doneness, turning once (allow 10 to 12 minutes total time for medium). Or, broil 3 inches from heat till desired doneness, turning once (allow 8 to 10 minutes total time for medium). Split each bread round to make a pocket; place a cooked meat patty inside. Spoon in some lettuce mixture. Makes 6 servings.

Cheesy Beef Chowder

     1 pound ground beef
     2 medium potatoes, peeled and cubed (2 cups)
    ½ cup chopped celery
    ¼ cup chopped onion
     2 tablespoons chopped green pepper
     1 tablespoon instant beef bouillon granules
    1½ cups water
    2½ cups milk
     3 tablespoons all-purpose flour
     1 cup shredded cheddar cheese (4 ounces)
       Shredded cheddar cheese (optional)
       Snipped parsley or chives (optional)

In a 3-quart saucepan brown ground beef; drain off fat. Stir in potatoes, celery, onion, green pepper, beef bouillon granules, and water. Cover and cook 15 to 20 minutes or till vegetables are tender.

Blend ½ *cup* of the milk with the flour. Add to saucepan along with remaining milk. Cook and stir till thickened and bubbly. Cook and stir 1 minute more. Add the 1 cup shredded cheese; heat and stir just till cheese melts. Garnish with additional shredded cheese and snipped parsley or chives, if desired. Makes 6 to 8 servings.

Cottage Cheese-Beef Bake

    3½ ounces medium noodles
     1 pound ground beef or ground pork
    ½ cup chopped onion
    ¼ cup chopped green pepper
     1 15-ounce can tomato sauce
    ½ teaspoon salt
    ½ teaspoon dried savory or marjoram, crushed
    ¼ teaspoon pepper
    1½ cups cream-style cottage cheese (12 ounces)
     1 3-ounce package cream cheese, softened
     1 egg
    ¼ cup grated Parmesan cheese

In a large saucepan cook noodles in a large amount of boiling salted water for 10 to 12 minutes or just till tender; drain. In skillet cook ground beef or ground pork, onion, and green pepper till meat is browned and vegetables are tender; drain off fat. Stir in tomato sauce, salt, savory or marjoram, pepper and the cooked noodles. Place *half* of the mixture in a 10x6x2-inch baking dish.

In a small mixer bowl combine cottage cheese, cream cheese, and egg; beat till fluffy. Spread over meat mixture in baking dish. Top with the remaining meat mixture. Sprinkle with Parmesan cheese. Bake, uncovered, in a 350° oven about 40 minutes or till heated through. Makes 6 servings.

Tortilla Enchilada Pies

     1 pound ground beef or ground pork
     1 medium onion, chopped
     1 10-ounce can (1¼ cups) enchilada sauce
     1 8¾-ounce can whole kernel corn, drained
    ⅓ cup sliced pitted ripe olives
     4 or 6 eight-inch flour tortillas
     1 16-ounce can refried beans
     4 or 6 slices tomato, halved
       Dairy sour cream (optional)
       Avocado slices (optional)

In a skillet cook ground beef or pork and onion till meat is brown and onion is tender; drain off fat. Stir in enchilada sauce, corn, and olives. Gently press *1 tortilla* in each of 4 or 6 individual casseroles or au gratin dishes, allowing tortilla to overlap sides of dish. Spread the refried beans in the bottom of each tortilla. Divide the meat mixture evenly among dishes.

Bake, uncovered, in a 350° oven for 30 minutes. Place 2 tomato half-slices atop meat in each dish. Return to oven; bake for 5 to 10 minutes more or till heated through. To serve, top each serving with a dollop of sour cream and an avocado slice, if desired. Makes 4 or 6 servings.

Manicotti

       8 manicotti shells
       1 pound ground beef or bulk Italian sausage
       2 cups water
       2 6-ounce cans tomato paste
     ½ cup chopped onion
     ⅓ cup snipped parsley
       1 large clove garlic, minced
       1 tablespoon dried basil, crushed
    1½ teaspoons salt
          Dash pepper
       2 beaten eggs
       3 cups ricotta or cream-style cottage cheese,
              drained
     ¾ cup grated Romano or Parmesan cheese
     ¼ teaspoon salt
          Dash pepper

Cook manicotti shells in a large amount of boiling salted water about 18 minutes or till tender; drain. Rinse shells in cold water; drain. Meanwhile, in large saucepan cook ground beef or sausage till browned; drain off fat. Stir in water, tomato paste, onion, *half* of the parsley, the garlic, basil, the 1½ teaspoons salt, and the dash pepper. Bring mixture to boiling; reduce heat. Simmer, uncovered, for 15 minutes, stirring mixture occasionally.

In a bowl combine eggs, ricotta or cottage cheese, *½ cup* of the Romano or Parmesan cheese, the ¼ teaspoon salt, dash pepper, and the remaining parsley. Stuff cooked manicotti shells with cheese mixture.

Pour *half* of the meat mixture into a 12x7½x2-inch baking dish. Arrange stuffed manicotti in baking dish; top with remaining meat mixture. Sprinkle with remaining Romano or Parmesan cheese. Bake, uncovered, in a 350° oven for 40 to 45 minutes or till heated through. Let stand 10 minutes before serving. Makes 6 to 8 servings.

Lasagna

       1 pound bulk pork sausage or ground beef
       1 medium onion, chopped (½ cup)
       1 clove garlic, minced
       1 16-ounce can tomatoes, cut up
       1 8-ounce can tomato sauce
       1 6-ounce can tomato paste
       2 teaspoons dried basil, crushed
       1 teaspoon salt
       1 tablespoon cooking oil
       8 ounces lasagna noodles
       2 beaten eggs
    2½ cups ricotta or cream-style cottage cheese
     ¾ cup grated Parmesan or Romano cheese
       2 tablespoons dried parsley flakes
       1 teaspoon salt
     ½ teaspoon pepper
       1 pound mozzarella cheese, thinly sliced

In a skillet cook meat, onion, and garlic till meat is brown. Drain off fat. Stir in the *undrained* tomatoes, tomato sauce, to-mato paste, basil, and the 1 teaspoon salt. Cover; simmer 15 minutes, stirring often.

Meanwhile, add the cooking oil to large amount of boiling salted water; cook noodles in the water for 10 to 12 minutes or just till tender. Drain and rinse the cooked lasagna noodles.

In bowl combine eggs, ricotta or cottage cheese, *½ cup* of the Parmesan or Romano cheese, the parsley, the 1 tea-spoon salt, and the pepper. Layer *half* of the noodles in a 13x9x2-inch baking dish; spread with *half* of the ricotta mixture. Add *half* of the mozzarella cheese and *half* of the meat sauce. Repeat layers. Sprinkle remaining Parmesan or Romano cheese atop.

Bake in a 375° oven for 30 to 35 minutes or till heated through. (Or, assemble ahead and refrigerate; bake in a 375° oven about 45 minutes or till heated through.) Let stand 10 minutes before serving. Makes 10 servings.

Pastitsio

This Greek-style casserole is layered with pasta, spiced meat, and a Parmesan-flavored custard—

       6 ounces elbow macaroni (1½ cups)
       1 beaten egg
     ⅓ cup grated Parmesan cheese
     ¼ cup milk
       1 pound ground lamb or ground beef
     ½ cup chopped onion
       1 8-ounce can tomato sauce
     ½ teaspoon salt
     ½ teaspoon ground cinnamon
     ⅛ teaspoon ground nutmeg
     ⅛ teaspoon pepper
       3 tablespoon butter or margarine
       3 tablespoon all-purpose flour
     ¼ teaspoon salt
    1½ cups milk
       1 beaten egg
     ¼ cup grated Parmesan cheese

Cook macaroni in a large amount of boiling salted water about 10 minutes or just till tender; drain. Combine cooked macaroni, 1 beaten egg, the ⅓ cup Parmesan cheese, and the ¼ cup milk; set aside.

In a skillet cook ground lamb or ground beef and onion till meat is browned and onion is tender; drain off fat. Stir in tomato sauce, the ½ teaspoon salt, the cinnamon, nutmeg, and pepper; set aside.

For sauce, in a saucepan melt butter or margarine; stir in flour and ¼ teaspoon salt. Add the 1½ cups milk all at once; cook and stir till thickened and bubbly. Remove from heat. Stir about half of the hot mixture into 1 beaten egg; return to remaining hot mixture in saucepan. Stir in the ¼ cup Parmesan cheese.

Place *half* of the macaroni mixture in an 8x8x2-inch baking dish. Spoon the meat mixture atop; add the remaining maca-roni mixture. Spread the sauce over all. Bake, uncovered, in 350° oven for 40 to 45 minutes. Let stand 10 minutes before serving. Makes 6 servings.

Meats & Main Dishes

Spaghetti Pie

The spaghetti forms the "crust" of this tasty meat pie—

- 6 ounces spaghetti
- 2 tablespoons butter or margarine
- 2 beaten eggs
- ⅓ cup grated Parmesan cheese
- 1 cup cream-style cottage cheese
- 1 pound ground beef or bulk pork sausage
- ½ cup chopped onion
- ¼ cup chopped green pepper
- 1 7½-ounce can tomatoes, cut up
- 1 6-ounce can tomato paste
- 1 teaspoon sugar
- 1 teaspoon dried oregano, crushed
- ½ teaspoon garlic salt
- ½ cup shredded mozzarella cheese

In saucepan cook spaghetti in a large amount of boiling salted water for 10 to 12 minutes or just till tender; drain (should have about 3 cups). Stir butter or margarine into hot spaghetti; stir in beaten eggs and Parmesan cheese. In a greased 10-inch pie plate form spaghetti mixture into a "crust." Spread with cottage cheese.

In skillet cook ground beef or sausage, onion, and green pepper till meat is browned and vegetables are tender. Drain off fat. Stir in *undrained* tomatoes, tomato paste, sugar, oregano, and garlic salt; heat through.

Turn meat mixture into spaghetti crust. Cover edges with foil. Bake in 350° oven for 20 minutes. Sprinkle with mozzarella cheese; bake about 5 minutes more or till cheese is melted. Makes 6 servings.

Beef-Stuffed Acorn Squash

- 1 medium acorn squash (1 pound)
  Salt
- ½ pound ground beef
- 2 tablespoons chopped onion
- 2 tablespoons chopped celery
- 2 tablespoons all-purpose flour
- ¼ teaspoon salt
- ¼ teaspoon ground sage
- ¾ cup milk
- ½ cup cooked rice
- ¼ cup shredded American cheese (1 ounce)

Cut squash in half; discard seeds as shown on page 108. Sprinkle squash with a little salt. Bake, cut side down, in 10x6x2-inch baking dish in a 350° oven for 45 to 50 minutes or till tender.

In skillet cook ground beef, onion, and celery till meat is brown. Drain off fat. Stir in flour, the ¼ teaspoon salt, and sage. Add milk. Cook and stir till thickened and bubbly. Cook and stir 1 minute more. Stir in cooked rice.

Turn squash cut side up in dish; fill with meat-rice mixture. Bake, uncovered, in a 350° oven for 30 minutes. Top with shredded cheese; bake 3 minutes more. Makes 2 servings.

Meat Loaf Wellington

- 1 beaten egg
- ¼ cup dry red wine
- ¼ cup water
- 2 cups soft bread crumbs
- 2 tablespoons finely chopped onion
- 1 teaspoon salt
- 1½ pounds ground beef
- 1 10-ounce package (6) frozen patty shells, thawed
- ¼ cup canned liver spread
- 1 beaten egg
  Wine and Olive Sauce

Combine 1 egg, wine, and water. Stir in bread crumbs, onion, and salt. Add meat; mix well. Pat into 8x4x2-inch loaf pan. Bake in 350° oven for 40 minutes. Drain off fat. Remove meat from pan. Increase oven temperature to 400°.

On a lightly floured surface press *3* patty shells together; roll to a 10x6-inch rectangle, cutting and patching as needed. Place pastry in shallow baking pan. Carefully transfer meat onto center of pastry. Spread top and sides of meat with liver spread. Press remaining patty shells together; roll to a 10x6-inch rectangle. Place over meat. Brush edges of bottom pastry with some of the remaining beaten egg. Seal top pastry to bottom; trim and reserve edges. Cut decorations from pastry trimmings; arrange atop loaf. Brush pastry with remaining beaten egg. Bake in a 400° oven for 30 to 35 minutes. Serve with Wine and Olive Sauce. Garnish with tomato roses, green onion brushes, or small cabbage flower as shown on pages 17-21, if desired. Makes 6 servings.

Wine and Olive Sauce: In a saucepan melt 2 tablespoons *butter or margarine*. Blend in 4½ teaspoons *cornstarch*. Stir in 1 cup *condensed beef broth*; cook and stir till bubbly. Stir in ¼ cup sliced pitted *ripe olives* and ¼ cup dry *red wine*; simmer for 5 minutes.

Taco Salad

1 pound ground beef
½ envelope onion soup mix (¼ cup)
¾ cup water
  Few dashes bottled hot pepper sauce
1 small head lettuce, torn into bite-size pieces
  (4 cups)
1 cup shredded cheddar cheese (4 ounces)
1 large tomato, cut into wedges
½ cup sliced pitted ripe olives
¼ cup chopped green pepper or chopped and
  seeded canned green chili peppers
  Guacamole (see recipe, page 38) or
  dairy sour cream (optional)
2 cups corn chips or broken tortilla chips
  Taco sauce (optional)

In a medium skillet brown beef; drain. Sprinkle dry onion soup mix over meat; stir in water. Simmer mixture, uncovered, about 10 minutes or till water evaporates. Stir in the hot pepper sauce.

Meanwhile, in a salad bowl combine lettuce, cheese, tomato, olives, and green pepper; toss well. Divide lettuce mixture among individual salad plates, if desired. Spoon meat mixture over lettuce; dollop with Guacamole or sour cream, if desired. Sprinkle with corn chips. Pass taco sauce, if desired. Makes 4 to 6 servings.

Beef-Macaroni Italiano

¾ cup elbow macaroni
1 tablespoon butter or margarine
2 tablespoons all-purpose flour
1 16-ounce can stewed tomatoes, cut up
1 8-ounce can tomato sauce
¼ cup dry red wine
½ envelope onion soup mix (¼ cup)
½ teaspoon dried oregano, crushed
¼ teaspoon salt
  Dash pepper
2 cups cubed cooked beef
½ cup shredded mozzarella cheese (2 ounces)
  Green pepper rings

In large kettle cook macaroni in large amount of boiling salted water till tender; drain. In saucepan melt butter; blend in flour. Stir in *undrained* stewed tomatoes, tomato sauce, wine, soup mix, oregano, salt, and pepper. Cook and stir till thickened and bubbly. Stir in cubed beef and cooked macaroni.

Spoon mixture into a 1½-quart casserole. Bake, uncovered, in a 350° oven for 20 minutes. Sprinkle with cheese; top with green pepper rings. Return to oven 5 minutes more or till cheese melts. Makes 4 or 5 servings.

Greek Salad

1 head curly endive, torn (6 cups)
½ medium head iceberg lettuce, torn (3 cups)
10 ounces cooked lamb or beef, cut into
  julienne strips (2 cups)
2 tomatoes, peeled and chopped
¾ cup cubed feta cheese
¼ cup sliced pitted ripe olives
¼ cup sliced green onion
⅔ cup olive oil or salad oil
⅓ cup white wine vinegar
½ teaspoon salt
¼ teaspoon dried oregano, crushed
⅛ teaspoon pepper
1 2-ounce can anchovy fillets, drained

In a mixing bowl toss together endive and lettuce; mound onto 6 individual salad plates. Arrange lamb or beef, tomatoes, feta cheese, olives, and onion atop salad greens.

To make dressing, in a screw-top jar combine oil, vinegar, salt, oregano, and pepper. Cover; shake well to mix. Pour dressing over salads. Top salads with the anchovy fillets. Makes 6 servings.

Cheddar Ham and Mac Salad

3 cups medium shell macaroni
2 cups cubed cheddar cheese
2 cups cubed fully cooked ham
½ cup chopped celery
½ cup chopped green pepper
¼ cup chopped onion
¼ cup snipped parsley
1¼ cups mayonnaise or salad dressing
1 cup dairy sour cream
½ cup sweet pickle relish
4 teaspoons vinegar
2 teaspoons prepared mustard
½ teaspoon salt
  Green pepper rings (optional)

In a large kettle cook macaroni in a large amount of boiling salted water till tender; drain. Cool to room temperature. Toss with cheese, ham, celery, green pepper, onion, and parsley.

In a mixing bowl combine mayonnaise or salad dressing and sour cream; stir in pickle relish, vinegar, mustard, and salt. Toss with macaroni mixture. Cover; chill several hours. Serve in lettuce-lined bowl. Garnish with green pepper rings as shown on page 99, if desired. Makes 6 servings.

for a Special Occasion

Seasoned Roast Lamb

    1   5- to 6-pound leg of lamb
    1   tablespoon olive oil
    1   tablespoon dried rosemary, crushed
    ½   cup dry white wine or vermouth
    ¼   cup grated Romano or Parmesan cheese

Remove excess fat and thin fat covering from surface of meat. Rub outside of meat with olive oil. Sprinkle with rosemary, 1 teaspoon *salt*, and ¼ teaspoon *pepper*; rub into meat.

Place meat on rack in shallow roasting pan. Insert meat thermometer in thickest portion of meat. Roast, uncovered, in a 400° oven for 1½ to 2 hours for medium-rare or till thermometer registers 145°. Remove meat; cover with foil to keep warm. Remove excess fat from pan, if necessary. Add wine to roasting pan, stirring and scraping crusty bits off bottom of pan. Cook and stir till bubbly. Continue cooking about 3 minutes or till slightly thickened. Sprinkle cheese over meat. Carve leg of lamb as shown on pages 28-29. Pass pan juices and sprinkle with additional cheese, if desired. Garnish with onion flower shown on page 16, if desired. Serves 10 to 12.

Seasoned Roast Beef: Trim excess fat from one 4- to 5-pound boneless *beef rib roast*. Prepare as directed above. Roast, uncovered, in a 400° oven for 1½ to 2 hours for medium-rare or till thermometer registers 145°. Continue as directed above. Carve roast, same as for rolled rib roast, shown on page 24.

Pork Crown Roast with Apricot Stuffing

    1   5½- to 6-pound pork rib crown roast
          (12 to 16 ribs)
    1   tablespoon sugar
    1   teaspoon instant chicken bouillon granules
    ¼   cup snipped dried apricots
    4   cups dry whole wheat bread crumbs (5½ slices)
    1   large apple, peeled, cored, and chopped
    ½   teaspoon finely shredded orange peel
    ½   teaspoon ground sage
    ¼   teaspoon ground cinnamon
    ½   cup chopped celery
    ¼   cup chopped onion
    ¼   cup butter or margarine
    ¼   cup orange juice
    1   tablespoon light corn syrup
    ½   teaspoon soy sauce

Place roast, bone tips up, on rack in shallow roasting pan. Season with a little salt and pepper. Make a ball of aluminum foil and press into cavity to hold open. Wrap bone tips with foil. Insert meat thermometer, making sure bulb does not touch bone. Roast in 325° oven 2½ hours.

Meanwhile, prepare stuffing. Dissolve sugar and bouillon granules in ¾ cup *hot water*; pour over apricots. Let stand 5 minutes. In large bowl combine bread cubes, apple, orange peel, sage, cinnamon, ½ teaspoon *salt*, and ⅛ teaspoon *pepper*. Cook celery and onion in butter or margarine till tender; add to bread mixture. Add apricot mixture; toss lightly to moisten. (If desired, add ¼ cup additional water for a moister stuffing.)

Remove all foil from roast. Pack stuffing lightly into center of roast, mounding high. Combine orange juice, corn syrup, and soy sauce; spoon some over meat. Roast, uncovered, 45 to 60 minutes more or till thermometer registers 170°; baste occasionally with orange juice mixture. Carefully transfer to platter. Garnish with onion flowers or fruit decorations shown on pages 16-21, if desired. Carve crown roast between ribs as shown on page 25. Makes 12 to 16 servings.

Chateaubriand with Béarnaise Sauce

    1   1½- to 2-pound center-cut beef tenderloin
    2   tablespoons butter or margarine, softened
    3   tablespoons tarragon vinegar
    1   teaspoon finely chopped green onion or shallot
    4   whole black peppercorns, crushed
    ¼   teaspoon dried tarragon, crushed
    ¼   teaspoon dried chervil, crushed
    ½   cup butter or margarine, softened
    4   egg yolks
    ¼   teaspoon dried tarragon, crushed

Place meat on rack in shallow roasting pan. Spread with 2 tablespoons butter. Insert meat thermometer. Roast in 425° oven for 40 to 45 minutes or till thermometer registers 140° (outside will be browned; the inside, rare). Remove to serving platter; keep warm. In a small heavy saucepan combine vinegar, green onion, peppercorns, the ¼ teaspoon tarragon, and the chervil. Simmer, uncovered, about 5 minutes or till liquid is reduced by half. Strain; stir in 1 tablespoon *cold water*.

Divide the ½ cup butter into *three portions*. Add one portion to vinegar mixture; stir in egg yolks. Cook and stir over *low* heat till butter melts. Add another portion of the butter and continue stirring. As mixture thickens and butter melts, add remaining butter; stir constantly. When butter is melted, remove from heat. Stir in the remaining ¼ teaspoon tarragon. Serve sauce with meat. Garnish with fluted mushrooms or green onion brushes shown on pages 16-18, if desired. Makes 5 or 6 servings.

Pictured: **Seasoned Roast Lamb.**

Meats & Main Dishes

Beef Wellington

- 1 4-pound beef tenderloin
- 2 cups all-purpose flour
- ½ teaspoon salt
- ⅔ cup shortening
- ⅓ to ½ cup cold water
- 1 4¾-ounce can liver pâté (⅔ cup)
- 1 beaten egg
- 1½ cups water
- 2 teaspoons instant beef bouillon granules
- ¼ cup all-purpose flour
- ⅓ cup burgundy
- ½ teaspoon dried basil, crushed

Place beef on rack in shallow roasting pan. Insert meat thermometer. Roast at 425° till thermometer registers 130°, about 45 minutes. Remove from pan; cool. Reserve drippings.

Stir together 2 cups flour and the ½ teaspoon salt; cut in shortening till size of small peas. Add the ⅓ to ½ cup cold water, 1 tablespoon at a time, tossing with fork till all is moistened. Form into ball. On floured surface roll to a 14x12-inch rectangle; spread with pâté to within ½ inch of edges.

Center meat atop pastry. Overlap long sides of pastry to cover roast. Brush on egg; seal. Trim excess pastry from ends; fold up. Brush on egg; seal. Place, seam down, on greased baking sheet. Reroll trimmings; make cutouts. Place on meat; brush remaining egg over pastry. Bake in a 425° oven for 35 minutes (meat will be rare). Heat and stir the reserved drippings with the 1½ cups water and bouillon granules till granules dissolve. Mix ½ cup *cold water* with ¼ cup flour; stir into hot mixture along with burgundy and basil. Cook and stir till mixture is bubbly. Cook and stir 1 minute more. Pass gravy. Garnish with green onion brushes or tomato roses as shown on pages 18-21, if desired. Serves 12.

Standing Rib Roast with Yorkshire Pudding

- 1 4-pound beef rib roast
- 4 eggs
- 2 cups milk
- 2 cups all-purpose flour
- 1 teaspoon salt

Place meat, fat side up, in a 15½x10½x2-inch roasting pan. Insert meat thermometer. Roast in 325° oven about 2¼ hours for rare or till thermometer registers 140°; about 3 hours for medium (160°); or about 3¼ hours for well-done (170°). Remove meat from pan. Cover with foil; keep warm. Reserve ¼ cup drippings in pan. Increase oven temperature to 400°.

Beat eggs at low speed of electric mixer for ½ minute. Add milk; beat 15 seconds. Add flour and salt; beat 2 minutes or till smooth. Pour over drippings in pan. Bake in 400° oven 35 to 40 minutes. Cut into squares; serve at once with roast. Carve roast as shown on page 25. Makes 10 servings.

Steak au Poivré

- 2 teaspoons whole black peppercorns
- 4 beef top loin steaks, cut 1 inch thick (2 pounds)
- 2 tablespoons butter or margarine
- 1 tablespoon olive oil or cooking oil
- ¼ cup cognac or other brandy
- ¼ cup beef broth

Coarsely crack the peppercorns with mortar and pestle. Slash fat edge of steaks at 1-inch intervals as shown on page 47. Sprinkle one side of each steak with ¼ teaspoon of the cracked peppercorns; rub over meat and press into surface. Repeat on other side of steaks. Let steaks stand at room temperature for 30 minutes.

In a 12-inch skillet or blazer pan of chafing dish, heat butter or margarine with olive oil. Cook steaks over medium-high heat to desired doneness, turning once. (Allow 12 minutes total cooking time for medium doneness.)

Add cognac or brandy to skillet, pouring over steaks. Carefully ignite; allow flames to subside. Remove steaks to hot platter; keep warm. Add beef broth to skillet. Bring to boiling; pour over steaks. Makes 4 servings.

Veal Marsala

- 1 pound veal leg round steak or sirloin steak, cut ¼ inch thick
- 3 tablespoons butter or margarine
- ¼ cup marsala or dry sherry
- 1 teaspoon instant chicken bouillon granules
- 1 4-ounce can sliced mushrooms, drained
- 1 tablespoon snipped parsley

Cut veal into 4 pieces. Place 1 piece of veal between 2 pieces of clear plastic wrap. Pound with meat mallet to about ⅛-inch thickness as shown on page 49. Remove plastic wrap; sprinkle with some *salt* and *pepper*. Repeat with remaining veal.

In large skillet cook *half* of the veal in hot butter or margarine over medium-high heat about 1 minute on each side. Remove to serving platter; keep warm. Add a little more butter, if necessary. Repeat with remaining veal. Keep veal warm. Add marsala or dry sherry, bouillon granules, and ½ cup *water* to drippings in skillet. Boil rapidly 3 to 4 minutes or till liquid is reduced to about ⅓ *cup*. Stir in sliced mushrooms and parsley. Pour over veal. Serve immediately. Serves 4.

Veal Piccata: Prepare Veal Marsala as above *except* omit the water, marsala or dry sherry, chicken bouillon granules, and mushrooms. Cook veal as directed above. To the skillet drippings add 3 tablespoons *lemon juice*, 2 tablespoons *butter or margarine*, and the 1 tablespoon snipped parsley. Heat and stir till butter melts; pour over veal.

Ham in Cottage Cheese Pastry

    1   5-pound fully cooked canned ham
    1   10-ounce package frozen chopped spinach,
          thawed and drained
    ½   cup grated Parmesan cheese
    ⅓   cup cooking oil
    ¼   cup very finely chopped almonds
    2   tablespoons finely chopped onion
    ¼   teaspoon salt
    1½ cups all-purpose flour
    ½   teaspoon salt
    ½   cup shortening
    ¾   cup cream-style cottage cheese, sieved
    1   beaten egg

Place ham on rack in shallow baking pan. Insert meat thermometer. Bake in 325° oven 1¼ to 1½ hours or till meat thermometer registers 140°. Remove ham from oven; use baster to remove drippings from pan. Remove rack from pan. Cool ham 20 minutes. Trim any excess fat from outside of ham.

Meanwhile, prepare the filling. Place spinach between a double thickness of paper toweling; press out excess moisture from spinach. In small mixer bowl combine spinach, Parmesan cheese, cooking oil, almonds, onion, and the ¼ teaspoon salt. Beat well, scraping sides of bowl constantly till mixture is the consistency of soft butter. Set aside.

To make pastry, in medium mixing bowl stir together flour and the ½ teaspoon salt. Cut in shortening till pieces are the size of small peas. Add cottage cheese. Toss with fork till all is moistened. Form into a ball. On a lightly floured surface roll out pastry to 15x12-inch rectangle. Spread spinach mixture atop the ham. Drape the pastry over the ham, covering top and sides with pastry. Mold pastry to the shape of the meat. Trim extra pastry at bottom; cut slits in top. Cut decorations from the pastry trimmings and arrange over the top.

Brush pastry with the beaten egg. Bake in a 450° oven for 10 to 15 minutes or till pastry is browned. Transfer to serving platter. Garnish with tomato roses or radish decorations shown on pages 19-21, if desired. Makes 12 to 15 servings.

Mock Gyros

    1   5- to 6-pound leg of lamb
    1   2-pound boneless beef round steak, tenderized
    1   tablespoon salt
    2   teaspoons dried thyme, crushed
    2   teaspoons ground coriander
    1   teaspoon pepper
    ½   cup cooking oil
    ½   cup lemon juice
    ¼   cup finely chopped onion
    4   cloves garlic, minced
    16 to 20 pita bread rounds
    2   medium tomatoes, chopped
    1   cup snipped parsley
    1   8-ounce carton plain yogurt

Bone and butterfly lamb as shown on page 45. With meat mallet, pound both lamb and beef to 16x12-inch rectangles, about ½ to ¾ inch thick (pound lamb only on cut surface).

Cut and patch meats where necessary to make surface even. Combine salt, thyme, coriander, and pepper; sprinkle *half* over the surface of each piece of meat. Pound in the seasoning mixture.

For marinade, combine oil, lemon juice, onion, and garlic. Pour half over lamb in shallow dish; add beef and remaining marinade. Cover and refrigerate several hours or overnight, turning occasionally.

Remove meats from marinade (most of the liquid should be absorbed). Place lamb, cut side up, on countertop or cutting board. Place beef atop lamb, fitting meat to edges. Pound meats together. Roll up meat, beginning at narrow end. Tie securely with string, first at center, then halfway between center and each end. Tie lengthwise. Finish securing roll by tying between crosswise strings.

Insert spit rod; adjust holding forks and test balance. Insert meat thermometer near center of meat, not touching spit rod. Place *hot* coals on both sides of a shallow foil drip pan. Attach spit so meat is over drip pan. Turn on motor and lower grill hood, or cover with foil tent. Grill for 2 to 2½ hours or till meat thermometer registers 140°. Remove from spit. Cut meat into thin slices, removing strings as you slice. Serve in bread rounds, adding tomatoes, parsley, and yogurt. Makes 16 to 20 sandwiches.

Stroganoff Meat Loaves for a Crowd

    2   beaten eggs
    1⅓ cups milk
    1   cup quick-cooking rolled oats
    ¾   cup chopped onion
    1   tablespoon Worcestershire sauce
    2   teaspoons salt
    ½   teaspoon pepper
    3   pounds ground beef
    3   4-ounce cans chopped mushrooms, drained
    1   cup dairy sour cream
    ½   teaspoon salt

In a large bowl combine eggs and milk. Stir in rolled oats, onion, Worcestershire sauce, 2 teaspoons salt, and pepper. Add ground beef; mix well. Pat about *one-quarter* of the meat mixture into each of the two 8x4x2-inch loaf pans; make a shallow depression lengthwise down centers of loaves.

In a small bowl combine chopped mushrooms, sour cream, and the ½ teaspoon salt. Divide mixture between the meat loaves, spreading *half* in the depression in *each* loaf. Cover loaves with the remaining meat mixture, pressing firmly to seal edges.

Bake meat loaves in a 350° oven for 1 to 1¼ hours or till done. Let stand 5 to 10 minutes before removing from pans. Garnish with fluted mushrooms or radish decorations shown on pages 16-20, if desired. Makes 2 meat loaves, 6 or 7 servings each.

Poultry

Roast Turkey with Stuffing

1 **10-pound turkey**
 Sage, Oyster, or Chestnut Stuffing, or
   Corn Bread-Sausage Stuffing (recipes this page)
 Cooking oil

Rinse turkey and pat dry with paper toweling. Rub inside of cavities with some salt. Spoon some of the *desired stuffing* loosely into the neck cavity; pull the neck skin to the back of turkey and fasten securely with a small skewer. Lightly spoon remaining stuffing into body cavity. If opening has a band of skin across tail, tuck drumsticks under band; if not, use string to tie legs securely to tail. Twist the wing tips under back.

Place turkey, breast side up, on a rack in a shallow roasting pan. Brush skin of turkey with cooking oil. Insert a meat thermometer in center of inside thigh muscle, making sure the bulb of the thermometer does not touch bone.

Roast, uncovered, in a 325° oven for 4 to 4½ hours or till meat thermometer registers 185° and drumstick moves easily in socket. When turkey is two-thirds done, cut band of skin or string between legs so thighs will cook evenly. Let stand 15 minutes before carving. Carve turkey in the traditional manner or as shown on page 29. Garnish with fruit decorations shown on pages 18-21, if desired. Makes 10 to 12 servings.

Sage Stuffing

1 **cup finely chopped celery**
1 **medium onion, chopped (½ cup)**
½ **cup butter or margarine**
1 **teaspoon poultry seasoning or ground sage**
8 **cups dry bread cubes**
¾ **to 1 cup chicken broth, water, or**
   Homemade Chicken Broth (see recipe, page 73)

In a saucepan cook celery and onion in butter till tender but not brown. Remove from heat; stir in poultry seasoning or sage, ½ teaspoon *salt*, and ⅛ teaspoon *pepper*. Place the dry bread cubes in a large mixing bowl. Add the celery mixture. Drizzle with enough broth or water to moisten, tossing lightly. Use to stuff one 10-pound turkey. Serves 10 to 12.

Oyster Stuffing: Prepare Sage Stuffing as directed above, *except* add 1 pint *shucked oysters*, drained and chopped, *or* two 8-ounce cans *whole oysters*, drained and chopped, with the seasonings. Reserve the drained oyster liquid if desired, and substitute it for part of the chicken broth or water. Continue as directed above.

Chestnut Stuffing: Prepare Sage Stuffing as directed above, *except* add 1 pound *fresh chestnuts*, roasted and coarsely chopped, *or* 12 ounces canned *unsweetened chestnuts*, coarsely chopped, with the seasonings. (To roast the fresh chestnuts, use a sharp knife to slash an ''X'' into each chestnut. Place on a baking sheet; bake in a 400° oven for 15 minutes. Cool and peel.) Continue as directed above.

Corn Bread-Sausage Stuffing

1 **cup all-purpose flour**
1 **cup yellow cornmeal**
¼ **cup sugar**
4 **teaspoons baking powder**
½ **teaspoon salt**
2 **slightly beaten eggs**
1 **cup milk**
¼ **cup bacon drippings or cooking oil**
1 **pound bulk pork sausage**
1 **medium onion, chopped (½ cup)**
½ **cup chopped green pepper**
½ **cup chopped celery**
¼ **cup snipped parsley**
2 **teaspoons poultry seasoning**
1 **to 1¼ cups chicken broth, water, or**
   Homemade Chicken Broth (see recipe, page 73)

For corn bread, stir together flour, cornmeal, sugar, baking powder, and salt. Combine eggs, milk, and bacon drippings or cooking oil. Add to dry mixture; stir just till combined. Turn mixture into a greased 9x9x2-inch baking pan. Bake in a 425° oven for 20 to 25 minutes. Cool. Crumble enough corn bread to make 6 cups.

In a skillet cook sausage, onion, green pepper, and celery till sausage is brown and vegetables are tender. Drain off fat. In a mixing bowl combine corn bread crumbs, parsley, poultry seasoning, and sausage mixture. Add enough of the chicken broth or water to moisten. Toss lightly to mix. Use to stuff one 10-pound turkey. (Any stuffing that does not fit in bird can be baked in a small casserole, covered, in a 325° oven about 30 minutes.) Makes 16 servings.

Curry-Stuffed Chicken

½ **cup chopped onion**
½ **cup chopped celery**
¼ **cup butter or margarine**
1 **teaspoon curry powder**
½ **teaspoon salt**
⅛ **teaspoon pepper**
5 **cups dry bread cubes**
1 **cup chicken broth or Homemade Chicken Broth**
   (see recipe, page 73)
1 **4- to 5-pound whole roasting chicken**
 Cooking oil

Cook onion and celery in butter till tender but not brown. Stir in curry powder, salt, and pepper. Combine with bread cubes; toss with enough of the broth to moisten. Rub neck and body cavities of chicken with salt; stuff loosely. Skewer neck skin to back. Tie legs to tail. Twist wings under back.

Place, breast up, on a rack in roasting pan. Brush with oil. Roast, uncovered, in 375° oven for 2 to 2½ hours or till done. Baste occasionally with pan drippings. Makes 4 servings.

Pictured: **Golden Stuffed Cornish Hens (see recipe, page 67).**

Poultry

Harvest Chicken

The flavor of the roast chicken is enhanced by a moist herb and vegetable stuffing–

½ cup shredded carrot
½ cup chopped celery
¼ cup chopped onion
¼ cup butter or margarine
½ teaspoon ground sage or poultry seasoning
¼ teaspoon salt
⅛ teaspoon ground cinnamon
Dash pepper
4 cups dry white or whole wheat bread cubes (about 6 slices bread)
1 cup finely chopped, peeled apple (1 medium)
¼ cup chopped walnuts (optional)
¼ to ½ cup chicken broth
1 4- to 5-pound whole roasting chicken
Cooking oil or melted butter or margarine

To prepare stuffing, in skillet cook carrot, celery, and onion in ¼ cup butter or margarine till tender but not brown. Stir in sage or poultry seasoning, salt, cinnamon, and pepper. In a large mixing bowl combine bread cubes, chopped apple, and walnuts, if desired. Drizzle with enough chicken broth to moisten. Toss lightly to mix.

Spoon some stuffing into neck cavity of chicken; skewer neck skin to back. Lightly spoon remaining stuffing into body cavity. (Bake any additional stuffing in a small covered casserole the last 20 to 30 minutes of roasting.) Tie legs securely to tail. Twist wing tips under back.

Place chicken, breast side up, on a rack in shallow roasting pan. Brush skin of bird with cooking oil or the melted butter or margarine. Roast, uncovered, in 375° oven for 2 to 2½ hours or till drumstick moves easily in socket. Brush dry areas of skin occasionally with pan drippings, cooking oil, or melted butter. Garnish with green onion brush or fruit decorations shown on pages 18-21, if desired. Makes 8 servings.

Roast Tarragon Chicken

1 3-pound broiler-fryer chicken
2 tablespoons lemon juice
½ teaspoon salt
2 tablespoons butter or margarine
1½ teaspoons dried tarragon, crushed

Brush chicken with lemon juice inside and out; rub with salt. Skewer neck skin to back; tie legs to tail. Twist wings under back. Place, breast side up, on a rack in a shallow roasting pan. Melt butter; stir in tarragon. Brush over chicken. Roast, uncovered, in a 375° oven for 1¼ to 1½ hours or till done. Baste occasionally with drippings. Makes 6 servings.

Turkey Breast with Orange-Wine Sauce

⅔ cup orange juice
⅓ cup dry white wine
2 tablespoons cooking oil
1 tablespoon snipped chives
1 clove garlic, minced
1 teaspoon instant chicken bouillon granules
¼ teaspoon ground allspice
⅛ teaspoon pepper
1 5- to 6-pound frozen breast of turkey, thawed
¼ cup all-purpose flour

Mix orange juice, wine, oil, chives, garlic, chicken bouillon granules, allspice, and pepper; set aside. Place thawed turkey breast on rack in shallow roasting pan; insert meat thermometer. Roast turkey in 325° oven for 2½ to 3 hours or till thermometer registers 185°, basting occasionally with orange mixture. Remove turkey to platter; let stand 15 minutes.

Pour pan juices into 4-cup measure; skim off fat. Add remaining wine mixture and enough *cold water* to make *2¼ cups* liquid; stir into flour. Cook and stir till thickened and bubbly; cook and stir 1 minute more. Pass wine sauce with slices of turkey. Makes 10 servings.

Oven Chicken with Vegetables

1 teaspoon salt
1 teaspoon onion powder
1 teaspoon poultry seasoning
½ teaspoon garlic powder
¼ teaspoon pepper
1 4- to 5-pound whole roasting chicken
4 to 6 medium potatoes, peeled and quartered
3 medium carrots, quartered
1 large onion, thinly sliced
½ cup water

In a small bowl combine salt, onion powder, poultry seasoning, garlic powder, and pepper. Rub chicken with some of the seasoning mixture. Rub cavity of chicken with additional salt, if desired. Skewer neck skin to back. Tie legs to tail; twist wing tips under back. Place chicken in roasting pan or Dutch oven. Arrange potatoes, carrots, and onion around chicken. Add the water and sprinkle with remaining seasoning mixture. Cover pan with foil or lid.

Bake in a 350° oven about 1¾ hours or till chicken and vegetables are tender. Skim off excess fat and pass juices. Makes 6 to 8 servings.

Granola-Stuffed Cornish Hen

    1   1- to 1½-pound Cornish game hen
    ¼   cup chopped onion
    1   tablespoon butter or margarine
    ½   cup cooked rice
    ½   cup granola
    ¼   cup raisins
    1   tablespoon orange juice
    ¼   teaspoon curry powder
    1   teaspoon cornstarch
    1   teaspoon brown sugar
    ¼   teaspoon instant chicken bouillon granules
    ¼   cup orange juice
    ½   teaspoon finely shredded orange peel

Halve the Cornish hen lengthwise as shown at right. Rinse hen in cold water. Pat dry with paper toweling.

For stuffing, in a saucepan cook onion in hot butter or margarine till tender but not brown. Stir in rice, granola, raisins, the 1 tablespoon orange juice, curry powder, and ¼ teaspoon *salt*. Toss gently to mix.

In a 1½-quart casserole or 9-inch pie plate, spoon the stuffing into 2 mounds. Place *each* hen half, cut side down, over a mound of stuffing. Bake, uncovered, in a 350° oven for 50 to 60 minutes or till the hen is done.

For sauce, in a small saucepan combine cornstarch, brown sugar, and bouillon granules. Stir in ⅓ cup *water*, the ¼ cup orange juice, and shredded orange peel. Cook and stir till thickened and bubbly. Cook and stir 2 minutes more.

To serve, carefully transfer the hen halves and the stuffing to plates, keeping stuffing intact under each hen half. Spoon some of the sauce over the hen halves; pass the remaining sauce. Makes 2 servings.

Golden Stuffed Cornish Hens

Pictured on page 64—

    6   slices bacon
    1   cup finely chopped carrot
    ¼   cup snipped parsley
    1   teaspoon snipped fresh savory or ¼ teaspoon
        dried savory, crushed
    3   cups dry bread cubes (4 slices)
    ½   teaspoon instant chicken bouillon granules
    ¼   cup hot water
    4   1- to 1½-pound Cornish game hens
        Cooking oil
    ½   cup dry red wine
    2   tablespoons butter or margarine, melted
    3   tablespoons orange juice
    2   tablespoons cornstarch
    2   tablespoons brown sugar
    1   teaspoon instant chicken bouillon granules

Cook bacon till crisp; drain, reserving *2 tablespoons* of the drippings. Crumble bacon; set aside.

Cook carrot in the reserved bacon drippings till tender; remove from heat. Stir in crumbled bacon, parsley, savory, and dash *pepper*. Stir in bread cubes. Dissolve the ½ tea-

spoon chicken bouillon granules in hot water; drizzle over bread mixture. Toss.

Season cavities of Cornish hens with salt. Lightly stuff hens with bread mixture. Secure neck skin to back with small skewers. Tie legs to tail. Twist wing tips under back. Place hens, breast side up, on a rack in a shallow roasting pan. Brush with cooking oil; cover loosely with foil. Roast in a 375° oven for 30 minutes.

Combine wine, melted butter, and orange juice. Uncover birds; brush with wine mixture. Roast, uncovered, about 1 hour longer or till drumstick can be twisted easily in socket brushing with wine mixture once or twice. Remove to a warm serving platter; keep warm.

Pour drippings into a large measuring cup. Skim fat from pan drippings; stir in remaining wine mixture. Add *water*, if necessary, to make *1½ cups* liquid. For sauce, in a small saucepan combine cornstarch, brown sugar, the 1 teaspoon chicken bouillon granules, and ¼ teaspoon *salt*. Add cooking liquid all at once. Cook and stir till bubbly. Cook and stir 2 minutes more. Garnish with celery leaves and carrot petals shown on page 19, if desired. Pass sauce with Cornish hens. Split Cornish hens lengthwise to serve. Makes 8 servings.

To Split Cornish Hens

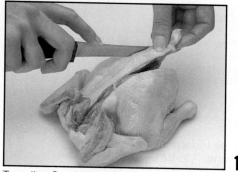

1

To split a Cornish hen for 2 servings, position the hen, breast side down, on a cutting board. Use a sharp boning knife to remove backbone, as shown.

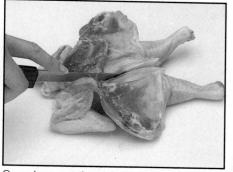

2

Open hen; cut through the breastbone to make two halves. Rinse with cold water; pat dry.

Poultry

Oven-Fried Chicken

3 cups corn flakes or ½ cup fine dry bread crumbs
¼ cup butter or margarine, melted
1 2½- to 3-pound broiler-fryer chicken, cut up*

For the crumb mixture, crush corn flakes finely enough to make 1 cup crumbs or use the ½ cup bread crumbs; set aside.

Rinse chicken pieces; pat dry with paper toweling. Season chicken with salt and pepper. Brush *each* piece with melted butter. Place crushed corn flakes or bread crumbs on a sheet of waxed paper; roll chicken in crumbs to coat. In a shallow baking pan, arrange chicken, skin side up and so pieces don't touch. Bake in a 375° oven about 50 minutes or till tender. *Do not turn chicken while cooking.* (Chicken is done when it is easily pierced with a fork. Test the thigh or breast at a point near the bone, since these parts require the most cooking time.) Makes 6 servings.

Potato Chip Chicken: Prepare Oven-Fried Chicken as above, *except* substitute 1½ cups crushed *potato chips or barbecue-flavored potato chips* for the crumb mixture. *Do not season chicken with salt.*

Parmesan Chicken: Prepare Oven-Fried Chicken as above, *except* substitute a mixture of ⅔ cup crushed *herb-seasoned stuffing mix*, ½ cup grated *Parmesan cheese*, and 3 tablespoons snipped *parsley* for the crumb mixture. *Do not season chicken with salt.*

Curry and Parsley Chicken: Prepare Oven-Fried Chicken as above, *except* substitute a mixture of ⅔ cup finely crushed *saltine crackers* (about 20 crackers), ¼ cup snipped *parsley*, 2 tablespoons *curry powder*, 1 teaspoon *onion salt*, and ⅛ teaspoon ground *ginger* for the crumb mixture. *Do not season chicken with salt.*

Chicken Italiano: Prepare Oven-Fried Chicken as above, *except* substitute a mixture of 1 cup coarsely crushed *40% bran flakes*, 2 teaspoons *Italian or onion salad dressing mix*, and ½ teaspoon *paprika* for the crumb mixture. *Do not season chicken with salt.*

*Note: Or, buy a whole broiler-fryer chicken and cut it up as shown on pages 32-33.

Chicken Country Captain

A colonial Southern favorite, this chicken dish is baked in a spicy sauce of curry, mace, paprika, currants, tomatoes, and green pepper—

½ cup chopped onion
½ cup chopped green pepper
1 clove garlic, minced
2 tablespoons butter or margarine
1 28-ounce can tomatoes, cut up
¼ cup dried currants or raisins
¼ cup snipped parsley
2 tablespoons curry powder
1 teaspoon salt
1 teaspoon ground mace
½ teaspoon sugar
⅛ teaspoon pepper
½ cup all-purpose flour
1½ teaspoons salt
¼ teaspoon pepper
¼ teaspoon paprika
2 2½- to 3-pound broiler-fryer chickens, cut up*
2 tablespoons cooking oil
2 tablespoons cold water
1 tablespoon cornstarch
Hot cooked rice
¼ cup sliced almonds (optional)

In a saucepan cook onion, green pepper, and garlic in butter or margarine till tender but not brown. Stir in *undrained* tomatoes, currants or raisins, parsley, curry powder, 1 teaspoon salt, mace, sugar and ⅛ teaspoon pepper. Simmer, uncovered, for 15 minutes.

In a plastic bag combine flour, 1 teaspoon salt, ¼ teaspoon pepper, and paprika. Add 2 or 3 chicken pieces at a time; shake to coat. In a large skillet lightly brown chicken pieces on all sides in hot oil about 15 minutes. Arrange chicken in a 13x9x2-inch baking dish; top with tomato mixture. Cover and bake in a 325° oven about 1 hour or till chicken is tender.

Remove chicken from baking dish; keep warm. Skim excess fat from tomato mixture; transfer tomato mixture to a medium saucepan. Stir cold water into cornstarch; add to tomato mixture. Cook and stir till thickened and bubbly. Cook and stir 2 minutes more. Serve chicken and sauce with rice. Garnish with almonds, if desired. Makes 12 servings.

*Note: Or, buy whole broiler-fryer chickens and cut them up yourself as shown on pages 32-33.

Orangy Chicken Vegetable Skillet

¼ cup all-purpose flour
2 tablespoons paprika
½ teaspoon salt
¼ teaspoon pepper
1 2½- to 3-pound broiler-fryer chicken, cut up*
2 tablespoons cooking oil
1 cup frozen small whole onions
½ cup coarsely chopped carrots
½ of a 6-ounce can (⅓ cup) frozen orange juice
    concentrate
½ cup water
½ teaspoon ground ginger
¼ cup water
1 tablespoon all-purpose flour
1 3-ounce can sliced mushrooms, drained
2 tablespoons snipped parsley
    Hot cooked rice

Stir together ¼ cup flour, paprika, salt, and pepper. Coat chicken pieces, 2 or 3 at a time, with seasoned flour mixture.

In a 12-inch skillet brown chicken pieces slowly in hot oil. Drain excess fat. Add onions and chopped carrots. Combine orange juice concentrate, the ½ cup water and the ginger; pour atop chicken. Bring to boiling. Reduce heat and simmer, covered, about 35 to 40 minutes. Remove chicken to platter; keep warm. Skim fat from pan juices. Blend the ¼ cup water with the 1 tablespoon flour; stir into pan juices. Cook and stir till thickened and bubbly. Add sliced mushrooms. Cook and stir 1 minute more. Pour atop chicken. Sprinkle with parsley. Serve with hot rice. Makes 4 to 6 servings.

*Note: Or, buy a whole boiler-fryer chicken and cut it up as shown on pages 32-33.

Popover Chicken Tarragon

1 2½- to 3-pound broiler-fryer chicken, cut up*
2 tablespoons cooking oil
    Salt
    Pepper
3 eggs
1½ cups milk
1 tablespoon cooking oil
1½ cups all-purpose flour
¾ to 1 teaspoon dried tarragon, crushed
¾ teaspoon salt

In a skillet brown broiler-fryer chicken in oil; season with salt and pepper. Place chicken in a well-greased 13x9x2-inch baking dish.

In a mixing bowl beat eggs, milk, and cooking oil. Stir together flour, tarragon, and salt. Add to egg mixture. Beat till smooth. Pour over chicken pieces in dish. Bake in a 350° oven for 55 to 60 minutes or till done. Makes 6 servings.

*Note: Or, buy a whole boiler-fryer chicken and cut it up as shown on pages 32-33.

Oven-Crisped Orange Chicken

1 beaten egg
½ of a 6-ounce can (⅓ cup) frozen orange juice
    concentrate, thawed
2 tablespoons soy sauce
½ cup fine dry bread crumbs
1 teaspoon paprika
3 tablespoons butter or margarine
1 2½- to 3-pound broiler-fryer chicken, cut up*

Combine beaten egg, orange juice concentrate, and soy sauce; stir to mix well. In a small bowl thoroughly combine bread crumbs, paprika, and ¼ teaspoon *salt*. Melt butter in a 13x9x2-inch baking pan. Dip chicken pieces in the orange-soy mixture, then coat with crumbs. Place chicken, skin side up and so pieces don't touch, in the baking pan. Sprinkle with any remaining crumb mixture. Bake, uncovered, in a 375° oven about 50 minutes or till tender. *Do not turn* chicken pieces while cooking. Makes 6 servings.

*Note: Or, buy a whole broiler-fryer chicken and cut it up as shown on pages 32-33.

Chicken with Pineapple

1 2½- to 3-pound broiler-fryer chicken, cut up*
2 tablespoons cooking oil or shortening
1 cup finely chopped onion
1 small green pepper, cut into thin strips
1 clove garlic, minced
2 medium tomatoes, peeled and coarsely
    chopped (1 cup)
¼ cup raisins (optional)
2 tablespoons lemon or lime juice
½ teaspoon dried oregano, crushed
1 8¼-ounce can pineapple chunks
1 tablespoon cornstarch

In large skillet brown chicken in hot oil or shortening about 15 minutes, turning as necessary to brown evenly. Season with 1 teaspoon *salt* and ⅛ teaspoon *pepper*. Remove chicken. In skillet drippings cook onion, green pepper, and garlic till onion is tender. Stir in tomatoes, raisins, lemon or lime juice, and oregano. Return chicken to skillet, placing meaty pieces toward center and remaining pieces around edge. Cover; simmer for 30 minutes. Add *undrained* pineapple. Simmer, uncovered, about 5 minutes more, or till chicken is tender.

Arrange chicken on heated serving platter. Remove fruit and vegetables from pan juices with slotted spoon and place on platter with chicken; cover and keep warm.

To make sauce, skim excess fat from pan juices. Blend together 2 tablespoons *cold water* and cornstarch; add to juices. Cook and stir till thickened and bubbly. Cook and stir 2 minutes more. Spoon sauce over chicken. Makes 4 servings.

*Note: Or, buy a whole broiler-fryer chicken and cut it up as shown on pages 32-33.

Poultry

Arroz con Pollo

Thread saffron are the orange filaments gathered from the purple crocus flower. This aromatic spice gives a yellow color and pleasant flavor to foods—

- 1 2½- to 3-pound broiler-fryer chicken, cut up*
- 2 tablespoons cooking oil
- 1½ cups long grain rice
- 1 cup chopped onion
- 2 cloves garlic, minced
- 1 7½-ounce can tomatoes, cut up
- 1 tablespoon instant chicken bouillon granules
- ¼ teaspoon thread saffron, crushed
- 1 cup frozen peas
- 1 2-ounce can sliced pimiento, drained and chopped

In 12-inch skillet brown chicken in hot oil about 15 minutes. Remove chicken from skillet. In the remaining pan drippings, cook and stir rice, onion, and garlic till rice is golden. Add 3 cups *water*, the *undrained* tomatoes, bouillon granules, saffron, 1 teaspoon *salt*, and ¼ teaspoon *pepper*. Bring to boiling; stir well. Arrange chicken atop rice mixture. Cover and simmer 30 to 35 minutes or till chicken is tender. Stir in peas and pimiento; cover and cook 5 minutes more. Garnish with lettuce leaf and pimiento strips, if desired. Serves 6.

*Note: Or, buy a whole boiler-fryer chicken and cut it up as shown on pages 32-33.

Herbed Chicken and Rice Bake

- ¾ cup brown rice
- 1⅔ cups beef broth
- 2 medium carrots, bias sliced
- 2 medium chicken breasts, split
- 2 tablespoons cooking oil
- ¼ cup sliced green onion
- ¼ cup dry white wine
- ½ teaspoon dried marjoram, crushed
- ½ teaspoon dried oregano, crushed
     Paprika or snipped parsley

In a medium saucepan combine brown rice and beef broth. Bring mixture to boiling; reduce heat and simmer, covered, for 35 minutes. Add carrots to saucepan. Cover and cook 15 minutes more or till rice is tender.

Meanwhile, brown chicken slowly in hot oil about 10 minutes. Remove rice from heat; stir in onion, wine, marjoram, oregano, and ⅛ teaspoon *pepper*. Turn rice mixture into a 10x6x2-inch baking dish. Top with chicken; sprinkle chicken with some *salt* and *pepper*. Cover; bake in 350° oven for 30 minutes; uncover and bake 15 minutes more or till chicken is done. Sprinkle with paprika or parsley. Makes 4 servings.

Pictured: **Arroz con Pollo.**

Chicken Dijon

- 2 whole medium chicken breasts (1½ pounds)
- 1 teaspoon onion salt
- ½ teaspoon lemon pepper
- 1 6-ounce package regular long grain and wild rice mix or 2 cups hot cooked rice
- 3 tablespoons butter or margarine
     Chicken broth
- ½ cup light cream
- 2 tablespoons all-purpose flour
- 1 tablespoon Dijon-style mustard

Halve whole chicken breasts lengthwise. Skin and bone chicken breasts as shown on page 72. Sprinkle chicken with onion salt and lemon pepper. Prepare long grain and wild rice mix according to package directions.

Meanwhile, in a skillet over medium heat cook chicken in butter or margarine about 20 minutes or till tender. Remove to a platter; keep warm. Measure pan juices; add enough chicken broth to make *1 cup* liquid. Return to skillet. Stir together light cream and flour; add to broth. Cook and stir till thickened and bubbly. Cook and stir 1 minute more. Stir in mustard. Spoon some sauce over chicken; pass remainder. Serve with the hot cooked rice. Makes 4 servings.

Chicken with Walnuts

- 1½ pounds whole chicken breasts
- 3 tablespoons soy sauce
- 2 teaspoons cornstarch
- 2 tablespoons dry sherry
- 1 teaspoon grated gingerroot
- 1 teaspoon sugar
- ½ teaspoon crushed red pepper
- 2 tablespoons cooking oil
- 2 medium green peppers, cut into ¾-inch pieces
- 4 green onions, bias sliced into 1-inch lengths
- 1 cup walnuts
     Hot cooked rice

Halve whole chicken breasts lengthwise. Skin and bone breasts as shown on page 72. Cut chicken into 1-inch pieces; set aside. In a small bowl blend soy sauce into cornstarch; stir in sherry, gingerroot, sugar, red pepper, and ½ teaspoon *salt*. Set aside.

Preheat a wok or large skillet over high heat; add cooking oil. Stir-fry green peppers and green onions in hot oil 2 minutes or till crisp-tender. Remove from wok. Add walnuts to wok; stir-fry 1 to 2 minutes or till just golden. Remove from wok. (Add more oil, if necessary.) Add *half* of the chicken to hot wok or skillet; stir-fry 2 minutes. Remove from wok. Stir-fry remaining chicken 2 minutes. Return all chicken to wok or skillet. Stir soy mixture; stir into chicken. Cook and stir till thickened and bubbly. Stir in vegetables and walnuts; cover and cook 1 minute more. Serve at once. Serve with hot cooked rice. Makes 4 to 6 servings.

Poultry

Chicken Paprikash

- 3 whole chicken breasts, halved lengthwise
- 2 tablespoons cooking oil
- 2 medium onions, sliced
- 1 tablespoon paprika
- ¼ cup dry white wine
- ½ teaspoon instant chicken bouillon granules
- ½ cup dairy sour cream
- 1 tablespoon all-purpose flour
  Hot cooked noodles
  Snipped chives or parsley (optional)

In 12-inch skillet brown chicken breasts in hot oil about 10 minutes. Drain off fat. Season chicken with some *salt* and *pepper*. Add onion to skillet. Blend in paprika. Stir in wine, chicken bouillon granules, and ¼ cup *water*. Bring to boiling. Reduce heat; cover. Simmer 20 minutes.

Remove chicken to serving platter; keep warm. Combine sour cream and flour; stir into liquid in skillet. Heat and stir till thickened; do not boil. Serve with chicken over noodles. Sprinkle with chives or parsley, if desired. Makes 6 servings.

Chicken with Mushrooms

- 4 whole large chicken breasts
- ¼ cup all-purpose flour
- 2 beaten eggs
- 2 tablespoons milk
- 1 cup fine dry bread crumbs
- ¼ cup cooking oil
- ½ cup sliced fresh mushrooms
- ¼ cup chopped onion
- 2 tablespoons butter or margarine
- 1 tablespoon all-purpose flour
- ½ teaspoon salt
- ¼ teaspoon pepper
- 1 cup milk
- ½ cup dairy sour cream

Halve whole chicken breasts lengthwise. Skin and bone chicken breasts as shown at right. Place chicken between two pieces of clear plastic wrap. Pound to ½-inch thickness; remove wrap. Coat chicken with the ¼ cup flour. Mix eggs and the 2 tablespoons milk; dip chicken in mixture to coat, then dip into crumbs. In a skillet fry the chicken in hot oil about 5 minutes on each side or till golden brown. Remove to platter; cover and keep warm.

Meanwhile, in a saucepan cook mushrooms and onion in butter or margarine till tender. Stir in the 1 tablespoon flour, salt, and pepper. Add the 1 cup milk; cook and stir till thickened and bubbly. Cook 1 minute more. Stir in sour cream. Heat through; do not boil. Pass with chicken. Garnish with snipped parsley or fluted mushroom decorations shown on page 16, if desired. Makes 8 servings.

To Bone a Chicken Breast

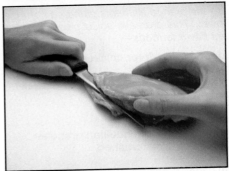

1

Remove skin from meat; discard. Hold breast half with bone side down. Insert a sharp boning knife close to bone.

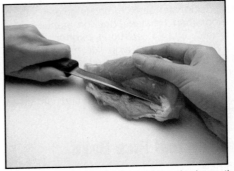

2

Begin cutting the meat away from the breastbone side of the chicken breast, as shown. Carefully cut as close to the bone as possible. Use fingers to gently pull the chicken meat away from bone as you cut.

3

Continue cutting the meat from the bone. Use a sawing motion, pressing the flat side of the knife blade against the rib bones. With the other hand, gently pull the meat away from the rib bones. Repeat steps 1, 2, and 3 with remaining chicken breasts.

Lemon Chicken and Zucchini

1½ pounds chicken breasts and thighs
¼ cup Homemade Chicken Broth (recipe below)
1 tablespoon cornstarch
2 tablespoons soy sauce
1 teaspoon sugar
2 tablespoons cooking oil
1 teaspoon grated gingerroot
3½ cups sliced zucchini
2 tablespoons lemon juice
Deep-Fried Rice Sticks (recipe at right)

Halve whole chicken breasts lengthwise. Skin and bone chicken breasts as shown on page 72. Skin and bone chicken thighs. Cut chicken into 1-inch pieces. Blend chicken broth into cornstarch; stir in soy sauce and sugar. Set aside.

Preheat a wok or large skillet over high heat; add cooking oil. Stir-fry gingerroot in hot oil for 30 seconds. Stir-fry *half* of the zucchini for 2 to 3 minutes or till crisp-tender. Remove zucchini. Stir-fry remaining zucchini 2 to 3 minutes. Remove from wok. (Add more oil, if necessary.) Add *half* the chicken to hot wok or skillet; stir-fry 2 minutes or till done. Remove chicken. Stir-fry remaining chicken 2 minutes. Return all chicken to wok or skillet. Stir broth mixture; stir into chicken. Cook and stir till thickened and bubbly. Add zucchini and lemon juice; cover and cook 1 minute more. Serve atop Deep-Fried Rice Sticks. Makes 4 to 6 servings.

Homemade Chicken Broth

1 5- to 6-pound stewing chicken, cut up* or two 2½- to 3-pound broiler-fryer chickens, cut up*
4 stalks celery with leaves, cut up
1 small onion, cut up
10 whole black peppercorns or ¼ teaspoon pepper
3 sprigs parsley or fresh coriander
2 slices gingerroot

In 5-quart Dutch oven combine chicken and enough *water* to cover (about 6 cups). Add remaining ingredients and 2 teaspoons *salt*. Cover; bring to boiling. Reduce heat; simmer 2 to 2½ hours for stewing chicken (about 1 hour for broiler-fryers) or till tender. Remove chicken; strain broth. Set chicken and broth aside to cool. When chicken is cool enough to handle, remove meat, discarding skin and bones. Store chicken and broth separately in tightly covered containers in refrigerator. Lift fat from broth when chilled. (Broth and chicken may be frozen separately in 1-cup portions. Use meat in recipes calling for cooked chicken.) Use broth as directed in recipes. Makes 4 cups broth and 4 cups cooked chicken.

Ingredient substitution: When recipe calls for Homemade Chicken Broth, you can substitute canned chicken broth or make bouillon (1 teaspoon instant chicken bouillon granules for each 1 cup boiling water).

*Note: Or, buy whole chickens and cut them up as shown on pages 32-33.

Deep-Fried Rice Sticks

Rice sticks are very fine, crisp rice noodles. Buy these packaged noodles, rolled in tight wads, at Oriental food stores or in the specialty food section of grocery stores—

2 ounces uncooked rice sticks
Cooking oil

Fry *uncooked* rice sticks, a few at a time, in deep hot cooking oil (375°) about 5 seconds or just till sticks puff and rise to top. Remove; drain on paper toweling. Keep warm in oven. (Store any uncooked rice sticks in a tightly closed plastic bag.)

Chicken Teriyaki Kabobs

½ teaspoon finely shredded orange peel
⅓ cup orange juice
¼ cup soy sauce
¼ cup dry sherry
2 tablespoons sliced green onion
2 teaspoons grated gingerroot or ½ teaspoon ground ginger
1 teaspoon toasted sesame seed
2 cloves garlic, minced
2 whole medium chicken breasts (1½ pounds)
¾ cup water
4 teaspoons cornstarch
Hot cooked rice

For marinade, in a bowl combine orange peel, orange juice, soy sauce, sherry, green onion, gingerroot or ginger, sesame seed, and garlic.

Halve whole chicken breasts lengthwise. Skin and bone as shown on page 72. Pound chicken slightly to flatten; cut lengthwise into ½- to ¾-inch-wide strips. Add chicken pieces to marinade. Cover; let stand 30 minutes at room temperature. Drain chicken, reserving the marinade. Thread chicken strips accordion style on wooden or metal skewers. Broil 4 to 5 inches from heat about 4 minutes per side, brushing occasionally with marinade. In a small saucepan combine ½ cup of the marinade, water, and cornstarch. Cook and stir till thickened and bubbly. Cook and stir 2 minutes more. Serve chicken and sauce over hot cooked rice. Makes 4 servings.

Poultry

Almond-Chicken Casserole

- 1 9-ounce package frozen French-style green beans
- 1 8-ounce package wide noodles
- 1 8-ounce carton plain yogurt
- ½ cup mayonnaise or salad dressing
- ¼ cup dry white wine
- ½ teaspoon salt
- ½ teaspoon dried parsley flakes
- ½ teaspoon dried dillweed
- ¼ teaspoon garlic powder
    Dash pepper
- 3 cups cubed cooked chicken
- 1 cup slivered almonds
- ⅓ cup grated Parmesan cheese

Cook beans and noodles separately, according to package directions; drain well. In a bowl combine yogurt, mayonnaise or salad dressing, white wine, salt, parsley, dillweed, garlic powder, and pepper.

In a 3-quart casserole layer *half* of the cooked noodles, green beans, cubed chicken, almonds, Parmesan cheese, and seasoned yogurt mixture; repeat layers. Bake, covered, in a 350° oven for 45 minutes or till heated through. Makes 6 to 8 servings.

Super Chicken Subs

- ½ cup dairy sour cream
- 2 tablespoons thinly sliced green onion
- 2 teaspoons prepared mustard
- ½ teaspoon dried basil, crushed
- ⅛ teaspoon garlic salt
- 4 individual French rolls
- 4 lettuce leaves
- 8 slices cooked chicken or turkey
- 4 slices American, Swiss, cheddar, or Monterey Jack cheese
- 2 medium tomatoes, peeled and thinly sliced
- 1 small cucumber, sliced
- 1 small green pepper, sliced crosswise into rings
- ¼ cup sliced pimiento-stuffed olives or pitted ripe olives
- ⅓ cup alfalfa sprouts (optional)

For sandwich spread, in a small mixing bowl combine sour cream, onion, mustard, basil, and garlic salt. Cover; chill thoroughly.

Split French rolls lengthwise, cutting to, but not through, the other side. Scoop out some of the center. Spread both halves of rolls generously with chilled spread mixture.

On the bottom half of each roll, arrange lettuce, chicken, cheese, and tomato. Top each with cucumber, green pepper, olives, and alfalfa sprouts, if desired. Place upper halves of rolls atop. Anchor sandwiches with wooden picks, if desired. Makes 4 sandwiches.

Chicken Divan

- 2 10-ounce packages frozen broccoli spears or two 8-ounce packages frozen cut asparagus
- ¼ cup butter or margarine
- ⅓ cup all-purpose flour
- ⅛ teaspoon ground nutmeg
- 1 cup light cream or milk
- 1 cup chicken broth or Homemade Chicken Broth (see recipe, page 73)
- ¼ cup dry white wine
- ⅓ cup shredded Swiss cheese
- 10 ounces sliced cooked chicken
- ¼ cup grated Parmesan cheese
    Paprika

Cook vegetable according to package directions; drain. Arrange crosswise in a 12x7½x2-inch baking dish.

For sauce, in a saucepan melt butter; stir in flour, nutmeg, ½ teaspoon *salt*, and ⅛ teaspoon *pepper*. Add cream and chicken broth all at once. Cook and stir till thickened and bubbly. Stir in wine. Add Swiss cheese; stir till melted.

Pour *half* of the sauce over broccoli or asparagus. Top with sliced chicken. Pour remaining sauce over all. Sprinkle Parmesan cheese and paprika atop. Bake in a 350° oven for 20 minutes or till heated through. Broil 3 or 4 inches from heat for 1 to 2 minutes or till golden. Makes 6 servings.

Chicken Enchilada Casserole

- 1 cup chopped onion
- ½ cup chopped green pepper
- 2 tablespoons butter or margarine
- 2 cups chopped cooked chicken or turkey
- 1 4-ounce can green chili peppers, rinsed, seeded, and chopped
- 3 tablespoons butter or margarine
- ¼ cup all-purpose flour
- 1 teaspoon ground coriander seed
- 2½ cups chicken broth or Homemade Chicken Broth (see recipe, page 73)
- 1 cup dairy sour cream
- 1½ cups shredded Monterey Jack cheese (6 ounces)
- 12 6-inch tortillas

In a large saucepan cook onion and green pepper in the 2 tablespoons butter till tender. Combine onion mixture in a bowl with chicken and chili peppers; set aside. For sauce, in same saucepan melt 3 tablespoons butter. Stir in flour, coriander, and ¾ teaspoon *salt*. Stir in chicken broth all at once; cook and stir till bubbly. Remove from heat; stir in sour cream and ½ *cup* of the shredded cheese. Stir ½ *cup* of the sauce into chicken mixture. Dip *each* tortilla into remaining sauce to soften; fill each with about ¼ *cup* of the chicken mixture. Roll up. Arrange rolls in 13x9x2-inch baking dish; pour remaining sauce over. Sprinkle with remaining cheese. Bake, uncovered, in 350° oven about 25 minutes or till bubbly. Serves 6.

Chicken-Cashew Salad

2 large potatoes, cooked, peeled, and diced (2 cups)
2½ cups cubed cooked chicken or turkey
1 cup frozen peas, thawed
½ cup chopped green pepper
½ cup chopped dill pickle
3 tablespoons sliced green onion
1 8-ounce carton dairy sour cream
1 8-ounce carton plain yogurt
½ teaspoon dillweed
¼ teaspoon salt
⅛ teaspoon pepper
¾ cup broken cashews
    Lettuce
    Hard-cooked egg (optional)

In a large bowl combine potatoes, chicken, peas, green pepper, dill pickle, and green onion; toss gently to combine. Combine sour cream, yogurt, dillweed, salt, and pepper; mix well. Add to chicken mixture, tossing gently till well combined. Cover and chill 2 to 3 hours.

To serve, gently toss chicken mixture with the cashews. Mound chicken salad on a lettuce-lined serving platter. If desired, garnish with additional cashews and the hard-cooked egg cut into wedges. Makes 6 to 8 servings.

Chicken-Broccoli Puff

1 10-ounce package frozen chopped broccoli
3 tablespoons butter or margarine
2 tablespoons all-purpose flour
1 teaspoon poultry seasoning
½ teaspoon salt
1 cup milk
½ cup shredded cheddar cheese (2 ounces)
2½ cups cubed cooked chicken
1 tablespoon chopped pimiento
3 egg yolks
⅛ teaspoon salt
1 teaspoon finely chopped green onion
¼ teaspoon celery seed
3 egg whites
1 tablespoon grated Parmesan cheese

Cook broccoli according to package directions; drain and set aside. In saucepan melt butter; stir in flour, poultry seasoning, and the ½ teaspoon salt. Add milk all at once. Cook and stir till thickened and bubbly. Stir in cheddar cheese till melted. Stir in broccoli, chicken, and pimiento; heat till bubbly. Cover; keep warm. In a small mixer bowl beat egg yolks and the ⅛ teaspoon salt about 4 minutes or till thick and lemon colored. Add green onion and celery seed. Wash beaters thoroughly.

Beat egg whites till stiff peaks form (tips stand straight). Fold egg yolk mixture into egg whites. Spoon *hot* chicken mixture into the bottom of an *ungreased* 9-inch quiche dish or 8x1½-inch round baking dish. Spread egg mixture over hot chicken mixture. Sprinkle grated Parmesan cheese atop. Bake in a 350° oven about 30 minutes or till the egg mixture is golden brown. Serve the puff immediately. Makes 6 servings.

Chicken-Vegetable Noodle Soup

Serve this delicious soup with hot, buttery French bread—

1 5- to 6-pound stewing chicken
6 cups water
⅓ cup chopped onion
2 teaspoons salt
¼ teaspoon pepper
1 bay leaf
1 16-ounce can tomatoes, cut up
1 16-ounce can cream-style corn
2 small zucchini, thinly sliced (about 2 cups)
1½ cups frozen or packaged noodles

Cut up whole chicken as shown on pages 32-33. In a large kettle combine water, chicken pieces, onion, salt, pepper, and bay leaf. Bring to boiling; reduce heat. Cover and simmer about 2 hours or till chicken is tender. Remove chicken from broth. Skim fat from broth; remove bay leaf. When chicken is cool enough to handle, remove skin and bones from chicken; discard skin and bones. Cube chicken; set aside. Add the *undrained* tomatoes, corn, and zucchini to broth. Bring mixture to boiling. Stir in noodles. Cover and simmer about 8 minutes or till noodles are nearly tender. Stir in cubed chicken. Cover and simmer about 5 minutes or till heated through. Serves 8.

Cheesy Chicken-Herb Pies

¼ cup chopped onion
¼ cup butter or margarine
¼ cup all-purpose flour
2 teaspoons instant chicken bouillon granules
½ teaspoon salt
¼ teaspoon dried thyme, crushed
¼ teaspoon ground sage
    Dash pepper
1⅓ cups milk
1 cup water
2 cups cubed cooked chicken or turkey
1 10-ounce package frozen mixed vegetables, cooked and drained
2 tablespoons snipped parsley
1 cup packaged biscuit mix
½ cup shredded American or cheddar cheese
¼ cup milk

Cook onion in butter or margarine till tender but not brown. Blend in flour, chicken bouillon granules, salt, thyme, sage, and pepper. Add the 1⅓ cups milk and the water. Cook and stir till thickened and bubbly. Cook and stir 1 minute more. Stir in cubed chicken or turkey, mixed vegetables, and parsley. Cook and stir till bubbly.

Meanwhile, for biscuit topper, combine biscuit mix and shredded cheese. Blend in the ¼ cup milk. Pour chicken mixture into five or six 10-ounce casseroles or one 1½-quart casserole. Drop biscuit batter by tablespoons atop hot filling in casseroles. Bake in a 400° oven for 15 to 20 minutes or till biscuits are lightly browned. Makes 5 or 6 servings.

for a Special Occasion

76

Poultry

Elegant Chicken a la King

 1 cup sliced fresh mushrooms
¼ cup chopped green pepper
¼ cup butter or margarine
 2 tablespoons all-purpose flour
¾ teaspoon salt
½ teaspoon paprika
2¼ cups light cream or milk
 2 beaten egg yolks
 3 cups cubed cooked chicken
 2 tablespoons chopped pimiento
 2 tablespoons dry sherry
 1 teaspoon lemon juice
 1 teaspoon onion juice or ⅛ teaspoon onion powder
 Baked patty shells or toast points

In a large saucepan cook mushrooms and green pepper in butter till tender but not brown. Stir in flour, salt, and paprika. Stir in light cream or milk; cook and stir till thickened and bubbly. Cook and stir 1 minute more. Stir about *1 cup* of the hot mixture into beaten egg yolks; return to mixture in saucepan. Cook and stir 1 minute over medium heat. Stir in chicken, pimiento, sherry, lemon juice, and onion juice or onion powder; heat through. Serve in patty shells or over toast points. Garnish with curly green onion top and pimiento cutout atop three green cabbage flower petals (see page 17, steps 2-3, for making cabbage petals), if desired. Serves 6.

Chicken Tetrazzini

 3 tablespoons butter or margarine
1½ cups sliced fresh mushrooms
¼ cup chopped green pepper
¼ cup all-purpose flour
¼ teaspoon salt
1½ cups light cream
 1 cup chicken broth or Homemade Chicken Broth
 (see recipe, page 73)
2½ cups cubed cooked chicken
 6 ounces spaghetti, cooked and well drained
 2 tablespoons dry sherry
¼ cup grated Parmesan cheese
¼ cup sliced almonds

In a large saucepan melt butter or margarine; add mushrooms and green pepper. Cook and stir till tender; stir in flour and salt. Add light cream and broth; cook and stir till thickened and bubbly. Cook and stir 1 minute more. Stir in chicken, spaghetti, and sherry. Heat through.

Turn into a 12x7½x2-inch baking dish. Sprinkle with Parmesan cheese and sliced almonds. Bake in a 400° oven for 10 to 15 minutes. Makes 5 or 6 servings.

Pictured: **Elegant Chicken a la King.**

Chicken-Cheese Crepes

 6 tablespoons butter or margarine
⅓ cup all-purpose flour
 Dash salt
 2 cups milk
 1 tablespoon instant chicken bouillon granules
 1 cup water
½ cup shredded Swiss cheese or brick cheese
¼ cup dry white wine
 2 tablespoons snipped parsley
 Several dashes bottled hot pepper sauce
 1 2½-ounce jar sliced mushrooms, drained
 1 10-ounce package frozen peas
 2 cups chopped cooked chicken or turkey
 2 tablespoons chopped pimiento
12 Main Dish Crepes (recipe below)
 Paprika

For cheese sauce, in a medium saucepan melt butter. Stir in flour and salt. Add milk, chicken bouillon granules, and water all at once. Cook and stir over medium heat till thickened and bubbly. Cook and stir 1 to 2 minutes more. Stir in cheese, wine, parsley, and hot pepper sauce. Remove *1 cup* of the cheese sauce; set aside. Stir drained mushrooms into remaining sauce.

For filling, cook peas according to package directions; drain. Combine peas, chicken or turkey, pimiento and the 1 cup reserved cheese sauce. Spread *¼ cup* filling over the *unbrowned* side of each crepe, leaving ¼-inch rim around edge. Roll up crepe. Place seam side down, in a 12x7½x2-inch baking dish. Repeat with remaining crepes. Pour the remaining cheese sauce over crepes. Sprinkle with paprika, if desired. Cover; bake crepes in a 375° oven for 18 to 20 minutes or till heated through. Let stand 10 minutes before serving. Makes 6 servings.

Main Dish Crepes

 1 cup all-purpose flour
1½ cups milk
 2 eggs
 1 tablespoon cooking oil
¼ teaspoon salt

In a mixing bowl combine flour, milk, eggs, oil, and salt. Beat with a rotary beater until blended. Heat a lightly greased 6-inch skillet. Remove from heat; spoon in about *2 tablespoons* of the batter. Lift and tilt skillet to spread batter evenly. Return to heat; brown on *one side only.* (Or, cook on an inverted crepe pan according to manufacturer's directions.) To remove, invert pan over paper toweling; remove crepe. Repeat with remaining batter to make 16 to 18 crepes, greasing skillet occasionally.

Poultry

Chicken Kiev

4 whole medium chicken breasts (3 pounds)
2 tablespoons snipped parsley
  1 to 2 tablespoons chopped green onion
1 ¼-pound stick of butter, chilled
⅓ cup all-purpose flour
1 beaten egg
½ cup fine dry bread crumbs
  Cooking oil or shortening for deep-fat frying

Halve whole chicken breasts lengthwise. Skin and bone chicken breasts as shown on page 72. Place 1 piece chicken between two pieces of clear plastic wrap. Working from center to edges, pound lightly with a meat mallet, forming a rectangle about ⅛ inch thick. Remove plastic wrap; sprinkle chicken with some parsley and onion. Season with some *salt* and *pepper*. Repeat with remaining chicken.

Cut chilled butter into 8 sticks, each about 2 to 2½ inches long. Place 1 of the sticks on each chicken piece. Fold in sides; roll up jelly roll style, pressing all edges together gently with your fingers to seal.

Place flour in a shallow dish. In another shallow dish combine egg and 1 tablespoon *water*. Roll chicken in flour to coat, then dip in egg mixture. Coat with crumbs. Cover; chill at least 1 hour. Fry chicken rolls, a few at a time, in deep hot oil (375°) for 5 minutes or till golden brown. Remove from hot oil with tongs or a slotted spoon; drain on paper toweling. Keep warm while frying remaining chicken rolls. Makes 8 servings.

Oven Chicken Kiev: Prepare Chicken Kiev as directed above, *except* omit deep-fat frying. Heat an additional ¼ cup *butter or margarine* in a large skillet. Fry chilled chicken rolls on all sides about 5 minutes or till brown. Transfer to a 12x7½x2-inch baking dish. Bake in a 400° oven for 15 to 18 minutes. Spoon pan drippings over individual servings.

Chicken Saltimbocca

3 whole medium chicken breasts (2¼ pounds)
6 thin slices boiled ham
6 thin slices Swiss cheese
1 medium tomato, peeled, seeded, and chopped
  Dried sage, crushed
⅓ cup fine dry bread crumbs
2 tablespoons grated Parmesan cheese
2 tablespoons snipped parsley
¼ cup butter or margarine, melted

Halve whole chicken breasts lengthwise. Skin and bone chicken breasts as shown on page 72. Place 1 piece of chicken, boned side up, between 2 pieces of clear plastic wrap. Working from the center to the edges, pound lightly with a meat mallet, forming a rectangle about ⅛ inch thick. Remove plastic wrap. Repeat with remaining chicken.

To assemble, place a ham slice and a cheese slice on *each* cutlet, trimming to fit within ¼ inch of edges. Top with

some chopped tomato; sprinkle lightly with sage. Fold in sides; roll up jelly roll style, pressing to seal. Combine bread crumbs, Parmesan cheese, and parsley. Dip chicken in butter, then roll in crumbs. Bake in a shallow baking pan in a 350° oven for 40 to 45 minutes. Remove to a serving platter. Stir mixture remaining in pan till smooth; spoon over chicken. Makes 6 servings.

Coq au Vin

4 slices bacon, cut up, or ¼ pound salt pork,
  finely chopped
2 2½- to 3-pound broiler-fryer chickens, cut up
2 tablespoons all-purpose flour
¾ teaspoon salt
¼ teaspoon pepper
2 cups burgundy
2 tablespoons cognac or brandy
2 tablespoons snipped parsley
½ teaspoon dried marjoram, crushed
½ teaspoon dried thyme, crushed
2 bay leaves
1 pound shallots or small whole onions, peeled (16)
2 cups fresh whole mushrooms
½ cup thinly sliced carrot
2 cloves garlic, minced
3 tablespoons all-purpose flour
3 tablespoons butter or margarine, softened
  Snipped parsley (optional)

In an 8-quart Dutch oven cook bacon or salt pork till crisp; remove from pan, reserving ¼ cup of the drippings. (If necessary, add cooking oil to drippings to measure ¼ cup liquid.)

Brown the chicken, half at a time, over medium heat about 15 minutes, turning as necessary to brown evenly. Remove from Dutch oven.

Stir 2 tablespoons flour, salt, and pepper into remaining drippings in pan. Add burgundy and cognac or brandy all at once. Cook and stir till thickened and bubbly. Stir in parsley, marjoram, thyme, and bay leaves.

Return chicken to Dutch oven along with shallots or onions, mushrooms, carrot, garlic, and bacon or salt pork. Simmer, covered, for 40 minutes or till chicken is tender.

Remove chicken and vegetables from Dutch oven; arrange on serving plate and keep warm. Discard bay leaves. Stir the 3 tablespoons flour into butter to make a smooth paste. Using a wire whisk, stir paste into hot sauce in Dutch oven. Cook and stir till thickened and bubbly. Cook and stir 1 minute more. To serve, top chicken with sauce. Sprinkle with additional snipped parsley, if desired. Makes 12 servings.

Spicy Barbecued Chicken

Be sure to brush all of the barbecue sauce on the chicken pieces during the last 10 minutes of grilling—

- ¼ **cup finely chopped onion**
- 1 **clove garlic, minced**
- 2 **tablespoons cooking oil**
- ¾ **cup catsup**
- ⅓ **cup vinegar**
- 1 **tablespoon Worcestershire sauce**
- 2 **teaspoons brown sugar**
- 1 **teaspoon celery seed**
- 1 **teaspoon dry mustard**
- ½ **teaspoon salt**
- ¼ **teaspoon pepper**
- ¼ **teaspoon bottled hot pepper sauce**
- 2 **2½- to 3-pound broiler-fryer chickens**

For barbecue sauce, in a saucepan cook chopped onion and minced garlic in cooking oil till onion is tender but not brown. Stir in catsup, vinegar, Worcestershire sauce, brown sugar, celery seed, dry mustard, salt, pepper, and bottled hot pepper sauce. Bring mixture to boiling. Reduce heat and simmer sauce, uncovered, for 10 minutes, stirring once or twice during cooking.

Meanwhile, cut the chicken into quarters as shown on pages 32-33, steps 1-7. Break the wing, hip, and drumstick joints of chicken so that the pieces will remain flat during grilling. Twist wing tips under back. Season chicken pieces with additional salt.

Place chicken pieces, bone side down, over *medium-hot* coals. Grill chicken for 25 minutes or till bone side is well browned. Turn chicken. Grill 20 to 25 minutes more or till chicken is tender. Brush chicken often with barbecue sauce during the last 10 minutes of grilling, using all of the sauce. Makes 12 servings.

Broccoli-Stuffed Cornish Hens

- ½ **of 10-ounce package (1 cup) frozen chopped broccoli**
- ¼ **cup chopped onion**
- ½ **cup cooked long grain rice**
- ¼ **cup shredded process Swiss cheese (1 ounce)**
- 1 **tablespoon butter or margarine, melted**
- ¼ **teaspoon salt**
  Dash pepper
- 2 **1- to 1½-pound Cornish game hens**
  Melted butter or margarine
- ¼ **cup orange marmalade**

Cook chopped broccoli according to package directions, *except* omit salt and add the chopped onion; drain well. Combine with cooked rice, shredded Swiss cheese, the 1 tablespoon butter or margarine, the salt, and pepper.

Rinse Cornish hens and pat dry with paper toweling. Lightly salt cavities. Stuff birds with the broccoli mixture. Secure neck skin to back with small skewers. Tie legs to tail. Twist wing tips under back.

Place on rack in a large roasting pan. Brush birds with a little melted butter or margarine. Cover loosely with foil and roast in a 375° oven for 30 minutes. Uncover; roast about 1 hour or till done, brushing with additional melted butter or margarine every half hour. In a saucepan melt the orange marmalade. Brush hens with marmalade during the last 5 minutes of roasting. Split hens lengthwise to serve. Serves 4.

Roast Turkey with Peanut Dressing

- 1½ **cups finely chopped celery**
- ¾ **cup finely chopped onion**
- ½ **cup snipped parsley**
- 1 **cup butter or margarine**
- 2 **cups salted peanuts, chopped**
- 1 **tablespoon ground sage**
- 1 **teaspoon pepper**
- ½ **teaspoon salt**
- 12 **cups soft bread crumbs**
- ½ **cup chicken broth**
- 1 **12- to 14-pound turkey**
  Cooking oil

In saucepan cook celery, onion, and parsley in butter or margarine till tender. Stir in chopped peanuts, sage, pepper, and salt. Place bread in large mixing bowl. Add the peanut mixture and chicken broth; toss to mix well.

Rinse turkey; pat dry with paper toweling. Spoon some of the bread crumb mixture into the neck cavity; pull the neck skin to the back of the turkey and fasten securely with a small skewer. Lightly spoon the remaining stuffing into body cavity.

If the opening has a band of skin across the tail, tuck drumsticks under band; if not, tie legs securely to tail. Twist wing tips under back, if desired. Place turkey, breast side up, on a rack in shallow roasting pan. Brush with a little cooking oil. Insert a meat thermometer in the center of the inside thigh muscle (bulb should not touch bone).

Roast, uncovered, in a 325° oven about 4½ to 6 hours or till meat thermometer registers 185° and the drumstick moves easily in socket. When turkey is two-thirds done, cut band of skin or string between legs so thighs will cook evenly. Let stand 15 minutes before carving. Carve turkey in the traditional manner or as shown on page 29. Makes 24 servings.

Fish and Asparagus Bundles

    4 fresh or frozen fish fillets
    ¾ pound fresh asparagus or one 8-ounce package
       frozen asparagus spears
    1 tablespoon butter or margarine
    2 tomatoes, peeled and cut up
    1 cup sliced fresh mushrooms
    ¼ cup thinly sliced celery
    ¼ cup chopped onion
    ¼ cup dry white wine
    1 clove garlic, minced
    ½ teaspoon dried mint, crushed
    ½ teaspoon dried basil, crushed
    ¼ teaspoon salt

Thaw fish, if frozen. Cut fresh asparagus into about 6-inch lengths. In a covered saucepan cook fresh asparagus in small amount of boiling water for 8 to 10 minutes or till almost tender. (Or, cook frozen asparagus according to package directions.) Drain.

Dot fillets with butter or margarine; sprinkle with a little salt. Place asparagus across fillets; roll up fillets and fasten with wooden picks as shown on page 82. Place fish rolls, seam side down, in 10-inch skillet. Add tomatoes, mushrooms, celery, onion, wine, garlic, mint, basil, and the ¼ teaspoon salt. Cover tightly; simmer for 7 to 8 minutes or till fish flakes easily when tested with a fork. Remove fish to platter; keep warm. Boil tomato mixture gently, uncovered, for 3 minutes or till slightly thickened. Spoon over fish rolls. Makes 4 servings.

Baked Fish with Mushrooms

    4 fresh or frozen fish fillets or steaks
    2 slices bacon
    1 cup sliced fresh mushrooms or one 6-ounce can
       sliced mushrooms, drained
    ½ cup green onion bias-sliced into 1-inch lengths
    3 tablespoons butter or margarine
    ¼ teaspoon dried tarragon, crushed
      Paprika

Thaw fish, if frozen. In a skillet cook bacon; reserve drippings. Crumble bacon; set aside. Cook mushrooms and onion in drippings till tender. Place fish in a 12x7½x2-inch baking dish; sprinkle with salt. Combine mushrooms, onion, butter and tarragon. Spread atop fish; sprinkle with paprika. Bake in a 350° oven 15 to 20 minutes or till fish flakes easily when tested with a fork. (Thin fillets will bake in less time.) Garnish with the crumbled bacon. Makes 4 servings.

Pictured: **Fish and Asparagus Bundles.**

Cioppino

    1 pound fresh or frozen fish fillets
    ½ large green pepper
    2 tablespoons finely chopped onion
    1 clove garlic, minced
    1 tablespoon cooking oil
    1 16-ounce can tomatoes, cut up
    1 8-ounce can tomato sauce
    ½ cup dry white or red wine
    3 tablespoons snipped parsley
    ½ teaspoon salt
    ¼ teaspoon dried oregano, crushed
    ¼ teaspoon dried basil, crushed
      Dash pepper
   12 ounces frozen shelled shrimp or two 4½-ounce
       cans shrimp, drained and deveined*
    1 6½-ounce can minced clams

Thaw fish, if frozen. Remove any skin from the fish fillets and cut fillets into 1-inch pieces; set aside. Cut green pepper into ½-inch squares (see directions, page 99).

In a 3-quart saucepan cook green pepper, onion, and garlic in oil till onion is tender but not brown. Add *undrained* tomatoes, tomato sauce, wine, parsley, salt, oregano, basil, and pepper. Bring to boiling. Reduce heat; cover and simmer for 20 minutes. Add the fish pieces, deveined shrimp, and *undrained* clams to tomato mixture. Bring just to boiling. Reduce heat; cover and simmer 5 to 7 minutes or till fish and shrimp are done. Makes 6 servings.

*Note: To devein shrimp, refer to directions on page 93.

Broiled Fish Fillets or Steaks

    2 pounds fresh or frozen fish fillets or steaks
    2 tablespoons butter or margarine, melted
      Salt
      Pepper

Thaw fillets or steaks, if frozen. Cut into 6 to 8 serving-size portions. Place fish in a single layer on greased cold rack of broiler pan or in greased baking pan. Tuck under any thin edges. Brush *1 tablespoon* of the butter or margarine over the fish. Sprinkle with salt and pepper.

Broil fish 4 inches from the heat till fish flakes easily when tested with a fork (allow 5 to 6 minutes for each ½ inch of thickness). Brush fish with remaining butter or margarine during cooking. If more than 1 inch thick, turn when half done. Makes 6 to 8 servings.

Broiled Whole Fish: Choose one 2-pound fresh or frozen *dressed fish.* Thaw the fish, if frozen; remove head, if desired. Rinse and dry fish. Combine 3 tablespoons *butter or margarine,* melted, and 1 tablespoon *lemon juice.* Place fish on greased cold rack of broiler pan or in greased baking pan. Brush fish inside and out with butter mixture; sprinkle inside and out with salt and pepper.

Broil 5 inches from the heat till fish flakes easily when tested with a fork (allow 5 to 6 minutes for each ½ inch of thickness). Turn fish once during cooking; brush with remaining butter mixture. Makes 6 servings.

Fish, Seafood & Eggs

Pan-Fried Fish

1 pound fresh or frozen fish fillets or
    steaks or three 10- to 12-ounce fresh or
    frozen pan-dressed trout or other fish
1 egg
2 tablespoons water
⅔ cup fine dry bread crumbs or cornmeal
½ teaspoon salt
    Dash pepper
    Shortening for frying

Thaw fish, if frozen. Cut fillets into 3 portions. Rinse pan-dressed fish; pat dry. In a shallow dish beat the egg; blend in water. In another dish combine bread crumbs or cornmeal, salt, and pepper. Dip fish into the egg mixture; coat both sides. Then roll fish in crumb mixture; coat evenly.

In a large skillet heat ¼ inch shortening. Add the fish in a single layer. If fillets have skin on, fry skin side last. Fry fish on one side 6 to 7 minutes or till brown. Turn and fry 6 to 7 minutes longer. Fish is done when both sides are brown and crisp and when fish flakes easily when tested with a fork. (Thin fillets will require less total cooking time than pan-dressed fish.) Drain. Makes 3 servings.

Fish and Chips

1 pound fresh or frozen fish fillets
3 medium potatoes (1 pound)
    Shortening or cooking oil for deep-fat frying
½ cup all-purpose flour
½ teaspoon salt
½ cup milk
1 egg
2 tablespoons cooking oil
½ cup all-purpose flour
    Malt vinegar (optional)

Thaw fish, if frozen. Cut fillets into 3 or 4 serving-size portions. Pat dry with paper toweling. Peel potatoes; cut lengthwise into ⅜-inch-thick strips. In saucepan or deep-fat fryer heat about 2 inches shortening or cooking oil to 375°. Fry potatoes ¼ at a time for 7 to 8 minutes or till golden brown. Remove from fat; drain on paper toweling. Keep warm in 325° oven while preparing fish.

In mixing bowl stir together ½ cup flour and salt. Add milk, egg, and the 2 tablespoons oil; beat till smooth. Place ½ cup flour in shallow bowl. Dip fish in flour, then in egg mixture. Fry fish in hot fat for 2 minutes on each side or till golden brown. Sprinkle fish and potatoes with salt. Sprinkle fish with vinegar, if desired. Makes 3 or 4 servings.

To Stuff a Fish Fillet

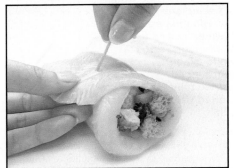

Lay a fish fillet flat on a cutting board. Place filling in center of the fillet. Bring ends of fish together and overlap atop the filling, as shown. Secure with wooden picks.

Marinated Fish Kabobs

1 pound fresh or frozen haddock fillets
3 tablespoons cooking oil
3 tablespoons dry sherry
3 tablespoons soy sauce
2 green onions, finely chopped
2 cloves garlic, minced
1 tablespoon brown sugar
1 teaspoon dry mustard
⅛ teaspoon pepper
6 mushroom caps
1 large green pepper
12 cherry tomatoes

Thaw fish, if frozen. Cut fish fillets into 1-inch pieces. For marinade, in a bowl combine oil, dry sherry, soy sauce, green onions, garlic, brown sugar, dry mustard, and pepper. Place fish pieces in marinade. Cover; marinate at room temperature for 1 hour.

Drain fish, reserving the marinade. Pour some boiling water over mushrooms in a bowl. Let stand 1 minute; drain. Cut green pepper into 1-inch squares. On 6 skewers alternate fish pieces, green pepper, cherry tomatoes, and whole mushrooms. Grill kabobs over *medium* coals for 8 to 10 minutes or till fish is done, turning and basting frequently with marinade. Makes 6 servings.

Herbed Fish Fillets

    1 pound fresh or frozen fish fillets
    3 tablespoons butter or margarine, softened
    1 tablespoon chopped green onion
    ½ teaspoon dried sage, crushed
    ¼ teaspoon dried thyme, crushed
    ⅛ teaspoon paprika
    ¼ teaspoon salt
    ⅛ teaspoon pepper
    1 tablespoon snipped parsley

Thaw fish, if frozen. Separate into fillets or cut into 4 serving-size portions. Place in greased shallow baking pan. Combine softened butter or margarine, green onion, sage, thyme, paprika, salt and pepper; spread over fish. Broil 4 inches from heat till fish flakes easily when tested with fork. (Allow 5 minutes for each ½ inch of thickness.) Baste occasionally with butter mixture during broiling. If fish fillets are more than 1 inch thick, turn when fish is half done. Sprinkle with parsley. Makes 4 servings.

To Fillet a Fish

1

On cutting surface, position back of fish toward you. Cut behind the pectoral fin and gill straight down to the backbone with a very sharp fillet knife, as shown. Angle the cut toward the top of the head.

2

Carefully run the end of the knife blade along one side of the backbone. The knife tip should scrape the rib bones without cutting them.

3

Push the knife through the flesh near the vent just behind the rib bones. Run knife along entire length of fish; cut the fillet free at the tail.

4

Carefully cut the flesh away from the rib cage. The knife blade should just graze the bones so little, if any, flesh is wasted.

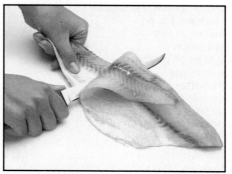

5

To skin the fillet, place fillet skin side down. Hold the tail firmly with fingers and cut between the flesh and skin with a sawing motion, peeling away skin. Repeat procedure with other side of fish.

Fish, Seafood & Eggs

Lemon-Marinated Salmon Steaks

    2 pounds fresh or frozen salmon steaks
    1 cup water
    ½ cup lemon juice
    ⅓ cup sliced green onion
    ¼ cup cooking oil
    3 tablespoons snipped parsley
    3 tablespoons chopped green pepper
    1 tablespoon sugar
    2 teaspoons dry mustard
    ½ teaspoon salt
    ⅛ teaspoon ground red pepper

Thaw fish, if frozen. Bring water to boiling in a 10-inch skillet or fish poacher with tight-fitting cover. Sprinkle salmon with a little *salt*. Place *half* of the fish on a greased rack in the skillet or poacher so fish does not touch water. Cover pan tightly and steam for 5 to 7 minutes or till fish flakes easily when tested with a fork. Carefully remove fish to a shallow dish. Repeat with remaining fish.

For marinade, in a screw-top jar combine lemon juice, green onion, cooking oil, parsley, green pepper, sugar, mustard, salt, and red pepper. Shake vigorously to blend. Pour over fish. Cover; chill several hours or overnight, spooning marinade over fish several times. Drain before serving and spoon vegetables from marinade over fish. Serves 6.

Spanish-Style Fish

    2 pounds fresh or frozen fish steaks
    2 medium tomatoes, sliced
    ½ small cucumber, sliced
    ¼ cup chopped onion
    ¼ cup chopped green pepper
    1 clove garlic, minced
    2 tablespoons butter
    2 tablespoons snipped parsley
    2 tablespoons lemon juice
    ½ teaspoon dried marjoram, crushed

Thaw fish, if frozen. Place fish steaks in greased baking dish. Arrange tomato and cucumber slices atop. In saucepan cook onion, green pepper, and minced garlic in butter till onion is tender but not brown. Remove from heat; stir in parsley, lemon juice, and marjoram. Spoon lemon mixture over fish. Bake in 375° oven about 25 minutes or till fish flakes easily when tested with a fork. Makes 6 servings.

Baked Fish a l'Orange

    2 pounds fresh or frozen halibut steaks
       or other fish steaks
    ½ cup finely chopped onion
    2 cloves garlic, minced
    2 tablespoons cooking oil
    2 tablespoons snipped parsley
    1 teaspoon salt
    ⅛ teaspoon pepper
    ½ cup orange juice
    1 tablespoon lemon juice
      Hard-cooked egg (optional)
      Paprika (optional)
      Orange slices (optional)

Thaw fish, if frozen. Arrange in a 12x7½x2-inch baking dish. Cook onion and garlic in oil till onion is tender but not brown. Stir in parsley, salt, and pepper. Spread mixture over fish. Combine orange and lemon juices; pour evenly over all.

Bake, covered, in a 400° oven for 20 to 25 minutes or till fish flakes easily with a fork. If desired, arrange hard-cooked egg wedges atop fish, sprinkle with paprika, and garnish with fruit decorations shown on pages 18-21. Makes 6 servings.

To Cut Fish into Steaks

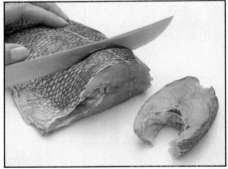

Place the dressed fish (head, tail, and fins removed) on a cutting board. Use a sharp slicing knife to cut 5/8- to 1-inch-thick cross-section slices (back to belly).

To Clean a Fish

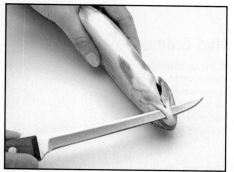

Position fish with backbone down on cutting surface. With a very sharp fillet knife, slice the throat connection (tissue that connects the lower jaw and the gill membrane).

1

With one hand, push thumb into the throat. With other hand, begin pulling gills and entrails toward the tail.

4

Lay fish on side with belly facing you. Insert knife tip in the vent and run knife toward gills. (Do not puncture the intestines.)

2

Pull entrails out with gills attached.

5

Run the blade tip up stomach to gills and cut tissue at the point of the gill attachment.

3

Open fish. With knife, remove dark blood line that runs along backbone, as shown. Rinse with cold water.

6

85

Fish, Seafood & Eggs

Trout Amandine

4 to 6 fresh or frozen pan-dressed trout
(about 8 ounces each)
1 beaten egg
¼ cup light cream or milk
½ cup all-purpose flour
2 tablespoons cooking oil
6 tablespoons butter or margarine
¼ cup sliced almonds
2 tablespoons lemon juice

Thaw fish, if frozen. Bone trout, if desired. Season. Combine egg and cream. Dip fish in flour, then in egg-cream mixture, and again in flour.

In a large skillet heat together the oil and *2 tablespoons* of the butter. Fry trout in hot oil mixture for 5 to 6 minutes on each side or till golden and fish flakes easily with fork. In a skillet cook almonds in remaining butter till nuts are golden brown. Remove from heat; stir in lemon juice. Place trout on a platter; pour almond mixture over. Makes 4 to 6 servings.

Luau Fish Bake

1 1- to 1½-pound fresh or frozen pan-dressed fish
½ cup sliced celery
¼ cup chopped green pepper
2 tablespoons chopped onion
3 tablespoons butter or margarine
1½ cups herb-seasoned stuffing mix
Lemon juice
1 tablespoon brown sugar
1 teaspoon cornstarch
2 tablespoons lemon juice
2 tablespoons soy sauce
2 tablespoons sliced green onion
1 tablespoon butter or margarine
1 clove garlic, minced

Thaw fish, if frozen. Cook celery, green pepper, and chopped onion in the 3 tablespoons butter or margarine till tender but not brown. For stuffing mixture combine vegetables, stuffing mix, and 3 tablespoons *water*.

Place fish on well-greased foil; season cavity with *salt* and brush with lemon juice. Stuff cavity with stuffing mixture. Seal foil around fish. Place in shallow baking pan. Bake in 350° oven for 30 minutes. Turn foil back; continue baking for 10 to 15 minutes or till fish flakes easily when tested with a fork.

Meanwhile, for sauce, in small saucepan combine brown sugar and cornstarch. Stir in the 2 tablespoons lemon juice, and soy sauce, and 2 tablespoons *water*. Add green onion, the 1 tablespoon butter or margarine, and garlic. Cook and stir till thickened and bubbly. Cook and stir 2 minutes more. Remove fish to warm serving platter. Pour sauce over fish. Makes 3 servings.

Baked Stuffed Salmon

1½ cups sliced fresh mushrooms
1 cup shredded carrot
¼ cup sliced green onion
¼ cup snipped parsley
¼ cup butter or margarine
1 6-ounce package regular long grain and wild rice mix
2½ cups water
2 teaspoons instant chicken bouillon granules
⅛ teaspoon pepper
1 5-pound dressed salmon
3 tablespoons butter or margarine, melted

In saucepan cook mushrooms, carrot, onion, and parsley in the ¼ cup butter or margarine till tender. Add the rice and seasonings from mix. Stir in water, bouillon granules, and pepper. Cover; cook over low heat about 25 minutes or till rice is tender and liquid is absorbed.

Rinse fish and pat dry. Place in greased 15½x10½x2-inch baking pan. Brush 3 tablespoons melted butter or margarine on inside and outside of fish. Stuff loosely with rice mixture. (Spoon extra rice mixture into small casserole. Bake, covered, last 30 to 40 minutes of baking time.) Bake stuffed fish, covered, in 350° oven about 1½ hours or till fish flakes easily when tested with a fork. Makes 8 servings.

Oven-Fried Fish

3 10- to 12-ounce fresh or frozen pan-dressed trout or other fish, or 1 pound fresh or frozen fish fillets or steaks
1 beaten egg
½ cup fine dry bread crumbs
Salt
Pepper
¼ cup butter or margarine, melted
1 tablespoon lemon juice

Thaw fish, if frozen. (If using fillet block, cut frozen block into 3 or 4 pieces.) Dip fish into beaten egg, then into bread crumbs. Place coated fish in a well-greased, shallow baking pan; season with some salt and pepper. Combine the melted butter or margarine and lemon juice; drizzle over fish.

Bake fish in a 500° oven until golden and fish flakes easily when tested with a fork. (Allow 5 to 6 minutes for each ½ inch of thickness.) Makes 3 or 4 servings.

Salmon Loaf

- 1 16-ounce can salmon, drained
- 2 cups soft bread crumbs (about 2½ slices)
- 2 tablespoons chopped green onion
- 1 tablespoon butter or margarine, melted
- ½ teaspoon salt
- ⅛ teaspoon pepper
- ½ cup milk
- 1 slightly beaten egg
  Cheese Sauce or Lemon-Chive Sauce, optional
  (see recipe, page 111)

Flake salmon, discarding skin and bones. In a bowl combine salmon, bread crumbs, chopped onion, butter or margarine, salt, and pepper. Mix well. Combine milk and egg; add to salmon mixture and mix thoroughly. Shape into a loaf in a greased shallow baking pan or in a greased 7½x3½x2-inch loaf pan.

Bake in a 350° oven for 35 to 40 minutes. If desired, serve slices of salmon loaf with Cheese Sauce or Lemon-Chive Sauce. Makes 3 or 4 servings.

Nutty Tuna-Noodle Bake

- 3 cups medium noodles (4 ounces)
- 2 tablespoons butter or margarine
- 2 tablespoons all-purpose flour
- 1⅓ cups milk
- 1 10¾-ounce can condensed
  cream of mushroom soup
- ¾ cup shredded American cheese
- 1 12½-ounce can tuna
- 1 8-ounce can peas and carrots
- 2 tablespoons chopped pimiento
- ½ cup chopped peanuts

Cook noodles according to package directions; drain well. Meanwhile, in a saucepan melt butter or margarine; stir in flour. Add milk and mushroom soup all at once. Cook and stir till thickened and bubbly. Remove from heat; stir in shredded cheese till melted. Drain and flake tuna. Drain peas and carrots. Stir tuna, peas and carrots, and pimiento into soup mixture. Fold cooked noodles into soup-tuna mixture. Turn into a 2-quart casserole. Sprinkle chopped peanuts over mixture. Bake, uncovered, in a 350° oven for 30 to 35 minutes or till heated through. Makes 6 servings.

Tuna Salad in Tomato Cups

- 1 6½- or 7-ounce can tuna, drained
  and flaked
- ½ cup sliced celery
- ¼ cup sliced pimiento-stuffed olives
- ¼ cup sliced green onion
- 1 tablespoon lemon juice
- ¼ teaspoon salt
  Dash pepper
- ½ cup mayonnaise or salad dressing
- 2 hard-cooked eggs, chopped
- 4 medium tomatoes, cored
  Salt
  Leaf lettuce

In bowl combine tuna, celery, olives, green onion, lemon juice, salt, and pepper. Gently fold in mayonnaise or salad dressing and chopped eggs; cover and chill.

With stem end down, cut *each* tomato into 4 to 6 wedges, cutting to, but not through, the stem end of the tomato. Spread wedges apart slightly; sprinkle lightly with some salt. Cover and chill.

To serve, place a chilled tomato on each individual lettuce-lined plate; fill each tomato with about ½ cup of the tuna mixture. Garnish with additional sliced pimiento-stuffed olives, if desired. Makes 4 servings.

Salad Niçoise

- 3 cups torn romaine
- 1 head bibb lettuce, torn (2 cups)
- 1 7-ounce can water-pack tuna, drained
- 1 10-ounce package frozen cut green beans,
  cooked, drained, and chilled
- 1 cup cherry tomatoes halved
- 1 small green pepper, cut into rings
- 1 small onion, sliced and separated into rings
- 3 hard-cooked eggs, cut into wedges
- 1 medium potato, cooked, chilled, and sliced
- ½ cup pitted ripe olives
- 1 2-ounce can anchovy fillets, drained

Line large platter with torn romaine and bibb lettuce. Break tuna into chunks; mound in center of torn lettuce. Arrange chilled green beans, tomatoes, green pepper, onion rings, egg wedges, potato, olives, and anchovy fillets atop the lettuce. Cover and chill. Just before serving, drizzle with Vinaigrette Dressing. Makes 6 to 8 servings.

Vinaigrette Dressing: In a screw-top jar combine ½ cup *salad oil or olive oil*; ⅓ cup *vinegar or lemon or lime juice*; ½ to 1 teaspoon *sugar or honey*; ½ teaspoon *salt*; ¾ teaspoon *dry mustard* (optional); ¾ teaspoon *paprika* (optional); and ½ teaspoon dried *thyme, or oregano, or basil,* crushed. Cover and shake well to mix. Chill. Shake again just before serving. Makes ¾ cup dressing.

Classic Cheese Strata

- 8 slices day-old bread
- 8 ounces American or Swiss cheese, sliced
- 4 eggs
- 2½ cups milk
- ¼ cup finely chopped onion
- ¾ teaspoon salt
- ½ teaspoon prepared mustard
  Dash pepper
  Paprika

Trim the crusts from *4 slices* of the bread. Cut the trimmed slices in half diagonally to make 8 triangles; set aside.

Arrange the trimmings and the remaining 4 slices of untrimmed bread to cover the bottom of a 9x9x2-inch baking pan. Place American or Swiss cheese slices over the bread in the baking pan. Arrange the reserved 8 bread triangles in 2 rows over the cheese. (Points will slightly overlap bases of adjacent triangles.)

Thoroughly beat the eggs; stir in the milk, finely chopped onion, salt, prepared mustard, and pepper. Pour the egg mixture over bread and cheese layers in the baking pan. Sprinkle with paprika. Cover and chill in refrigerator several hours or overnight. Bake, uncovered, in a 325° oven for 1¼ hours or till a knife inserted near center comes out clean. Let stand 10 minutes before serving. Makes 6 servings.

Vegetable Welsh Rarebit

- 1 10-ounce package frozen cut broccoli
- ¼ cup chopped onion
- 2 tablespoons butter or margarine
- 3 tablespoons all-purpose flour
- ½ teaspoon dry mustard
- ¼ teaspoon salt
- ⅛ teaspoon ground red pepper
- 1½ cups milk
- 1½ teaspoons Worcestershire sauce
- 2 cups shredded cheddar cheese (8 ounces)
- 1 8-ounce can water chestnuts, drained and sliced
- 12 slices bread, toasted and quartered

Cook broccoli according to package directions; drain well. In a medium saucepan cook chopped onion in butter or margarine till tender but not brown. Stir in flour, dry mustard, salt, and ground red pepper. Add milk and Worcestershire sauce all at once. Cook and stir till mixture is thickened and bubbly. Cook and stir 1 minute more.

Add shredded cheese, stirring till melted. Add cooked broccoli and water chestnuts. Heat through. Spoon the cheese mixture over the toasted bread. Makes 6 servings.

Scalloped Eggs and Bacon

- ¼ cup chopped onion
- 2 tablespoons butter or margarine
- 2 tablespoons all-purpose flour
- 1½ cups milk
- ½ cup shredded American cheese
- ½ cup shredded Swiss cheese
- 6 hard-cooked eggs, sliced
- 10 to 12 slices bacon, crisp-cooked and crumbled
- 1½ cups crushed potato chips

Cook onion in butter till tender but not brown. Stir in flour. Add milk all at once. Cook and stir till thickened and bubbly. Cook and stir 1 minute more. Add cheeses; stir till melted. Place *half* of the sliced eggs in bottom of a 10x6x2-inch baking dish; pour *half* of the cheese sauce over. Sprinkle with *half* of the potato chips and *half* of the bacon. Repeat layers. Bake in 350° oven for 15 to 20 minutes. Makes 6 servings.

Eggs a la Suisse

- 3 tablespoons chopped green pepper
- 2 tablespoons chopped onion
- 2 tablespoons butter or margarine
- 2 tablespoons all-purpose flour
- 1 tablespoon horseradish mustard
- ⅛ teaspoon dried oregano, crushed
- ⅛ teaspoon dried thyme, crushed
- 1 cup milk
- 6 eggs
- 3 English muffins, split and toasted
- 6 slices cheddar cheese (4 ounces)
- 6 slices Swiss cheese (4 ounces)
  Paprika

For sauce, in a saucepan cook green pepper and onion in butter till tender. Stir in flour, horseradish mustard, oregano, thyme, ¼ teaspoon *salt*, and ¼ teaspoon *pepper*. Add milk all at once. Cook and stir till thickened and bubbly. Cook and stir 1 minute more. Cover and keep warm.

Lightly grease a 12-inch skillet. In the skillet heat 1½ inches of water to boiling; reduce heat to simmer. Break 1 of the eggs into a sauce dish; carefully slide egg into simmering water. Repeat with remaining eggs, keeping them separate in the skillet. Simmer, uncovered, over low heat for 3 to 5 minutes or to desired doneness. (Do not let water boil.)

Meanwhile, top each muffin half with a slice *each* of cheddar and Swiss cheese. Broil till cheese melts. When eggs are done, lift out with a slotted spoon; place one egg on each cheese-topped muffin half. Spoon sauce over each. Sprinkle paprika atop. Makes 6 servings.

Garden Frittata Parmesan

     2 cups fresh broccoli flowerets, chopped, or
          one 10-ounce package frozen chopped broccoli
     8 beaten eggs
    ¼ cup grated Parmesan cheese
    ¼ cup milk
     1 tablespoon all-purpose flour
    ½ teaspoon dried basil or thyme, crushed
    ¼ teaspoon salt
    ¼ teaspoon pepper
     1 tablespoon cooking oil
     6 thin tomato slices
         Cooking oil
     1 tablespoon grated Parmesan cheese
         Dairy sour cream
         Snipped chives

In a saucepan cook fresh broccoli in boiling salted water, covered, 8 to 10 minutes. (Or, cook frozen broccoli according to package directions.) Drain well.

Combine eggs, the ¼ cup Parmesan cheese, milk, flour, basil or thyme, salt, and pepper; mix well. Add broccoli. In a 10-inch oven-going skillet or omelet pan, heat the oil; swirl to coat the bottom and sides of the pan. Pour the broccoli-egg mixture into the hot skillet. Cook over medium-low heat, lifting edges occasionally to allow the uncooked portion to flow underneath. Cook about 4 minutes, or till edges begin to set and bottom is lightly browned. Place pan under the broiler, 4 to 5 inches from the heat, for 2 minutes or till set. Top with tomato slices; brush tomato slices lightly with oil. Sprinkle with the 1 tablespoon Parmesan cheese. Broil about ½ minute more or till tomatoes are heated. Cut into wedges to serve. Top each serving with a dollop of sour cream; sprinkle with chives. Serves 4.

Classic Quiche Lorraine

     8 slices bacon
     1 medium onion, thinly sliced
     4 beaten eggs
     1 cup light cream
     1 cup milk
     1 tablespoon all-purpose flour
    ½ teaspoon salt
         Dash ground nutmeg
    1½ cups shredded Swiss cheese
         Pastry for Single-Crust Pie (see recipe, page 129)

In a skillet cook bacon till crisp; drain, reserving *2 tablespoons* of the drippings. Crumble bacon; set aside. Cook onion in reserved drippings till tender; drain. Stir together eggs, cream, milk, flour, salt, and nutmeg. Stir in the bacon, onion, and Swiss cheese; mix well.

Prepare Pastry for Single-Crust Pie. To keep crust in shape, line the unpricked pastry shell with a double thickness of heavy-duty foil. Bake in a 450° oven for 5 minutes. Remove foil. Bake 5 to 7 minutes more or till pastry is nearly done. Remove from oven; reduce oven temperature to 325°.

Pour cheese mixture into *hot* pastry shell. If necessary, cover edge of crust with foil to prevent overbrowning. Bake in a 325° oven for 45 to 50 minutes or till a knife inserted near center comes out clean. Let stand 10 minutes before serving. Makes 6 servings.

Cheese Soufflé

     6 tablespoons butter or margarine
    ⅓ cup all-purpose flour
    ½ teaspoon salt
         Dash ground red pepper
    1½ cups milk
     3 cups shredded cheddar cheese (12 ounces)
     6 egg yolks
     6 egg whites

Attach a foil collar to a 2-quart soufflé dish. For collar, measure enough foil to go around dish plus a 2- to 3-inch overlap. Fold foil into thirds lengthwise. Lightly butter one side. With buttered side in, position foil around dish, letting collar extend 2 inches above top of dish; fasten with tape. Set aside.

In a saucepan melt butter or margarine; stir in flour, salt, and red pepper. Add milk all at once. Cook and stir till thickened and bubbly. Cook and stir 1 to 2 minutes more. Remove from heat. Add shredded cheese, stirring till cheese is melted. Beat egg yolks till thick and lemon colored. *Slowly* add cheese mixture, stirring constantly. Cool slightly.

Using clean beaters, beat egg whites till stiff peaks form (tips stand straight). Gradually pour cheese-yolk mixture over beaten whites, folding to blend. Pour into the ungreased 2-quart soufflé dish. Bake in a 300° oven about 1½ hours or till a knife inserted near center comes out clean. Gently peel off collar; serve soufflé immediately. Makes 6 servings.

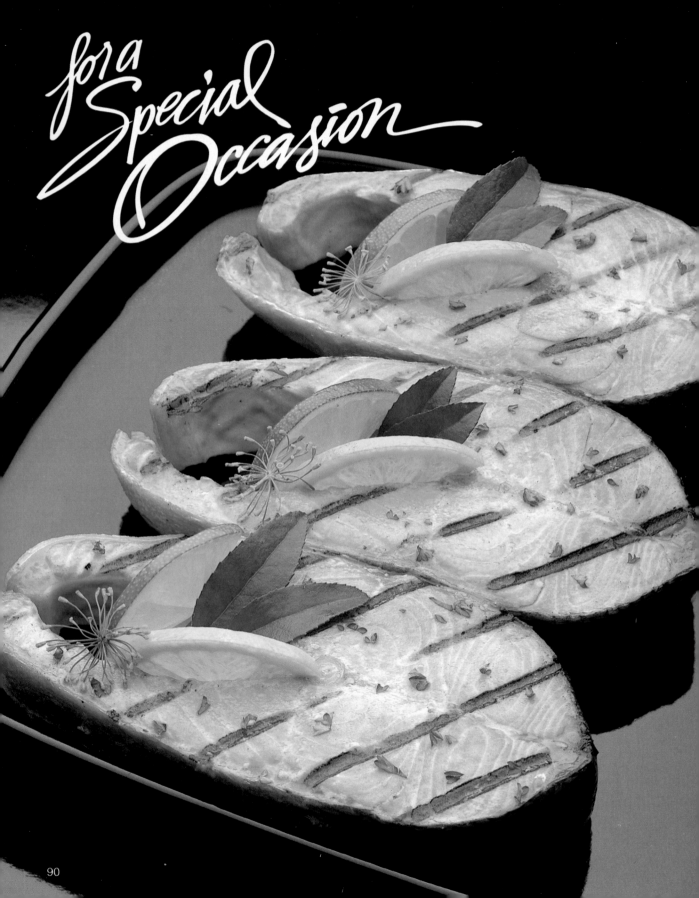

for a *Special Occasion*

Grilled Salmon Steaks

- 3 fresh or frozen salmon steaks or other fish steaks (1 to 1½ inches thick)
- ½ cup cooking oil
- ¼ cup snipped parsley
- ¼ cup lemon juice
- 2 tablespoons grated onion
- 1 teaspoon dry mustard
- ¼ teaspoon salt
  Dash pepper

Thaw fish steaks, if frozen. Place fish in a shallow dish. Combine oil, parsley, lemon juice, onion, mustard, salt, and dash pepper. Pour over fish. Marinate, covered, in the refrigerator 6 hours. Drain, reserving marinade. Place fish in a well-greased wire grill basket. Grill over *medium-hot* coals 8 to 10 minutes or till fish is lightly browned. Baste with marinade and turn. Brush again with marinade; grill 8 to 10 minutes more or till fish flakes easily when tested with a fork. Garnish with dillweed and lemon and lime slices, if desired. Serves 6.

Red Snapper with Wild Rice Stuffing

- 1 3-pound fresh or frozen red snapper or other fish (with head and tail)
- 1 4-ounce package (⅔ cup) wild rice
- 1 cup sliced fresh mushrooms
- ¼ cup butter or margarine
- 1 cup frozen peas, thawed
- 2 tablespoons sliced green onion
- 2 tablespoons chopped pimiento
- ½ teaspoon finely shredded lemon peel
- 2 tablespoons lemon juice
- 1 teaspoon salt
- ⅛ teaspoon pepper
- 2 tablespoons butter or margarine, melted
  Lemon slices (optional)
  Green onions (optional)

Thaw fish, if frozen. Cook rice according to package directions. Cook mushrooms in the ¼ cup butter or margarine till tender. For stuffing combine cooked rice, cooked mushrooms, peas, green onion, pimiento, lemon peel, lemon juice, salt, and pepper. Toss lightly.

Sprinkle fish cavity with salt. Fill fish cavity with stuffing, patting stuffing to flatten evenly. Tie or skewer fish closed; place in a greased large shallow baking pan. Brush some of the 2 tablespoons melted butter over fish. Bake in 350° oven for 45 to 60 minutes or till fish flakes easily when tested with a fork, brushing occasionally with remaining melted butter. Carefully lift fish to warm platter. Remove string or skewers. Garnish with fruit decorations and green onion brushes as shown on pages 18-21, if desired. Makes 6 servings.

Pictured: **Grilled Salmon Steaks.**

Canadian Bacon-Filled Gougère

A gougère is made from an egg, flour, and cheese mixture and resembles a giant cream puff when baked. The golden crust is filled with a saucy meat and vegetable mixture—

  Butter or margarine
- 1 cup water
- 6 tablespoons butter or margarine
- ½ teaspoon salt
  Dash pepper
- 1 cup all-purpose flour
- 4 eggs
- 2 cups shredded mozzarella cheese (8 ounces)
- 1 tablespoon butter
- 2 cups sliced fresh mushrooms
- ¼ cup sliced green onion
- 1 tablespoon cornstarch
- 1 8-ounce can tomatoes, drained and cut up
- 2 tablespoons dry white wine
- 2 tablespoons catsup
- ½ teaspoon Worcestershire sauce
- 2 cups Canadian-style bacon cut into bite-size strips

Butter a 12x7½x2-inch baking dish. In saucepan combine water, the 6 tablespoons butter, salt, and pepper, bring to boiling. Add flour, cook and stir over medium heat till mixture forms a ball that doesn't separate. Remove from heat.

Cool 5 minutes. Add eggs, one at a time, beating by hand after each addition till smooth. Stir in *1¾ cups* of the cheese. Spread mixture over the bottom and up the sides of baking dish. Bake in a 400° oven 20 minutes.

Meanwhile, in a saucepan melt the 1 tablespoon butter. Add the sliced mushrooms and green onion. Cook and stir till mushrooms are tender.

Stir in cornstarch. Add tomatoes, dry white wine, catsup, and Worcestershire sauce. Cook and stir till mixture is thickened and bubbly. Cook and stir 2 minutes more. Stir in Canadian-style bacon.

Pour vegetable-bacon mixture into partially baked crust; sprinkle with the remaining cheese. Bake 15 to 20 minutes more or till puffed and golden. Makes 6 servings.

Fish, Seafood & Eggs

Stuffed Flounder Fillets

An elegant entrée for a special occasion—

- 2 **pounds fresh or frozen flounder fillets (8 fillets)***
- 1 **3-ounce can chopped mushrooms**
- ¼ **cup chopped onion**
- ¼ **cup butter or margarine**
- 1 **7-ounce can crab meat, drained, flaked, and cartilage removed**
- ½ **cup coarsely crushed saltine crackers**
- 2 **tablespoons snipped parsley**
- ½ **teaspoon salt**
  Dash pepper
- 3 **tablespoons butter or margarine**
- 3 **tablespoons all-purpose flour**
- ¼ **teaspoon salt**
  Milk
- ⅓ **cup dry white wine**
- 1 **cup shredded Swiss cheese (4 ounces)**
  Paprika

Thaw fish, if frozen. Drain mushrooms, reserving liquid. In a skillet cook onion in ¼ cup butter or margarine about 3 minutes or till tender but not brown. Stir drained mushrooms into skillet with flaked crab, cracker crumbs, parsley, the ½ teaspoon salt, and the pepper. Spread filling lengthwise over flounder fillets. Fold fillets over filling, tucking fish under. Place the filled fish fillets, seam side down, in a 12x7½x2-inch baking dish.

In a saucepan melt 3 tablespoons butter or margarine. Blend in flour and the ¼ teaspoon salt. Add enough milk to mushroom liquid to make 1½ cups total liquid. Add liquid mixture with wine to saucepan. Cook and stir till sauce is thickened and bubbly. Pour sauce over fillets. Bake, uncovered, in a 400° oven about 30 minutes or till fish flakes easily when tested with a fork. Sprinkle with Swiss cheese and paprika. Return to oven. Bake 5 minutes longer or till cheese is melted. Makes 8 servings.

*Note: If fish fillets are in pieces, press fish together to form 8 whole pieces.

Citrus Buttered Lobster

- 4 **6- to 8-ounce frozen lobster tails**
- ¼ **cup butter or margarine, melted**
- 1 **tablespoon lemon juice**
- 1 **teaspoon finely shredded orange peel**
- ¼ **teaspoon salt**
  Dash ground ginger
  Dash paprika
  Lemon wedges

Partially thaw lobster tails. Butterfly lobster tails as shown at right. Spread tail open, butterfly-style, so lobster meat is on top. Place tails on broiler pan, shell side down. Combine melted butter, lemon juice, orange peel, salt, ginger, and

paprika; brush some over lobster. Broil 4 inches from the heat 15 to 20 minutes or till meat loses its translucency and can be flaked easily when tested with a fork. Loosen meat from shell by inserting a fork between shell and meat. Brush lobster meat with butter mixture before serving. Serve with lemon wedges. Makes 4 servings.

To Butterfly Lobster Tails

For broiling and grilling, butterfly lobster tails so they will cook evenly. To do so, partially thaw frozen lobster tails.

Cut through the center of the hard top shell with a sharp chef's knife or kitchen shears. Cut through meat with a sharp knife, but *do not cut through the undershell*. Spread the meat open in the shell.

If you prefer to leave the lobster tails intact, thaw them, then cut off the thin undershell membrane with kitchen shears. Bend the tail back to crack the shell, or insert long skewers lengthwise between the shell and the meat to prevent curling.

Broiled Shrimp

- 2 **pounds fresh or frozen large shrimp in shells**
- ¼ **cup butter or margarine, melted**
- 2 **tablespoons lemon juice**
  Dash bottled hot pepper sauce

Thaw shrimp, if frozen. Remove shells and devein as shown on page 93. Combine melted butter or margarine, lemon juice, and hot pepper sauce. Brush some of the butter mixture over shrimp.

To broil in the oven, place shrimp on a well-greased broiler rack and broil 4 to 5 inches from heat for 4 minutes. Turn and brush with butter mixture. Broil 2 to 4 minutes more or till shrimp are done. To broil on an outdoor grill, thread shrimp on skewers and grill over *hot* coals for 4 minutes. Turn and brush with butter mixture. Grill 4 to 5 minutes more or till shrimp are done. Makes 6 servings.

Batter-Fried Stuffed Shrimp

24 fresh or frozen large shrimp in shells
 2 tablespoons finely chopped celery
 2 tablespoons finely chopped green pepper
 1 clove garlic, minced
 2 tablespoons butter or margarine
 1 tablespoon all-purpose flour
¼ cup milk
 1 7-ounce can crab meat drained, cartilage removed,
    and chopped
½ cup soft bread crumbs
½ teaspoon Worcestershire sauce
½ teaspoon lemon juice
¼ teaspoon salt
⅛ teaspoon pepper
    Shortening or cooking oil for deep-fat frying
 1 cup all-purpose flour
½ teaspoon sugar
½ teaspoon salt
 1 slightly beaten egg
 1 cup ice water
 2 tablespoons cooking oil
    Lemon wedges

Thaw shrimp, if frozen. Remove shells. Butterfly shrimp, as shown at right. Spread shrimp open, split side up.

In a saucepan cook the celery, green pepper, and garlic in butter or margarine till tender; stir in 1 tablespoon flour. Add milk all at once; cook and stir till thickened and bubbly. Cook and stir 1 minute more. Remove from heat.

Stir in the crab meat, bread crumbs, Worcestershire sauce, lemon juice, the ¼ teaspoon salt, and the pepper. Press crab mixture onto slit shrimp, packing firmly. Place on tray lined with paper toweling; chill at least 1 hour.

In a saucepan or deep-fat fryer heat 2 inches of shortening or cooking oil to 360°.

Meanwhile, in a mixing bowl stir together 1 cup flour, the sugar, and ½ teaspoon salt. Mix slightly beaten egg, ice water, and the 2 tablespoons oil; stir into dry ingredients just till moistened (a few lumps should remain). Keep batter cool by placing the bowl in a larger bowl filled with ice cubes; use immediately.

Pat shrimp dry; dip into batter. Fry a few at a time in deep hot fat for 4 to 5 minutes or till golden. Drain on paper toweling; keep warm in 325° oven while frying remainder. Serve with lemon wedges, if desired. Makes 4 servings.

To Shell, Devein & Butterfly Shrimp

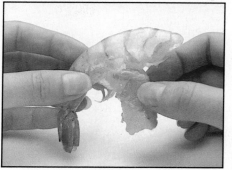

1

To shell shrimp, open the shell lengthwise down the body. Hold the shrimp in one hand and carefully peel back the shell starting with the head end. Leave the last section of the shell and tail intact. Then, either cut the body portion of the shell off, leaving the tail shell in place, or gently pull on the tail portion of the shell and remove the entire shell.

2

Remove the sandy black vein in shrimp by making a shallow slit with a sharp paring knife along the back of the shrimp. Look for the vein that appears as a dark line running down the center of the back. If it is present, use the tip of the knife to scrape it out and discard it.

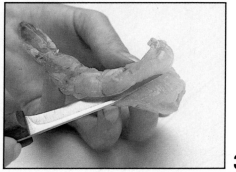

3

To butterfly the shrimp, after removing the sandy black vein, make a deeper slit in the shrimp's back. Cut almost but not all the way through the shrimp. The sides of the shrimp will open out to resemble a butterfly.

Salads

Choose-a-Fruit Salad Platter

    8 cups desired fresh fruits*
      Lemon juice
      Lettuce
      Spicy Nectar Dressing and/or
        Strawberry-Cheese Dressing

If necessary, brush fruits with lemon juice to prevent browning. On a large lettuce-lined platter arrange desired fruits.
Serve with Spicy Nectar Dressing and/or Strawberry-Cheese
Dressing. Makes 8 to 12 servings.
  Spicy Nectar Dressing: In a small mixer bowl combine 1
cup *dairy sour cream*, ½ cup *apricot nectar*, ½ cup *salad oil*,
2 tablespoons *sugar*, ½ teaspoon *ground cinnamon*, ½ teaspoon *paprika*, and dash *salt*. Beat till smooth. Cover and
chill. Makes 2 cups dressing.
  Strawberry-Cheese Dressing: In a small mixer bowl
combine one 3-ounce package *cream cheese*, softened; ½
of a 10-ounce package (½ cup) frozen *strawberries*, thawed;
1 tablespoon *sugar*; 1 tablespoon *lemon juice*; and dash *salt*.
Beat till smooth. Add ½ cup *salad oil* in a slow stream,
beating till thick. Cover and chill. Makes 1½ cups dressing.
  ***Fruit Options:** Choose any combination of the following:
Peeled and sliced or cut up avocados, bananas, kiwifruit,
mangoes, melons, papayas, peaches, or pineapple; sliced or
cut up apples, apricots, nectarines, pears, plums, or starfruit;
peeled and sectioned oranges, tangerines, or grapefruit; berries (halve large strawberries); halved and pitted dark sweet
cherries; or grapes.

Carrot-Pineapple Toss

    ½ cup raisins
      Boiling water
    1 8- or 8¼-ounce can pineapple chunks, drained
    2 cups coarsely shredded carrot
    ½ cup mayonnaise or salad dressing
    1 teaspoon lemon juice (optional)

Place raisins in bowl; cover with boiling water. Let stand 5
minutes; drain well. Mix pineapple chunks with the shredded
carrot and raisins. Cover and chill. Just before serving, fold in
mayonnaise or salad dressing. Sprinkle with lemon juice, if
desired. Makes 4 servings.

Rainbow Compote

    ½ cup honey
    2 tablespoons lemon juice
    1 tablespoon finely snipped candied ginger
        (optional)
    1 teaspoon finely shredded orange peel
    4 oranges, peeled and sliced crosswise
  1½ cups blueberries
    2 cups cubed honeydew melon
  1½ cups halved strawberries
      Whole strawberries

Combine honey, lemon juice, candied ginger, and orange
peel. Pour dressing over orange slices in bowl; cover and
refrigerate for several hours. Chill the remaining fruits.
  Drain oranges, reserving dressing. Arrange orange slices
in bottom of compote. Top with a layer of blueberries, a layer
of melon cubes, and a layer of halved strawberries. Pour the
reserved dressing over fruit. Garnish with additional whole
strawberries, if desired. Makes 10 servings.

Strawberry-Banana Soufflé Salads

    1 10-ounce package frozen sliced strawberries,
        thawed
    1 13-ounce package strawberry-flavored gelatin
    ¼ teaspoon salt
    1 cup boiling water
    2 tablespoons lemon juice
    ¼ cup mayonnaise or salad dressing
    ¼ cup chopped walnuts
    2 ripe medium bananas, sliced
      Lettuce

Drain strawberries, reserving syrup; set strawberries aside.
Add enough water to syrup to measure ¾ cup liquid. Dissolve gelatin and salt in boiling water. Stir in reserved strawberry syrup mixture and lemon juice. Add mayonnaise or
salad dressing; beat with a rotary beater. Chill till partially set
(the consistency of unbeaten egg whites).
  Whip gelatin mixture till fluffy. Fold in the reserved strawberries and the nuts. Divide banana slices among 6 individual
molds. Divide gelatin mixture among molds. Chill till firm.
Unmold onto a lettuce-lined platter. Serve with additional
mayonnaise or salad dressing, if desired. Makes 6 servings.

Pictured: **Choose-a-Fruit Salad Platter.**

Tropical Fruit Salad

¼ cup mayonnaise or salad dressing
1 tablespoon sugar
½ teaspoon lemon juice
   Dash salt
½ cup whipping cream
1 large red apple, chopped (1 cup)
1 large yellow delicious apple, chopped (1 cup)
1 large banana, sliced
1 cup sliced celery
½ cup broken walnuts
   Lettuce
½ cup toasted flaked coconut
   Unpeeled apple slices

In a mixing bowl blend together mayonnaise or salad dressing, sugar, lemon juice, and salt. Whip the cream till soft peaks form; fold into the mayonnaise mixture. Gently fold in the red and yellow apple, banana, celery, and walnuts. Cover and chill.

   Line salad bowl with lettuce; spoon in the chilled fruit mixture. Garnish with toasted coconut. Top with additional apple slices, if desired. Makes 6 servings.

Cherry-Cider Salad

2 cups apple cider or apple juice
1 6-ounce package cherry-flavored gelatin
1 16-ounce can pitted dark sweet cherries
½ cup thinly sliced celery
½ cup chopped walnuts
1 3-ounce package cream cheese, softened
1 8½-ounce can (1 cup) applesauce
   Leaf lettuce

Bring apple cider or juice to boiling. Dissolve gelatin in boiling cider. Drain cherries, reserving syrup. Halve cherries and set aside. Add enough water to reserved syrup to measure 1½ cups liquid; stir into gelatin. Set aside 2 cups of the gelatin mixture; keep at room temperature. Chill remaining gelatin till partialy set. Fold cherries, celery, and walnuts into partially set gelatin. Pour into 6½-cup ring mold. Chill till almost firm.

   Gradually add reserved gelatin to softened cream cheese, beating till smooth. Stir in applesauce. Spoon cream cheese mixture over cherry layer in mold. Chill till firm. Unmold on lettuce-lined platter as shown at right. Serve with mayonnaise or salad dressing sprinkled with additional walnuts, if desired. Makes 10 to 12 servings.

To Unmold Gelatin Salads

1

To unmold gelatin salads, dip the mold just to the rim in warm water for a *few seconds*. Tilt slightly to ease gelatin away from sides of mold and to let in air.

   With the tip of a narrow metal spatula, loosen gelatin from the outside and center of the ring mold by running the spatula around the edges.

2

Center an upside-down serving plate over the mold. Holding tightly, invert plate and mold together. Shake mold gently to let in air, loosening the gelatin all the way around.

3

Lift off the mold, being careful not to tear the gelatin. If the salad doesn't slide out easily, repeat steps 1 and 2.

   If desired, garnish salad with lettuce. Use a wide spatula to lift up the edges of the salad; slide lettuce leaves under.

Fresh Spinach Salad

  1 pound fresh spinach leaves, torn (12 cups)
  3 cups sliced fresh mushrooms
  1 8-ounce can water chestnuts, drained and sliced
  4 hard-cooked eggs, chilled and cut into wedges
  6 slices bacon
  ⅓ cup cooking oil
  ¼ cup sugar
  ¼ cup catsup
  ¼ cup vinegar
  2 teaspoons Worcestershire sauce

In a large salad bowl arrange spinach, mushrooms, water chestnuts, and eggs. In a skillet cook bacon till crisp; drain, reserving drippings in pan. Crumble bacon over spinach. To bacon drippings add cooking oil, sugar, catsup, vinegar, and Worcestershire sauce. Bring to boiling; pour over salad and toss to mix. Serve immediately. Makes 8 to 10 servings.

Create-a-Tossed Salad

  6 cups torn salad greens*
1½ cups desired salad ingredients*
    Desired salad dressing
    Salad Garnish*

In large salad bowl combine choice of torn salad greens and a combination of 2 or more desired salad ingredients. Cover; chill till serving time. Toss salad lightly with desired salad dressing. Arrange a Salad Garnish atop. Makes 6 servings.

*Salad green suggestions: Choose 2 or more of the following: iceberg lettuce, romaine, curly endive, leaf lettuce, spinach, Bibb lettuce, Boston lettuce, escarole, watercress, Chinese cabbage, Swiss chard, mustard greens, beet tops, kale leaves, dandelion greens, or fennel.

*Salad ingredient suggestions: Choose 2 or more from the following categories:

Fresh vegetables: tomato wedges, sliced cucumber, sliced fresh mushrooms, chopped or sliced celery, sliced radishes, shredded carrot, sliced cauliflower flowerets, onion rings, green pepper strips or rings, sliced zucchini, halved cherry tomatoes, chopped red cabbage, bean sprouts, or sliced water chestnuts.

Cooked vegetables: chopped broccoli, brussels sprouts, peas, beans (garbanzo, cut green, lima, pinto, kidney), or artichoke hearts.

Salad highlighters: sliced avocado, sliced pitted ripe or pimiento-stuffed olives, anchovy fillets, coarsely chopped or sliced hard-cooked egg, snipped chives, sliced green onion, alfalfa sprouts, cubed tofu, or raisins.

Cheeses: cheddar, Monterey Jack, Swiss, Muenster, colby, American, brick, or Gruyère cheese cut into julienne strips or cubes, or crumbled feta or blue cheese.

*Salad Garnishes: Top the salad with 1 or more of the following: croutons, toasted pumpkin seeds, peanuts, broken pecans or walnuts, crumbled crisp-cooked bacon, parsley sprigs, sieved hard-cooked egg yolk, or carrot curls.

To Cut Lettuce or Cabbage

Hold a quarter head of lettuce or cabbage firmly against cutting surface. With a sharp chef's knife, cut into long, coarse shreds. Cut crosswise into desired size pieces.

To Assemble a Salad Bowl

In a large salad bowl arrange the large, uncut leaves so leafy edges surround top edge of bowl

Fill in with the cut-up lettuce, assorted vegetables, and croutons. Add dressing just before serving; toss to coat.

Salads

Caesar Salad

      Garlic Olive Oil and Caesar Croutons
  3 medium heads romaine, torn into bite-size pieces
      (18 cups)
  2 to 3 tablespoons wine vinegar
  1 lemon, halved
  2 eggs
      Dash Worcestershire sauce
      Whole black pepper
  ⅓ cup grated Parmesan cheese
      Rolled anchovy fillets (optional)

One or more days before serving the salad, prepare Garlic Olive Oil. Several hours before serving, prepare Caesar Croutons. Chill a large salad bowl and dinner plates.

At serving time, place torn romaine in the chilled salad bowl. Drizzle romaine with about ⅓ *cup* of the Garlic Olive Oil and the vinegar; squeeze lemon over.

To coddle eggs, place eggs in shell in a saucepan of boiling water. Remove the saucepan from heat and let stand 1 minute. Remove eggs; let cool slightly. Break coddled eggs over romaine. Add Worcestershire; sprinkle with some *salt*. Grind a generous amount of pepper over all; sprinkle with Parmesan. Toss salad lightly till dressing is combined and the romaine is well coated. Add Caesar Croutons; toss once or twice. Serve immediately on the chilled dinner plates. Garnish with anchovies, if desired. Makes 8 to 10 servings.

Garlic Olive Oil: Slice 6 cloves *garlic* lengthwise into quarters; combine with 1 cup *olive or salad oil*. Store in a covered jar in the refrigerator. Remove garlic before using oil.

Caesar Croutons: Brush both sides of three ½-inch-thick slices firm-textured *white bread or French bread* with some Garlic Olive Oil. Cut bread into ½-inch cubes. Spread out on baking sheet. Bake in 250° oven about 1 hour or till croutons are dry and crisp. Sprinkle with some grated *Parmesan cheese*. Cool. Store croutons in covered jar in refrigerator.

Spinach-Orange Toss

  6 cups torn fresh spinach (8 ounces)
  1 11-ounce can mandarin orange sections, drained
  1 cup sliced fresh mushrooms
  3 tablespoons salad oil
  1 tablespoon lemon juice
  ½ teaspoon poppy seed
  ¼ teaspoon salt
  ¾ cup toasted slivered almonds

Place torn spinach in a large salad bowl. Add mandarin orange sections and sliced fresh mushrooms. Toss lightly; cover and chill.

For dressing, in a screw-top jar combine salad oil, lemon juice, poppy seed, and salt. Cover and shake well. Chill. Shake again and pour the dressing over the spinach-orange mixture. Toss salad lightly to coat. Sprinkle toasted almonds over top. Serve immediately. Makes 6 servings.

To Remove the Midrib from Romaine

With a sharp chef's knife, cut lengthwise along both sides of the heavy midrib (thick vein) of each leaf. Discard the midribs.

To Score and Slice Cucumbers

Cut a small V-shaped wedge the length of the *unpeeled* cucumber with the tip of a sharp paring knife. Repeat procedure around the outside of cucumber, keeping strips evenly spaced. Slice scored cucumber crosswise into thin slices.

To Chop Parsley

Gather parsley into tight ball. Slice across parsley with chef's knife. Draw pieces together in a heap; continue chopping.

Creamy Coleslaw

    4 cups shredded cabbage
    ½ cup shredded carrot
    ¼ cup finely chopped green pepper
    2 tablespoons finely chopped onion
    ½ cup mayonnaise or salad dressing
    1 tablespoon vinegar
    2 teaspoons sugar
    1 teaspoon celery seed

In large bowl combine cabbage, carrot, green pepper, and onion. For dressing, stir together mayonnaise, vinegar, sugar, celery seed, and ¼ teaspoon *salt*. Pour dressing over cabbage mixture; toss lightly to coat. Cover; chill. Serves 8.

Fruited Coleslaw: Prepare Creamy Coleslaw as above *except* substitute 2 medium *apples*, chopped; 2 medium *oranges*, peeled and coarsely chopped; and ⅓ cup *raisins* for the carrot, green pepper, and onion. Continue as directed.

Bulgur-Cabbage Salad

    1 cup bulgur wheat
    2 cups coarsely shredded cabbage
    1 cup frozen peas, thawed
    1 cup chopped tomato
    ¼ cup olive or salad oil
    ¼ cup lemon juice
    ¼ teaspoon dried dillweed
      Lettuce leaves

In a mixing bowl combine uncooked bulgur and 2 cups *warm water*; let stand 1 hour. Drain bulgur well, pressing out excess water. Stir in the shredded cabbage and the peas. Stir together the chopped tomato, olive oil or salad oil, lemon juice, and the dillweed. Stir oil mixture into bulgur-cabbage mixture. Cover and chill till serving time. To serve, spoon the salad into a lettuce-lined bowl. Makes 8 servings.

To Core Cabbage or Lettuce

Remove and discard any discolored or wilted outer leaves of cabbage or lettuce. To loosen and remove the core, use a sharp boner/utility knife to cut a 1-inch-deep circle at base of cabbage, as shown. Twist the core and lift out; discard.

To Cut Green Peppers

For green pepper rings, make a thin slice from the top of the green pepper with a sharp chef's knife. Scrape out the seeds and inside membrane; rinse with cold water. Slice crosswise into rings.

For strips, halve green pepper lengthwise. Scrape out seeds and membrane; rinse. Continue cutting each portion into strips of desired widths.

For cubes, cut strips crosswise into desired size cubes.

To Bias-Slice Vegetables

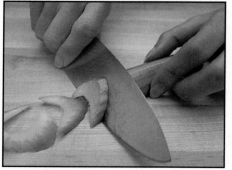

Place stalk of celery or a carrot on cutting board. Hold vegetable firmly with one hand; use the other to hold a sharp chef's knife or cleaver at an angle while you cut the food into slices.

The pieces cut this way have a greater surface area, so they will cook more quickly. That's why this cut is often used for firmer vegetables used in stir-frying. The additional surface area not only speeds cooking, but also adds visual appeal.

Salads

Garden-Fresh Tomato Aspics

    8 large tomatoes
    1 3-ounce package lemon-flavored gelatin
    2 tablespoons catsup
    1 tablespoon lemon juice
    2 teaspoons prepared horseradish
 1½ teaspoons Worcestershire sauce
  ½ teaspoon salt
       Dash pepper
  ¾ cup finely chopped celery
  ¼ cup finely chopped onion
  ¼ cup finely chopped green pepper
       Salt
       Spinach leaves
       Mayonnaise or salad dressing

Prepare tomato shells, as shown at right, by scooping out the pulp; *reserve pulp*. To drain, invert tomato shells on paper toweling. Place the reserved pulp in blender container. Cover; blend till pureed. Sieve to remove seeds. Measure *2 cups* of the tomato puree.

In a saucepan combine tomato puree and gelatin. Bring to boiling; stir to dissolve gelatin. Remove from heat; stir in catsup, lemon juice, horseradish, Worcestershire sauce, the ½ teaspoon salt, and the pepper. Chill till partially set.

Fold celery, onion, and green pepper into the gelatin mixture. Sprinkle insides of tomato shells with some salt; place upright on tray. Fill with gelatin mixture. Chill till firm. Serve individual tomato aspics on spinach leaves with mayonnaise, if desired. Makes 6 servings.

Creamy Potato Salad

    6 medium potatoes (2 pounds)
    1 cup thinly sliced celery
  ½ cup finely chopped onion
  ⅓ cup chopped sweet pickle
 1¼ cups mayonnaise or salad dressing
    2 teaspoons sugar
    2 teaspoons celery seed
    2 teaspoons vinegar
    2 teaspoons prepared mustard
 1½ teaspoons salt
    2 hard-cooked eggs, coarsely chopped

In a covered saucepan cook potatoes in boiling salted water for 25 to 30 minutes or till tender; drain well. Peel and cut up potatoes into a large bowl as shown at right. Add celery, onion, and sweet pickle. Combine mayonnaise or salad dressing, sugar, celery seed, vinegar, prepared mustard, and salt. Add mayonnaise mixture to potatoes. Toss lightly to coat potato mixture. Carefully fold in the chopped eggs. Cover and chill thoroughly. Makes 8 servings.

To Make Tomato Cups

To make tomato cups, cut a thin slice from top of tomato with a sharp parer/boning knife. Scoop out the center with a teaspoon, as shown. Remove as much liquid from the inside of the tomato shell as possible to prevent the filling from becoming too wet. Discard tomato pulp. Drain tomato shells, upside down, on paper toweling.

To Cut Potatoes

On a cutting board cut peeled potatoes lengthwise into quarters with a sharp chef's knife. Slice the potatoes crosswise into ¼-inch-thick pieces. (For smaller pieces, cut each potato quarter in half lengthwise, then slice crosswise into pieces.)

Chilled Pasta Salad

   4 ounces linguine
   1 cup thinly sliced fresh mushrooms
   1 carrot, shredded (½ cup)
   ¼ cup sliced green onion
   6 cherry tomatoes, halved
   2 tablespoons salad oil
   2 tablespoons soy sauce
   2 tablespoons lemon juice
   ½ teaspoon sesame oil
   1 small clove garlic, minced
     Few drops bottled hot pepper sauce
   2 tablespoons sesame seed, toasted

Cook linguine according to package directions. Rinse with cold water; drain well. In a bowl combine linguine, sliced mushrooms, shredded carrot, green onion, and halved cherry tomatoes.

For dressing, in a screw-top jar combine salad oil, soy sauce, lemon juice, sesame oil, minced garlic, and hot pepper sauce. Cover and shake well. Pour dressing over linguine mixture and toss to coat. Cover and refrigerate for 3 to 24 hours, stirring occasionally.

Before serving, toss mixture well. Sprinkle with toasted sesame seed. Garnish with parsley or green onion brush shown on page 18, if desired. Makes 6 servings.

Curried Layered Vegetable Salad

   6 cups torn lettuce
   1 pint cherry tomatoes, halved
   1 10-ounce package frozen peas, thawed
   1 medium cucumber or zucchini, thinly sliced*
   ½ cup dairy sour cream
   ½ cup mayonnaise or salad dressing
   1 tablespoon snipped parsley
   1 tablespoon milk
   1 teaspoon curry powder
   ½ teaspoon sugar
   6 slices bacon, crisp-cooked and crumbled

In large bowl layer in order *3 cups* of the lettuce, the tomatoes, peas, remaining 3 cups lettuce, and cucumber or zucchini. Combine sour cream, mayonnaise, parsley, milk, curry, and sugar; spread atop cucumber, sealing to edge of bowl. Cover and chill up to 48 hours. Wrap and chill crumbled bacon. Just before serving, sprinkle with bacon. Makes 10 servings.

*Note: Make decorated slices of cucumber or zucchini as shown on page 98, if desired.

Gazpacho Salad

   3 medium tomatoes, cut into eighths
   1 medium cucumber, thinly sliced
   1 medium green pepper, coarsely chopped
   2 small onions, sliced and separated into rings
   3 tablespoons snipped parsley
   ¼ cup salad oil
   2 tablespoons lemon juice
   1 tablespoon white wine vinegar
   1 teaspoon dried basil, crushed
   1 clove garlic, minced
     Few drops bottled hot pepper sauce
     Plain croutons

In bowl combine tomatoes, cucumber, green pepper, onions, and parsley. For dressing, in a screw-top jar combine oil, lemon juice, vinegar, basil, garlic, pepper sauce, and ½ teaspoon *salt*. Cover; shake well. Pour dressing over the tomato mixture. Toss lightly to coat vegetables. Cover; chill for 2 to 3 hours, stirring occasionally. Serve with croutons sprinkled atop individual servings, if desired. Makes 4 to 6 servings.

Fresh Asparagus-Mushroom Vinaigrette

   ¾ pound fresh asparagus or one 8-ounce package frozen asparagus spears
   ½ cup salad oil
   2 tablespoons white wine vinegar
   2 tablespoons lemon juice
   2 teaspoons snipped fresh dill or ½ teaspoon dried dillweed
  1½ teaspoons sugar
   1 teaspoon paprika
   ½ teaspoon dry mustard
   3 medium tomatoes, peeled and thinly sliced
   1 cup sliced fresh mushrooms
   1 small onion, thinly sliced and separated into rings
     Lettuce

Wash fresh asparagus and scrape off scales with a sharp knife. Break off woody bases as shown on page 103. Cook, covered, for 8 to 12 minutes or till asparagus spears are crisp-tender. (Or, cook frozen asparagus according to package directions.) Drain asparagus.

For dressing, in screw-top jar combine salad oil, vinegar, lemon juice, dill, sugar, paprika, dry mustard, and ½ teaspoon *salt*. Cover and shake well. Place asparagus, tomatoes, mushrooms, and onion in shallow dish. Pour dressing over all. Cover; refrigerate several hours or overnight, spooning dressing over vegetables occasionally.

To serve, lift vegetables from dressing with slotted spoon. Arrange vegetables on lettuce-lined platter or transfer to serving bowl; spoon some of the dressing over vegetables. Pass remaining dressing. Makes 6 servings.

Vegetables, Soups, & Sauces

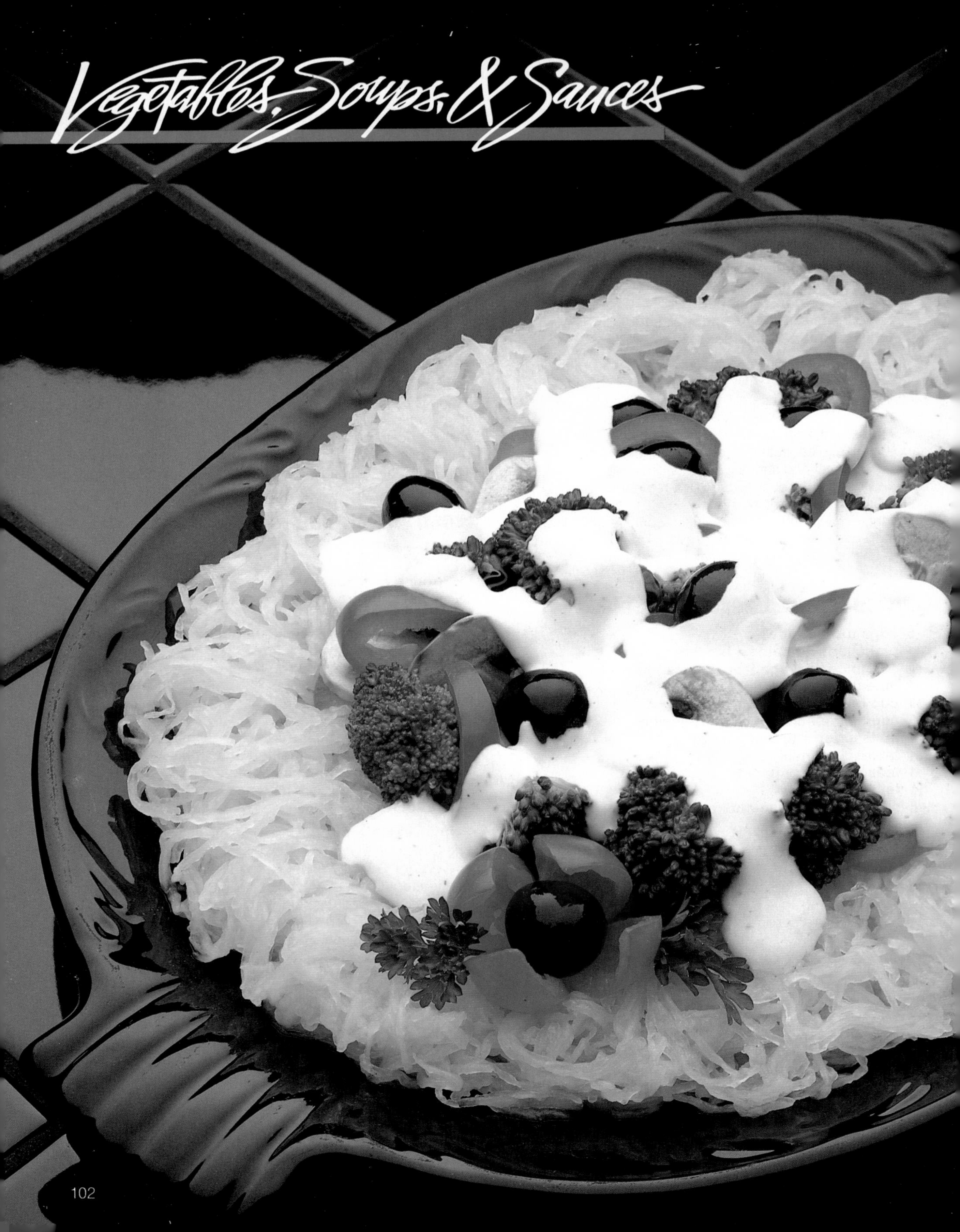

Artichokes with Butter Sauce

> 2 artichokes (about 10 ounces each)
> ¼ cup butter or margarine
> 1 tablespoon snipped parsley
> 1 tablespoon lemon juice

Trim stems of artichokes. Remove loose outer leaves; trim or snip off sharp leaf tips as shown at right. Cook artichokes in a large amount of boiling salted water 20 to 30 minutes or till a leaf pulls out easily. Drain upside down. Melt butter; stir in parsley and lemon juice. Turn artichokes right side up and serve with the butter sauce. Makes 2 servings.

Note: To eat, pull off one leaf at a time and dip the base of the leaf in butter sauce. Turn the leaf upside down and draw through the teeth, eating only the tender flesh. Discard remainder of leaf. Continue removing leaves until the fuzzy 'choke' appears. Scoop out and discard the 'choke.' Eat the remaining heart with a fork, dipping each piece in melted butter sauce.

Asparagus with Orange Cream Sauce

> 1 pound asparagus
> ¼ cup butter or margarine, softened
> 2 egg yolks
> ¼ teaspoon finely shredded orange peel
> 1 teaspoon orange juice
> Dash salt
> Dash white pepper
> ¼ cup dairy sour cream

Prepare asparagus spears as shown in photo at right. In saucepan cook asparagus spears in a small amount of boiling salted water for 10 to 15 minutes or till tender. Drain well.

Meanwhile, divide butter or margarine into 3 portions. In a small, heavy saucepan combine egg yolks and *1 portion* of the butter. Cook and stir over *low* heat till butter melts. Add another portion of the butter and continue stirring. As mixture thickens and butter melts, add remaining butter, stirring constantly. When butter is melted, remove from heat. Stir in orange peel, orange juice, salt, and white pepper. Return to *low* heat. Cook and stir 2 to 3 minutes or till thickened. Remove from heat at once. Blend hot orange mixture into sour cream. Spoon over asparagus spears. Garnish with additional finely shredded orange peel, if desired. Makes 4 or 5 servings.

To Prepare Artichokes

1

On cutting board firmly hold artichoke with one hand. Remove stem end with a sharp chef's knife.

2

Trim about 1 inch of the sharp leaf tips with knife, as shown. Brush cut edges with lemon juice to prevent browning.

To Prepare Asparagus

Wash fresh asparagus spears in cold water and scrape off scales with a small, sharp knife. Remove woody bases by breaking stalks, as shown. (Stalks will snap easily where the tender parts begin.)

Pictured: **Spaghetti Squash Vegetable Platter (see recipe, page 109).**

Asparagus-Mushroom Casserole

    4 cups fresh mushrooms, halved
    1 cup chopped onion
    ¼ cup butter or margarine
    2 tablespoons all-purpose flour
    1 teaspoon instant chicken bouillon granules
    ½ teaspoon salt
    ½ teaspoon ground nutmeg
    1 cup milk
    2 8-ounce packages frozen cut asparagus, cooked
       and drained
    ¼ cup chopped pimiento
 1½ teaspoons lemon juice
    ¾ cup soft bread crumbs (1 slice)
    1 tablespoon butter or margarine, melted

In a saucepan cook mushrooms and onions, covered, in the ¼ cup butter or margarine 10 minutes or till tender. Remove vegetables, leaving butter in skillet. Set vegetables aside.

Blend flour, chicken bouillon granules, salt, nutmeg, and dash **pepper** into skillet. Add milk all at once. Cook and stir till thickened and bubbly. Stir in mushrooms and onion, cooked asparagus, pimiento, and lemon juice. Turn into a 1½-quart casserole. Combine bread crumbs and the melted butter or margarine; sprinkle atop casserole. Bake, uncovered, in a 350° oven for 35 to 40 minutes. Makes 8 to 10 servings.

Green Beans Supreme

    1 pound green beans or two 9-ounce packages
       frozen French-style green beans
    1 small onion, sliced
    1 tablespoon snipped parsley
    3 tablespoons butter or margarine
    2 tablespoons all-purpose flour
    ½ teaspoon finely shredded lemon peel
    ½ teaspoon salt
    ½ cup milk
    1 cup dairy sour cream
    ½ cup shredded American cheese (2 ounces)
    ¼ cup fine dry bread crumbs

Cut fresh beans French style, as shown at right. Cook beans, covered, in a small amount of boiling salted water 10 to 12 minutes or till crisp-tender. (Or, cook frozen beans according to package directions.) Drain well.

In a saucepan cook onion and parsley in *2 tablespoons* of the butter till onion is tender. Blend in flour, lemon peel, salt, and dash **pepper**. Add milk; cook and stir till thickened and bubbly. Cook and stir 1 minute more. Stir in sour cream and the cooked green beans; heat till just bubbly. Spoon mixture into a 1-quart casserole. Sprinkle with shredded cheese.

Melt remaining 1 tablespoon butter; toss with bread crumbs and sprinkle atop beans. Broil 4 to 5 inches from heat 1 to 2 minutes till cheese melts and crumbs brown. Serves 8.

To Prepare Green or Wax Beans

Wash beans in cold water. Cut off ends and remove strings, if present. Leave beans whole, French cut, or snap into pieces.

1

To French cut beans, use the special cutter attached to the vegetable peeler, as shown, or use a small, sharp chef's knife to slice beans end to end.

2

For cut beans, use a sharp knife to slice the beans crosswise into 1-inch pieces, as shown. Or, to snap beans, grasp each bean between fingers and snap into 1-inch pieces.

To Cut Broccoli Spears

Wash broccoli and remove the outer leaves and tough part of stalks. With a sharp chef's knife, cut broccoli stalks lengthwise into uniform spears, following the branching lines.

Broccoli-Onion Deluxe

- 1 pound broccoli or two 10-ounce packages frozen cut broccoli
- 2 cups frozen small whole onions or 3 medium onions, quartered
- ¼ cup butter or margarine
- 2 tablespoons all-purpose flour
- ¼ teaspoon salt
  Dash pepper
- 1 cup milk
- 1 3-ounce package cream cheese
- ½ cup shredded American cheese (2 ounces)
- 1 cup soft bread crumbs

Cut buds off fresh broccoli; set aside. Cut remaining stalks into 1-inch pieces. Cook broccoli pieces in boiling salted water for 5 minutes. Add the reserved broccoli buds; cook 5 minutes more. (Or, cook frozen broccoli according to package directions.) Drain well. Cook frozen or fresh onions in boiling salted water till tender. Drain well.

In a saucepan melt *half* of the butter or margarine. Blend in flour, salt, and pepper. Add milk all at once. Cook, stirring constantly, till thickened and bubbly. Reduce heat; blend in cream cheese till smooth.

Place vegetables in a 1½-quart casserole. Pour sauce mixture over and mix lightly. Top with shredded American cheese. Melt the remaining butter; toss with bread crumbs. Sprinkle crumbs atop casserole. Bake in a 350° oven 40 to 45 minutes or till heated through. Makes 6 servings.

To Chop Onions

Cut the peeled onion in half through the root. Place one of the halves, flat side down, on cutting board. Hold onion with the fingertips tucked under. With a sharp chef's knife, cut vertical slices from one end to the other, up to, but not through, the root end.

Then, cut onion crosswise, up to the root end, to release the pieces of chopped onion, as shown.

Glazed Carrots

- 1 pound carrots, bias sliced ¼ inch thick or cut into julienne strips (see photo below)
- 2 tablespoons butter or margarine
- 2 tablespoons sugar
- ⅛ teaspoon ground cinnamon or ground ginger

In a saucepan cook carrots in a small amount of boiling salted water 8 to 10 minutes or till tender; drain. In the same saucepan combine butter, sugar, and cinnamon or ginger. Cook and stir 1 minute. Add carrots; cook over low heat about 5 minutes or till carrots are shiny and well glazed, stirring often. Stir in ⅓ cup *raisins*, if desired. Makes 4 servings.

Garden Vegetable Stir-Fry

- 2 medium carrots
- 2 cups green beans bias-sliced into 1-inch lengths*
- 2 cups sliced cauliflower
- 1½ teaspoons cornstarch
- 2 tablespoons soy sauce
- 1 tablespoon dry sherry
- 2 teaspoons sugar
- 2 tablespoons cooking oil
- 1 medium onion, cut into thin wedges
- 1 cup sliced zucchini

Cut carrots into thin sticks as shown below. In a covered saucepan cook carrots and beans in boiling salted water for 3 minutes. Add cauliflower. Cover and cook 2 minutes more; drain well. In small bowl blend 2 tablespoons *water* into cornstarch; stir in soy, sherry, sugar, and dash *pepper*. Set aside.

Preheat a wok or large skillet over high heat; add oil. Stir-fry onion in hot oil for 1 minute. Add carrots, beans, cauliflower, and zucchini; stir-fry 2 minutes or till vegetables are crisp-tender. Stir soy mixture; stir into vegetables. Cook and stir 3 to 4 minutes or till bubbly. Serve at once. Makes 6 servings.

*Note: To bias-slice green beans, see page 99.

To Julienne Vegetables

"Julienne" means to cut food into long, narrow strips resembling matchsticks. On a cutting board divide vegetable crosswise into desired lengths with a sharp chef's knife. Cut each portion lengthwise into pieces ⅛ to ¼ inch thick. Place the pieces flat side down. Cut into thin lengthwise strips ⅛ to ¼ inch thick.

Saucy Brussels Sprouts

- 2 **pints brussels sprouts**
- ½ **cup chopped onion**
- 2 **tablespoons butter or margarine**
- 1 **tablespoon all-purpose flour**
- 1 **tablespoon brown sugar**
- ½ **teaspoon dry mustard**
- ½ **cup milk**
- 1 **cup dairy sour cream**

Cook brussels sprouts, covered, in a small amount of boiling salted water 10 to 15 minutes or till crisp-tender; drain well.

Meanwhile, in a medium saucepan cook onion in butter till tender but not brown. Blend in flour, brown sugar, mustard, and 1 teaspoon *salt*. Stir in milk. Cook, stirring constantly, till thickened and bubbly. Cook and stir 1 minute more. Stir in sour cream. Add cooked brussels sprouts; stir gently to combine. Cook till heated through; do not boil. Serves 6 to 8.

German-Style Cabbage Bake

- 6 **cups shredded cabbage**
- 1 **large onion, sliced (1 cup)**
- 1 **cup dairy sour cream**
- 2 **tablespoons all-purpose flour**
- 1 **tablespoon prepared mustard**
- 1 **teaspoon caraway seed**
    Paprika

In a saucepan bring ½ cup *water* and ½ teaspoon *salt* to boiling. Add cabbage and onion. Cook, covered, 7 to 8 minutes or till crisp-tender. Drain, reserving cooking liquid. Add enough *water* to the cooking liquid to make ¾ *cup* liquid.

In same saucepan stir together sour cream, flour, mustard, caraway seed, ½ teaspoon *salt*, and ⅛ teaspoon *pepper*. Stir in reserved cooking liquid. Fold in cabbage and onion.

Turn mixture into a 1½-quart casserole. Bake, covered, in a 350° oven about 20 minutes or till heated through, stirring once. Sprinkle generously with paprika. Makes 6 servings.

Corn-Mushroom Bake

- ¼ **cup all-purpose flour**
- 1 **17-ounce can cream-style corn**
- 1 **3-ounce package cream cheese, cut into cubes**
- ½ **teaspoon onion salt**
- 1 **17-ounce can whole kernel corn, drained**
- 1 **4-ounce can mushroom stems and pieces, drained**
- ½ **cup shredded Swiss cheese**
- 1½ **cups soft bread crumbs**
- 2 **tablespoons butter or margarine, melted**

In a saucepan stir flour into cream-style corn. Add cream cheese and onion salt; heat and stir till cream cheese melts. Stir in whole kernel corn, mushrooms, and Swiss cheese.

Turn mixture into a 1½-quart casserole. Toss soft bread crumbs with melted butter or margarine; sprinkle crumbs atop casserole. Bake vegetables in a 350° oven for 40 minutes or till heated through. Makes 6 to 8 servings.

Cauliflower with Cheese and Mushroom Sauce

- 1 **medium head cauliflower**
- 1½ **cups sliced fresh mushrooms (4 ounces) or one 4-ounce can sliced mushrooms, drained**
- 2 **tablespoons butter or margarine**
- 2 **tablespoons all-purpose flour**
    Dash white pepper
- 1 **cup milk**
- 1 **cup shredded American cheese (4 ounces)**
- 1 **teaspoon prepared mustard**
- 1 **tablespoon snipped parsley**

Cook whole cauliflower, covered, in a small amount of boiling salted water 15 to 20 minutes or till just tender. (Or, cut into flowerets, as shown below, and cook for 10 to 15 minutes.) Drain cauliflower thoroughly; keep warm.

Meanwhile, cook fresh mushrooms in butter 4 minutes or till tender. (Or, if using canned mushrooms, set them aside and melt butter.) Blend flour, pepper, and ¼ teaspoon *salt* into butter. Add milk all at once. Cook, stirring constantly, till bubbly. Cook and stir 1 minute more. Stir in cheese and mustard. (If using canned mushrooms, stir into sauce.) Heat till cheese melts. Place whole cauliflower on platter. Spoon some sauce over; pass remaining. (Or, pour all sauce over flowerets in a serving bowl.) Sprinkle with parsley. Serves 6.

To Cut Cauliflower into Flowerets

Rinse head of cauliflower under cold water and remove outer green leaves. Remove woody stem with a sharp paring knife. With knife, loosen the small pieces called "flowerets"; pull apart with finger. Divide into desired size pieces.

Eggplant Parmigiana

¼ cup all-purpose flour
½ teaspoon salt
1 medium eggplant, peeled and cut into
　　½-inch slices
1 beaten egg
½ cup cooking oil
⅓ cup grated Parmesan cheese
　　Homemade Tomato Sauce
1 6-ounce package sliced mozzarella cheese

Combine flour and salt. Dip eggplant slices into beaten egg, then in flour mixture. In a large skillet brown eggplant in hot oil; drain well on paper toweling. Place *1 layer* of eggplant in 10x6x2-inch baking dish, cutting slices to fit. Sprinkle with *half* the Parmesan cheese. Top with *half* the Homemade Tomato Sauce and *half* the mozzarella cheese.

Cut remaining mozzarella cheese into triangles. Repeat eggplant, Parmesan cheese, Homemade Tomato Sauce, and mozzarella layers. Bake in a 400° oven 15 to 20 minutes or till heated through. Makes 6 servings.

Homemade Tomato Sauce: In a saucepan cook ⅓ cup chopped *onion*; ¼ cup finely chopped *celery*; ½ clove *garlic*, minced; and 1 teaspoon dried *parsley flakes* in 2 tablespoons *olive oil or cooking oil* till onion and celery are tender but not brown. Stir in one 14-ounce can peeled *Italian-style tomatoes*; ⅓ cup *tomato paste*; ½ teaspoon *salt*; ½ teaspoon dried *oregano*, crushed; ¼ teaspoon *pepper*; and 1 *bay leaf*. Simmer gently, uncovered, for 45 to 50 minutes. Remove bay leaf; discard.

Mushroom-Spinach Sauté

2 pounds fresh spinach
2 cups sliced fresh mushrooms
2 tablespoons butter or margarine
⅓ cup whipping cream
2 tablespoons dry white wine
½ teaspoon salt
¼ teaspoon ground nutmeg
　　Dash pepper

Wash, drain, and chop spinach. In a saucepan cook sliced mushrooms in butter or margarine till tender. Stir chopped spinach into mushrooms. Cover and cook 5 minutes or till spinach is wilted. Stir in cream, wine, salt, nutmeg, and pepper. Heat through; serve at once. Makes 6 servings.

Creamed Peas and New Potatoes

1½ pounds (about 15) tiny new potatoes
1 to 1½ cups fresh peas (1 to 1½ pounds in shell)
　　or one 10-ounce package frozen peas
3 tablespoons sliced green onion
4 teaspoons butter or margarine
4 teaspoons all-purpose flour
　　Dash salt
1 cup milk

Scrub potatoes; peel off narrow strip of peel around center of each. Cook in boiling salted water 15 to 20 minutes; drain.

Meanwhile, cook peas and onion in small amount of boiling salted water 10 to 12 minutes; drain. In a medium saucepan melt butter or margarine. Stir in flour and salt. Add milk. Cook, stirring constantly, till mixture is thickened and bubbly. Cook and stir 1 minute more. Fold in cooked peas. Pour over potatoes in serving bowl. Makes 6 servings.

Scalloped Tomatoes

2 pounds tomatoes, peeled and cut up (6 medium),
　　or one 28-ounce can tomatoes, cut up
1 cup celery
½ cup chopped onion
2 tablespoons all-purpose flour
1 tablespoon sugar
½ teaspoon salt
½ teaspoon dried marjoram, crushed
　　Dash pepper
¼ cup water
2 tablespoons butter or margarine
4 slices bread, toasted
2 tablespoons grated Parmesan cheese

In a saucepan combine fresh or canned tomatoes, celery, and onion. Cover and bring to boiling; reduce heat. Simmer, covered, till celery is tender, about 10 minutes. Combine flour, sugar, salt, marjoram, and pepper. Blend in water; stir into tomatoes. Cook, stirring constantly, till thickened and bubbly. Stir in butter till melted.

Cut *3 slices* of the toast into cubes; stir into tomato mixture. Pour into a 1½-quart casserole or a 10x6x2-inch baking dish. Bake in a 350° oven for 30 minutes. Cut the remaining slice of toast into 4 triangles. Arrange triangles down center of tomato mixture, overlapping slightly. Sprinkle with Parmesan cheese. Bake 20 minutes longer. Serve scalloped tomatoes in sauce dishes. Makes 6 servings.

Twice-Baked Potatoes Supreme

    4 medium baking potatoes
    ½ cup dairy sour cream
    ½ teaspoon salt
      Dash pepper
    1 tablespoon snipped chives, sliced green
        onion tops, or parsley
      Paprika (optional)

Scrub; prick into the potatoes with a fork. Bake in 425° oven for 40 to 60 minutes or till done. Prepare potato shells as shown below. Reserving potato shells, scoop out the insides and add to potato portions from top slices. Mash potato. Beat in sour cream, salt, and pepper till fluffy.

Pile mashed potato mixture into potato shells. Place in 10x6x2-inch baking dish. Bake in 425° oven 20 to 25 minutes or till heated through. Sprinkle with paprika, if desired. Garnish each potato with chives, green onion tops, or parsley. Makes 4 servings.

Note: If potatoes are made ahead and chilled, add 5 to 10 minutes to the baking time.

To Prepare Twice-Baked Potatoes

Let the baked potatoes stand till cool enough to handle. Cut a lengthwise slice from the top of each potato with a sharp chef's knife. Carefully peel the skin off the slice cut from the top of each potato. Discard skin and place potato in bowl.

Using a spoon, scoop out the inside of the potato, as shown, and add to potato portions in bowl. Set potato shells aside while preparing filling mixture. Pile mashed potato mixture into the reserved potato shells; bake as recipe directs.

Zucchini with Cheese Stuffing

    3 medium zucchini
    2 tablespoons chopped onion
    1 tablespoon butter or margarine
    1 cup shredded provolone cheese (4 ounces)
    1 4-ounce can chopped mushrooms, drained
    2 tablespoons all-purpose flour
    2 tablespoons grated Parmesan or Romano cheese
    2 tablespoons dairy sour cream
    ½ teaspoon dried basil, crushed

Cut off ends of zucchini; halve lengthwise. Cook zucchini in small amount of boiling salted water 5 to 10 minutes or till crisp-tender. Drain; scoop out pulp, leaving ¼-inch shell. Chop enough zucchini pulp to make about *¾ cup*; set aside.

In small skillet cook onion in butter till tender. Combine provolone cheese, mushrooms, flour, Parmesan cheese, sour cream, basil, the reserved zucchini pulp, cooked onion, and ½ teaspoon *salt*. Fill zucchini shells with cheese mixture; arrange in 10x6x2-inch baking dish. Bake in 350° oven 20 to 25 minutes or till heated through. Makes 6 servings.

Acorn Squash with Maple Syrup

    2 acorn squash
    4 teaspoons butter or margarine
    ¼ cup pure maple syrup or maple-flavored syrup
      Ground cinnamon and ground allspice
    ¼ cup coarsely chopped walnuts

Halve squash lengthwise and remove seeds, following directions below. Place halves, cut side down, in a 13x9x2-inch baking pan. Cover with foil. Bake in 350° oven 40 minutes. Turn squash cut side up; halve. Add ½ *teaspoon* of the butter and 1½ *teaspoons* of maple syrup to *each* squash portion. Sprinkle *each* lightly with some cinnamon, allspice, and *salt*. Sprinkle *each* with walnuts. Bake, uncovered, 20 minutes more or till tender. Makes 4 servings.

To Cut Acorn Squash

Cut squash in half lengthwise with a sharp knife. Use a spoon to remove seeds and strings in the center cavity, as shown.

Spaghetti Squash Vegetable Platter

This colorful vegetable side dish is pictured on page 102—

- 1 small spaghetti squash (about 2½ pounds)
- 2 cups sliced fresh mushrooms
- 1 clove garlic, minced
- 1 tablespoon butter or margarine
- 1 small red or green sweet pepper, cut into strips
- 2 cups broccoli flowerets
- ½ cup halved pitted ripe olives
- 1 tablespoon butter or margarine
- 1 tablespoon all-purpose flour
- ½ teaspoon dried basil, crushed
- ⅔ cup light cream or milk
- 1 cup ricotta cheese or cream-style cottage cheese
- 2 tablespoons grated Parmesan cheese
- 2 tablespoons butter or margarine, melted

Quarter squash; remove seeds and strings. Place in a large saucepan or Dutch oven with about 2 inches water. Bring to boiling; cover and simmer 20 to 30 minutes or till tender.

In a saucepan cook mushrooms and garlic in the 1 tablespoon butter or margarine till tender. Cook over low heat till about *2 tablespoons* liquid remains. Add green pepper and broccoli. Cook, covered, 2 to 3 minutes or till vegetables are crisp-tender. Add olives; cover. Set vegetables aside.

To prepare cheese sauce, in a medium saucepan melt 1 tablespoon butter. Stir in flour, basil, and ¼ teaspoon *salt*. Add cream all at once; cook and stir till bubbly. Cook and stir 1 minute more. Remove from heat; stir in ricotta or cottage cheese and the Parmesan cheese. Place sauce in a blender or food processor container. Cover; blend or process till smooth. Return to saucepan and heat through; do not boil.

When squash is cooked, shred pulp, using two forks to separate into strands. Pile squash onto a serving platter; toss with the 2 tablespoons melted butter or margarine. Arrange vegetables atop. Drizzle cheese sauce over all. Garnish with cherry tomatoes and ripe olives, if desired. Makes 8 servings.

Stuffed Pattypan Squash

- 6 pattypan squash
- 4 slices bacon
- ⅓ cup finely chopped onion
- ¾ cup seasoned fine dry bread crumbs
- ½ cup milk

Cook whole squash in boiling salted water 15 to 20 minutes or till just tender. Drain; cool. Cut a small slice from stem end of *each* squash. Scoop out pulp, leaving ½-inch shell. Finely chop pulp; set aside. Sprinkle shells with some *salt*. In a skillet cook bacon till crisp. Drain, reserving *2 tablespoons* of the drippings. Crumble bacon; set aside. Cook onion in reserved drippings till tender. Stir in crumbs, milk, and squash pulp. Fill shells; top with bacon. Place in 12x7½x2-inch baking dish. Bake, covered, in 350° oven 30 to 35 minutes. Serves 6.

Wild Rice Bake

- 1 cup wild rice
- 2½ cups beef broth
- ¾ cup sliced fresh mushrooms
- ¾ cup sliced celery
- 2 tablespoons sliced green onion
- 1 tablespoon butter or margarine
- 2 teaspoons all-purpose flour
- ¼ teaspoon ground nutmeg
- ¼ teaspoon ground coriander
- ½ cup dairy sour cream
- ¼ cup milk

Run cold water over *uncooked* rice in a strainer for 1 to 2 minutes, lifting rice with fingers to rinse well. Combine rice and beef broth. Bring to boiling; reduce heat. Cover; simmer 40 minutes. In a skillet cook mushrooms, celery, and onion in butter for 5 minutes. Stir in flour, nutmeg, and coriander. Add sour cream and milk. Cook and stir till thickened and bubbly. Cook and stir 1 minute more. Add to *undrained* rice; transfer to a 1½-quart casserole. Cover and bake in 325° oven 20 minutes. Let stand 10 minutes. Stir before serving. Serves 6.

Beer-Cheese Soup

- ½ cup shredded carrot
- ¼ cup finely chopped onion
- ¼ cup butter or margarine
- 3 tablespoons all-purpose flour
- 1 teaspoon instant chicken bouillon granules
- ¼ teaspoon dry mustard
- ⅛ teaspoon ground ginger
- 3 cups milk
- 1½ cups shredded cheddar cheese (6 ounces)
- ½ cup beer
  Snipped parsley, croutons, or popcorn (optional)

In a medium saucepan cook carrot and onion in butter till tender. Stir in flour, chicken granules, mustard, ginger, ½ teaspoon *salt*, and ⅛ teaspoon *pepper*. Add milk all at once. Cook and stir over medium heat till bubbly. Cook and stir 1 minute more. Reduce heat. Add cheese and beer; continue cooking and stirring till cheese is melted and soup is heated through. Sprinkle servings with parsley, if desired. Serves 4.

French Onion Soup

- 1½ pounds onions, thinly sliced (6 cups)
- ¼ cup butter or margarine
- 3 10½-ounce cans condensed beef broth
- 1 teaspoon Worcestershire sauce
  6 to 8 slices French bread, toasted
  Shredded Swiss cheese

In large saucepan cook onions, covered, in butter 20 minutes or till tender. Add broth, Worcestershire, ¼ teaspoon *salt*, and dash *pepper*; bring to boiling. Sprinkle toasted bread with cheese; place under broiler till cheese is lightly browned. Ladle soup into bowls and float bread atop. Serves 6 to 8.

Vegetables, Soups, & Sauces

Cream of Vegetable Soup

1½ cups Homemade Chicken Broth
　　(see recipe, page 73)
½ cup chopped onion
　　Desired vegetable and seasonings
　　(see chart below)
2 tablespons butter or margarine
2 tablespoons all-purpose flour
¼ teaspoon salt
　　Few dashes white pepper
1 cup milk

In a saucepan combine chicken broth, chopped onion, and *one* of the vegetable-seasoning combinations from the chart. (Or, substitute an equal amount of frozen vegetable, if desired.) Bring mixture to boiling. Reduce heat; cover and simmer for the time indicated in the chart or till vegetable is tender. (Remove bay leaf if using broccoli.)

Place *half* of the vegetable mixture in a blender container or food processor. Cover and blend 30 to 60 seconds or till smooth. Pour into a bowl. Repeat with remaining vegetable mixture; set all aside.

In the same saucepan melt the butter. Blend in flour, salt, and pepper. Add the milk all at once. Cook and stir till mixture is thickened and bubbly. Cook and stir 1 minute more. Stir in the blended vegetable mixture. Cook and stir till soup is heated through. Season to taste with additional salt and pepper. Makes 3 or 4 servings.

Vichyssoise

2 leeks, sliced
1 small onion, sliced
2 tablespoons butter or margarine
3 small potatoes, peeled and thinly sliced (2½ cups)
2 cups Homemade Chicken Broth
　　(see recipe, page 73)
1 teaspoon salt
1½ cups milk
　　White pepper
1 cup whipping cream
　　Snipped chives (optional)

Trim green tops from leeks; thinly slice the white portion of leeks (measure about ⅔ cup). In a medium saucepan cook leeks and onion in butter or margarine till vegetables are tender but not brown. Stir in sliced potatoes, chicken broth, and salt. Bring to boiling; reduce heat. Cover; simmer for 35 to 40 minutes or till potatoes are very tender.

Place *half* of the mixture in a blender container or food processor. Cover; blend till smooth. Pour into a bowl. Repeat with remaining mixture. Return all to saucepan; stir in milk. Season to taste with additional salt and white pepper. Bring to boiling, stirring frequently. Cool. Stir in whipping cream. Cover; chill thoroughly before serving. Garnish with snipped chives, if desired. Makes 4 to 6 servings.

Vegetable	Seasonings	Cooking Time	Yield
2 cups cut asparagus	1 teaspoon lemon juice ⅛ teaspoon ground mace	8 minutes	3½ cups
1½ cups cut green beans	½ teaspoon dried savory, crushed	20 to 30 minutes	3 cups
2 cups cut broccoli	½ teaspoon dried thyme, crushed 1 small bay leaf Dash garlic powder	10 minutes	3½ cups
1 cup sliced carrots	1 tablespoon snipped parsley ½ teaspoon dried basil, crushed	12 minutes	3½ cups
2 cups sliced cauliflower	½ to ¾ teaspoon curry powder	10 minutes	3½ cups
1½ cups chopped celery	2 tablespoons snipped parsley ½ teaspoon dried basil, crushed	15 minutes	3 cups
1 cup sliced fresh mushrooms	⅛ teaspoon ground nutmeg	5 minutes	2⅔ cups
2½ cups chopped onions	½ teaspoon Worcestershire sauce 1 small clove garlic, minced	5 minutes	4 cups
1½ cups shelled peas	¼ cup shredded lettuce 2 tablespoons diced fully cooked ham ¼ teaspoon dried sage, crushed	8 minutes	3½ cups
1 cup sliced potatoes	½ teaspoon dried dillweed	10 minutes	3 cups
2 cups chopped spinach	⅛ teaspoon dried thyme, crushed Dash ground nutmeg	3 minutes	2½ cups.
4 medium tomatoes, peeled, 　quartered and seeded	¼ teaspoon dried basil, crushed	15 minutes	3⅓ cups
1½ cups cut unpeeled zucchini	Several dashes ground nutmeg	5 minutes	3⅓ cups

Classic Hollandaise Sauce

4 **egg yolks**
½ **cup butter or margarine, cut into thirds and at room temperature**
2 **to 3 tablespoons lemon juice**
    Dash white pepper

Place egg yolks and *one-third* of the butter in the top of a double boiler. Cook, stirring rapidly, over boiling water till butter melts. (Water in the bottom of the double boiler should not touch the top pan.) Add one-third more of the butter and continue stirring rapidly. As butter melts and mixture thickens, add the remaining butter, stirring constantly. When butter is melted remove pan from water; stir rapidly for 2 more minutes. Stir in lemon juice, 1 teaspoon at a time; stir in white pepper, and dash *salt*. Heat again over boiling water, stirring constantly, for 2 to 3 minutes or till thickened. Remove from heat at once. Serve with vegetables, poultry, fish, or eggs. Makes about 1 cup sauce.

Note: If sauce curdles, immediately beat in 1 to 2 tablespoons *boiling water*.

Fresh Mint Sauce

¼ **cup cold water**
1½ **teaspoons cornstarch**
¼ **cup snipped fresh mint leaves**
3 **tablespoons light corn syrup**
1 **tablespoon lemon juice**
1 **drop green food coloring (optional)**

In small saucepan blend water into cornstarch; add mint leaves, corn syrup, and lemon juice. Cook, stirring constantly, till thickened and bubbly. Cook and stir 2 minutes more. Strain. Stir in green food coloring, if desired. Serve with roast lamb. Makes about ½ cup.

Teriyaki Marinade

¼ **cup cooking oil**
¼ **cup soy sauce**
¼ **cup dry sherry**
1 **teaspoon ground ginger**
1 **clove garlic, minced**
2 **tablespoons molasses**

To make marinade, combine oil, soy sauce, dry sherry, ginger, and garlic. Place chicken, beef, or pork in a baking dish or a plastic bag set in a deep bowl. Pour marinade over meat. Cover dish or close bag; refrigerate for 4 to 6 hours or overnight. Turn bag or spoon marinade over meat occasionally to coat evenly. Drain, reserving marinade. Stir molasses into the reserved marinade. Use to baste meat during the last 10 minutes of barbecuing or roasting. Makes about 1 cup marinade (enough for 2 pounds meat).

White Sauce and Variations

2 **tablesoons butter or margarine**
2 **tablespoons all-purpose flour**
1 **cup milk**

In a small saucepan melt butter or margarine. Stir in flour, ¼ teaspoon *salt*, and dash *pepper*. Add milk all at once. Cook and stir over medium heat till thickened and bubbly. Cook and stir 1 minute more. Makes about 1 cup.

Almond Sauce: Prepare White Sauce as above, *except* toast ¼ cup slivered *almonds* in the melted butter. Add 1 teaspoon instant *chicken bouillon granules*. Continue as directed. Serve with vegetables or fish.

Blue Cheese Sauce: Prepare White Sauce as above, *except* over low heat stir ¼ cup *dairy sour cream* and ¼ cup crumbled *blue cheese* into the cooking sauce. (Do not boil.) Serve with vegetables.

Cheese Sauce: Prepare White Sauce as above, *except* add ¼ cup additional *milk*. Continue as directed. Over low heat stir 1 cup shredded *cheddar, Swiss, American, or Gruyère cheese* into the cooked sauce, stirring to melt. Serve with vegetables.

Confetti Sauce: Prepare White Sauce as above. Stir 2 tablespoons finely chopped *green pepper or parsley*, 1 tablespoon finely chopped pitted *ripe or green olives*, and 1 tablespoon finely chopped *pimiento* into the cooked sauce. Serve with vegetables, beef, or fish.

Cucumber or Zucchini Sauce: Prepare White Sauce as above. Stir ½ cup shredded or finely chopped, unpeeled *cucumber or zucchini* into the cooked sauce. Serve with fish or seafood.

Curry Sauce: Prepare White Sauce as above, *except* add 1 teaspoon *curry powder* to the melted butter; cook 1 minute. Continue as directed. If desired, stir 1 tablespoon chopped *chutney* into the cooked sauce. Serve with fish or poultry.

Herb-Garlic Sauce: Prepare White Sauce as above, *except* cook 1 clove *garlic*, minced, in the butter or margarine for 1 minute. Continue as directed. Stir in ½ teaspoon dried *basil*, crushed, and ½ teaspoon dried *tarragon*, crushed, into the cooked sauce. Serve with vegetables.

Herb Sauce: Prepare White Sauce as above. Stir ½ *teaspoon* of one of the following herbs or spices into the cooked white sauce: dried *basil*, crushed; *caraway seed*; *celery seed*; dried *marjoram*, crushed; dried *oregano*, crushed; dried *sage*, crushed; or dried *thyme*, crushed. Serve with vegetables or poultry.

Lemon-Chive Sauce: Prepare White Sauce as directed above. Stir 1 tablespoon snipped *chives* and 2 teaspoons *lemon juice* into the cooked sauce. Serve with vegetables or fish.

Mexicali Sauce: Prepare White Sauce as above. Stir 2 tablespoons seeded, chopped *green chili peppers* and ½ teaspoon *chili powder* into the cooked sauce. Serve with beef or pork.

Parmesan or Romano Sauce: Prepare White Sauce as above. Stir ¼ cup grated *Parmesan cheese or Romano cheese* into the cooked sauce. Serve with vegetables, beef, sausage, poultry, pork, or burgers.

Brioche

1 package active dry yeast
¼ cup warm water (110° to 115°)
½ cup butter or margarine
⅓ cup sugar
4 cups all-purpose flour
½ cup milk
4 eggs

Soften yeast in the ¼ cup warm water. Cream butter, sugar, and ½ teaspoon *salt*. Add *1 cup* of the flour and the milk to creamed mixture. Separate *one* of the eggs; set egg white aside. Add yolk and remaining 3 eggs to creamed mixture.

Add softened yeast; beat well. Stir in the remaining flour till smooth. Turn into greased bowl. Cover; let rise in warm place till double (about 2 hours). Refrigerate overnight. Stir down and turn out onto lightly floured surface. Divide dough into *quarters*; set *one portion* aside. Divide each of the remaining quarters into 8 pieces, making a total of 24. With floured hands, form each piece into a ball, tucking under edges. Place each in a greased muffin cup. Divide reserved dough into 24 pieces; shape into small balls.

With floured finger, make an indentation in each large ball. Press a small ball into each indentation. Blend reserved egg white and 1 tablespoon *water*; brush over rolls. Cover; let rise till nearly double (40 to 45 minutes). Bake in 375° oven about 15 minutes, brushing again after 7 minutes. Makes 24.

To use individual brioche pans: prepare dough and divide into quarters as above; set *one* aside. Divide each remaining quarter into 6 pieces, making a total of 18. Form into balls; place in 18 greased, individual brioche pans. Divide reserved dough into 18 pieces; shape into balls and place one atop each larger ball. Let rise; bake for 15 to 18 minutes, brushing rolls again with egg white mixture after 8 minutes. Makes 18.

Sally Lunn

1 cup milk
1 package active dry yeast
6 tablespoons butter or margarine
¼ cup sugar
2 eggs
3 cups all-purpose flour

In saucepan heat milk just till warm (110° to 115°). Add to yeast, stirring to dissolve; set aside. In small mixer bowl cream together butter, sugar, and 1 teaspoon *salt*. Add eggs, one at a time, beating well after each addition. With a wooden spoon stir the flour and yeast-milk mixture alternately into creamed mixture. Beat till smooth; do not over-beat. Cover; let rise in warm place till almost double (about 1 hour). Beat batter down; pour into greased 10-cup Turk's-head mold or fluted tube pan. Let rise till almost double (about 30 minutes). Bake in a 350° oven about 40 minutes. Makes 1.

Pictured: **Assortment of homemade Bagels.**

Bagels

4½ to 4¾ cups all-purpose flour
2 packages active dry yeast
1½ cups warm water (110° to 115°)
3 tablespoons sugar
1 tablespoon sugar

In mixer bowl combine *1½ cups* of the flour and the yeast. Combine warm water, the 3 tablespoons sugar, and 1 table-spoon *salt*. Pour over flour mixture. Beat at low speed of electric mixer ½ minute, scraping sides of bowl constantly. Beat 3 minutes at high speed. Stir in as much remaining flour as you can mix in with a spoon. Turn out onto floured surface. Knead in enough remaining flour to make a moderately stiff dough that is smooth and elastic (6 to 8 minutes total). Cover; let rest 10 minutes. Cut into 12 portions; shape each into a smooth ball. Punch a hole in center of each with a floured finger. Pull gently to make hole as shown below. Place on greased baking sheet. Cover; let rise 20 minutes. Broil 5 inches from heat 3 to 4 minutes, turning once (tops should not brown). Heat 1 gallon *water* and 1 tablespoon sugar to boiling; reduce heat. Cook 4 or 5 bagels at a time in boiling water 7 minutes, turning once; drain. Place on greased baking sheet. Bake in 375° oven 25 to 30 minutes. Makes 12 bagels.

Light Rye Bagels: Prepare as above, *except* substitute 1¼ cups *rye flour* for 1¼ cups of the all-purpose flour.

Whole Wheat Bagels: Prepare Bagels as above, *except* substitute 1¼ cups *whole wheat flour* for 1¼ cups of the all-purpose flour.

Herb Bagels: Prepare Bagels as above, *except* add 2 teaspoons dried *marjoram*, crushed; *or* 1 teaspoon dried *dillweed*; *or* 1 teaspoon dried *tarragon*, crushed; *or* ½ tea-spoon *garlic powder* to the flour-yeast mixture.

Parmesan Bagels: Prepare Bagels as above, *except* stir ¼ cup grated *Parmesan cheese* into the flour-yeast mixture.

Onion Bagels: Prepare Bagels as above. Cook ½ cup finely chopped *onion* in 3 tablespoons *butter or margarine* till tender and golden but not brown. Brush onion-butter mixture over tops of bagels after first 15 minutes of baking.

Poppy Seed or Sesame Seed Bagels: Prepare Bagels as above. Before baking, brush tops with beaten *egg*; sprinkle with *poppy seed or toasted sesame seed*.

To Shape Bagels

Pull dough gently with both hands to make a 1½- to 2-inch hole. While pulling, try to keep each bagel in a uniform shape.

Breads

Pull-Apart Onion Rolls

2¼ to 2¾ cups all-purpose flour
 1 package active dry yeast
 ¾ cup milk
 2 tablespoons butter or margarine
 1 tablespoon sugar
 ½ teaspoon salt
 1 egg
 2 teaspoons minced dried onion
 2 teaspoons water
 3 tablespoons butter or margarine, melted
 1 tablespoon grated Parmesan cheese
 1 tablespoon sesame seed
 ½ teaspoon paprika
 ¼ teaspoon garlic salt

In large mixer bowl combine *1 cup* of the flour and the yeast. In saucepan heat together milk, 2 tablespoons butter or margarine, sugar, and salt just till warm (115° to 120°) and butter is almost melted, stirring occasionally. Add to flour mixture in bowl; add egg. Beat at low speed of electric mixer for ½ minute, scraping sides of bowl constantly. Beat 3 minutes at high speed. With a wooden spoon stir in as much of the remaining flour as you can. Turn out onto lightly floured surface. Knead in enough of the remaining flour to make a moderately stiff dough that is smooth and elastic (6 to 8 minutes total). Shape into a ball. Place in lightly greased bowl; turn once. Cover; let rise in warm place till double (about 45 minutes). Punch down. Cover; let rest 10 minutes.

Meanwhile, prepare onion butter. In bowl combine minced dried onion and water; let stand 5 minutes. Stir in the 3 tablespoons melted butter or margarine, Parmesan cheese, sesame seed, paprika, and garlic salt.

Roll dough to an 8-inch square. Spread with onion butter. Cut into sixteen 2-inch squares. Arrange squares, onion side up, in greased 1½-quart casserole, layering as necessary to fill. Cover; let rise till nearly double (about 45 minutes). Bake in 350° oven for 25 to 30 minutes covering with foil after first 15 minutes of baking to prevent overbrowning. Cool in dish 5 minutes; carefully turn out. Serve warm. Makes 16 rolls.

Dinner Rolls

4 to 4½ cups all-purpose flour
 1 package active dry yeast
 1 cup milk
 ⅓ cup sugar
 ⅓ cup butter, margarine, or shortening
 2 eggs

In large mixer bowl combine *2 cups* of the flour and the yeast. In saucepan heat milk; sugar; butter, margarine, or shortening; and 1 teaspoon *salt* just till warm (115° to 120°) and butter is almost melted; stir constantly. Add to flour mixture; add eggs. Beat at low speed of electric mixer for ½ minute, scraping bowl constantly. Beat 3 minutes at high speed.

Stir in as much of remaining flour as you can mix in with a spoon. Turn out onto lightly floured surface. Knead in enough of the remaining flour to make a moderately stiff dough that is smooth and elastic (6 to 8 minutes total). Shape into a ball. Place in a lightly greased bowl; turn once to grease surface. Cover; let rise in warm place till double (about 1 hour).

Punch down; divide dough in half. Cover; let rest 10 minutes. Shape into desired rolls (see below and instructions at right). Cover; let rise till nearly double (about 30 minutes). Bake in a 375° oven for 12 to 15 minutes or till done. Makes 2 to 2½ dozen rolls.

Refrig-a-Rise Rolls: Prepare Dinner Roll dough. After adding the remainder of the flour, place dough in a lightly greased bowl, turning once to grease surface. Cover loosely and refrigerate at least 2 hours or till needed. (Use within 3 to 4 days.) About 1½ to 2 hours before serving, shape into desired rolls (see instructions at right). Cover; let rise in a warm place till double (1 to 1¼ hours). Bake as above.

Brown-and-Serve Rolls: Prepare Dinner Rolls as directed above. Shape into desired rolls as shown at right. Cover; let rise till nearly double (about 30 minutes). Bake in a 325° oven about 10 minutes; do not brown. Remove from pans; cool. Wrap, label, and freeze. To serve, open packages containing desired number of rolls. Thaw rolls in opened package at room temperature for 10 to 15 minutes. Unwrap completely. Bake on ungreased baking sheets in a 400° oven about 10 minutes or till golden. Serve warm.

Hamburger Buns: Prepare Dinner Rolls as directed above; let rise till double. Punch dough down; divide into 12 portions. Cover; let rest 10 minutes. Shape each into an even circle, folding edges under. Press flat between hands. Place on a greased baking sheet; press to 3½-inch circles. Cover; let rise till nearly double (about 30 minutes). Bake in a 375° oven for 12 to 15 minutes or till golden. Remove rolls from sheet; cool on wire rack. Makes 12 buns.

Frankfurter Buns: Prepare Dinner Rolls as directed; let rise till double. Punch dough down; divide into 12 portions. Cover; let rest 10 minutes. Shape into rolls about 5½ inches long, tapering ends. Place on greased baking sheet. Cover; let rise till nearly double (about 30 minutes). Bake in a 375° oven for 12 to 15 minutes or till golden. Remove rolls from baking sheet; cool on wire racks. Makes 12 buns.

To Shape Dinner Rolls

1

To make Butterhorns, on lightly floured surface roll each ball to a 12-inch circle. Brush with melted butter. Cut each circle into 12 wedges with the dough cutter/scraper, as shown.

2

To shape rolls, begin at wide end of wedge and roll toward point, as shown.

3

To make Parker House Rolls, on lightly floured surface roll out each half of dough to ¼-inch thickness. Cut with floured 2½-inch round cutter. Brush with melted butter. Make an *off-center* crease in each round. Fold so large half overlaps slightly, as shown (dough crawls back during baking so that top half is shorter).

4

To make Shortcut Cloverleaves, divide each half of dough into 12 pieces. Shape each piece into a ball, pulling edges under to make a smooth top. Place one ball in each greased muffin cup, smooth side up.

Using scissors dipped in flour, snip top in half, then snip again, making 4 points, as shown.

Breads

Cinnamon-Raisin Graham Bread

2 to 2½ cups all-purpose flour
1 package active dry yeast
2 teaspoons ground cinnamon
¼ teaspoon ground ginger
1 cup milk
¾ cup water
¼ cup molasses
3 tablespoons butter or margarine
3 cups graham flour
1 cup raisins

In a large mixer bowl stir together *2 cups* of the all-purpose flour, the yeast, cinnamon, and ginger. In a saucepan combine milk, water, molasses, and butter; add ½ teaspoon *salt*, if desired. Heat and stir mixture till warm (115° to 120°) and butter is almost melted. Add to flour mixture. Beat at low speed of electric mixer for ½ minute, scraping sides of bowl constantly. Beat 3 minutes at high speed. Stir in graham flour and raisins. Stir in as much remaining all-purpose flour as you can. Turn out onto floured surface. Knead in enough remaining all-purpose flour to make a moderately stiff dough that is smooth and elastic (8 to 10 minutes total). Shape into a ball. Place in a greased bowl; turn. Cover; let rise till double (about 1 hour). Punch down; divide dough in half. Cover; let rest 10 minutes. Shape into two round loaves; place in two greased 9-inch pie plates or on greased baking sheets. Press to flatten to a 6-inch diameter. Cover; let rise till double (about 30 minutes). Bake in 375° oven 25 to 30 minutes. Cool. Makes 2.

Swedish Limpa

3¼ to 3¾ cups all-purpose flour
2 packages active dry yeast
1 tablespoon caraway seed
½ teaspoon fennel seed (optional)
2 cups warm water (115° to 120°)
½ cup packed brown sugar
2 tablespoons finely shredded orange peel
1 tablespoon cooking oil
2½ cups rye flour

In a large mixer bowl combine *2½ cups* of the all-purpose flour, the yeast, caraway seed, and fennel seed. Stir together water, brown sugar, orange peel, oil, and 1 teaspoon *salt*. Add to flour mixture. Beat at low speed of electric mixer for ½ minute, scraping bowl. Beat 3 minutes at high speed. With a wooden spoon stir in rye flour and as much remaining all-purpose flour as you can. Turn out onto floured surface. Knead in enough remaining flour to make a moderately stiff dough that is smooth and elastic (6 to 8 minutes total). Place in greased bowl; turn once. Cover; let rise in warm place till double (1¼ to 1½ hours). Punch down; divide in half. Cover; let rest 10 minutes. Shape into two 4½-inch round loaves on greased baking sheet. Cover; let rise till nearly double (about 40 minutes). Bake in 350° oven 40 to 45 minutes. Cool. Makes 2.

Cheese Braid

4 to 4½ cups all-purpose flour
1 package active dry yeast
1½ cups milk
2 tablespoons sugar
1 egg
2 cups shredded American cheese (8 ounces)
2 tablespoons chopped pimiento (optional)

In large mixer bowl combine *2 cups* flour and the yeast. Heat and stir milk, sugar, and 1½ teaspoons *salt* just till warm (115° to 120°). Add to flour mixture; add egg and cheese. Beat at low speed of electric mixer ½ minute, scraping bowl. Beat 3 minutes at high speed. Stir in pimiento, if desired. With a wooden spoon stir in as much remaining flour as you can. Turn out onto lightly floured surface. Knead in enough remaining flour to make a moderately stiff dough that is smooth and elastic (6 to 8 minutes total). Shape into a ball. Place in greased bowl; turn once. Cover; let rise in warm place till double (about 1½ hours).

Punch down; divide into 6 portions. Cover; let rest 10 minutes. Roll each portion into a rope 15 inches long. On greased baking sheets, shape into two braids using 3 ropes for each (see below). Cover; let rise till nearly double (35 to 45 minutes). Bake in 375° oven 15 to 20 minutes. Cool. Makes 2.

To Braid Bread Dough

Line up the three ropes, 1 inch apart, on a greased baking sheet. Braid loosely, beginning in the middle and working toward ends, as shown. (Working from the middle is easier and helps avoid stretching the dough, which results in an uneven loaf.)

Gently straighten on the baking sheet. Pinch ends of ropes together and tuck the sealed portion under the braid. If desired, brush with a little milk and lightly sprinkle with sugar for a crusty top, or brush with a mixture of beaten egg white and water for a shiny top.

Pita Bread

1 package active dry yeast
1¼ cups warm water (110° to 115°)
3¼ to 3¾ cups all-purpose flour
¼ cup shortening
1½ teaspoons salt

In large mixer bowl soften yeast in warm water. Add *2 cups* of the flour, the shortening, and salt. Beat at low speed of electric mixer for ½ minute, scraping sides of bowl. Beat 3 minutes at high speed. With a wooden spoon stir in as much of the remaining flour as you can mix in with a spoon. Turn out onto lightly floured surface. Knead in enough of the remaining flour to make a moderately soft dough that is smooth and elastic (3 to 5 minutes total). Cover; let rest in a warm place about 15 minutes. Divide into 12 equal portions. Roll each between floured hands into very smooth balls. Cover with plastic wrap or a damp cloth; let rest 10 minutes. Using fingers, gently flatten balls without creasing dough. Cover; let rest 10 minutes. (Keep dough pieces covered till ready to use.)

On well-floured surface lightly roll one piece of dough at a time into a 7-inch round, *turning dough over once*. Do not stretch, puncture, or crease dough. Work with enough flour so dough does not stick. Place on a baking sheet.

Bake two at a time in 450° oven about 3 minutes or till dough is puffed and softly set. Turn over with spatula as shown below. Bake about 2 minutes more or till dough begins to lightly brown. Repeat with remaining dough, baking one batch before rolling and baking the next batch.

To serve, slice bread in half crosswise and generously fill each pocket with desired filling. (Allow any extra bread to just cool before wrapping for storage.) Makes 12 pita rounds.

Whole Wheat Pita Bread: Prepare Pita Bread as above, *except* substitute 2 cups *whole wheat flour* and 1¼ to 1¾ cups *all-purpose flour* for the 3¼ to 3¾ cups all-purpose flour.

Party Pita Bread: Prepare Pita bread as above, *except* divide the dough into 24 equal portions. Roll into 4-inch rounds and bake about 2 minutes on each side. To serve, slice bread partway along one side and fill with desired filling.

To Turn Pita Bread

After baking pita bread rounds till dough is puffed and softly set, carefully turn over with a large turner, as shown. Continue baking till dough begins to lightly brown.

Soft Pretzels

4 to 4½ cups all-purpose flour
1 package active dry yeast
1½ cups milk
¼ cup sugar
2 tablespoons cooking oil
1½ teaspoons salt
3 tablespoons salt
2 quarts boiling water
1 slightly beaten egg white
    Sesame seed or coarse salt

In mixer bowl combine *2 cups* of the flour and the yeast. In a saucepan heat milk, sugar, oil, and 1½ teaspoons salt just till warm (115° to 120°); stir constantly. Add to flour mixture. Beat at low speed of electric mixer for ½ minute, scraping bowl. Beat 3 minutes at high speed. With a wooden spoon stir in as much of the remaining flour as you can. Turn out onto lightly floured surface. Knead in enough of the remaining flour to make a moderately stiff dough that is smooth and elastic (6 to 8 minutes total). Shape into a ball. Place in lightly greased bowl; turn once to grease surface. Cover; let rise in warm place till double (about 1½ hours).

Punch down; turn out onto lightly floured surface. Cover; let rest 10 minutes. Roll into a 12x8-inch rectangle. Cut into 16 strips, each 12 inches long and ½ inch wide. Roll each into a rope 16 inches long. Shape into pretzels as shown below. Let rise, uncovered, 20 minutes. Dissolve 3 tablespoons salt in the boiling water. Lower 3 or 4 pretzels at a time into boiling water; boil for 2 minutes, turning once. Remove with slotted spoon to paper toweling; let stand a few seconds, then place ½ inch apart on well-greased baking sheet. Brush with mixture of egg white and 1 tablespoon *water*. Sprinkle lightly with sesame seed or coarse salt. Bake in 350° oven 25 to 30 minutes or till golden brown. Makes 16 pretzels.

To Shape Pretzels

To shape a piece of dough into a pretzel isn't difficult, but it takes a little practice to master the technique.

Start by shaping one rope of dough into a circle, overlapping about 4 inches from each end and leaving ends free. Take one end of dough in each hand and twist at the point where dough overlaps. Carefully lift ends across to the opposite edge of circle, as shown. Tuck ends under edge to make a pretzel shape; moisten and press ends to seal.

Breads

Whole Wheat Butterhorns

2½ to 3 cups all-purpose flour
   2 packages active dry yeast
1¾ cups water
  ⅓ cup packed brown sugar
   3 tablespoons shortening
   2 tablespoons honey
   2 teaspoons salt
   2 cups whole wheat flour
   6 tablespoons butter or margarine, softened
  ½ cup very finely chopped walnuts or filberts
    Butter or margarine, melted

In a large mixer bowl combine *1½ cups* of the all-purpose flour and the yeast. In saucepan heat water, brown sugar, shortening, honey, and salt just till warm (115° to 120°) and shortening is almost melted; stir constantly. Add to flour mixture. Beat at low speed of electric mixer for ½ minute, scraping sides of bowl constantly. Beat 3 minutes at high speed. With a wooden spoon stir in the whole wheat flour and as much of the remaining all-purpose flour as you can. Turn out onto lightly floured surface. Knead in enough of the remaining all-purpose flour to make a moderately stiff dough that is smooth and elastic (6 to 8 minutes total). Shape into a ball. Place dough in a lightly greased bowl; turn once to grease surface. Cover and let rise in warm place till double (about 1½ hours).

Punch down; turn out onto lightly floured surface. Divide dough into 3 equal portions; shape each into a ball. Cover and let rest 10 minutes.

On lightly floured surface, roll one ball of dough into a 12-inch circle; spread with *2 tablespoons* of the softened butter and sprinkle with *one-third* of the nuts. Cut circle into 12 wedges. To shape rolls, begin at wide end of wedge and roll toward point (see photo on page 115). Place rolls, point down, 2 to 3 inches apart on greased baking sheet. Repeat with remaining dough, butter, and nuts. Cover rolls; let rise in warm place till nearly double (20 to 30 minutes). Brush with melted butter. Bake in a 400° oven for 10 to 12 minutes or till golden brown. Remove from baking sheet; cool on wire racks. Brush again with melted butter or margarine, if desired. Makes 36 rolls.

Basic Sweet Rolls

   4 to 4½ cups all-purpose flour
   1 package active dry yeast
   1 cup milk
  ⅓ cup sugar
  ⅓ cup butter, margarine, or shortening
   2 eggs

In mixer bowl combine *2 cups* flour and the yeast. In saucepan heat milk, sugar, butter, and 1 teaspoon *salt* just till warm (115° to 120°); stir constantly. Add to flour mixture; add eggs. Beat at low speed of electric mixer ½ minute. Beat 3 minutes

at high speed of electric mixer. Stir in as much of the remaining flour as you can mix in with a wooden spoon. Turn dough out onto floured surface. Knead in enough of remaining flour to make a moderately stiff dough that is smooth and elastic (6 to 8 minutes total). Shape into a ball in lightly greased bowl; turn once. Cover; let dough rise in warm place till double (about 1 hour). Punch down; divide in half. Cover; let rest 10 minutes. Shape and bake rolls as directed below. Makes 24.

Caramel-Pecan Rolls: Prepare Basic Sweet Roll dough as directed as above. Divide dough in half. Roll one *half* into a 12x8-inch rectangle. Melt 3 tablespoons *butter or margarine*; brush *half* over dough. Combine ½ cup *granulated sugar* and 1 teaspoon *ground cinnamon*; sprinkle *half* over dough. Roll up jelly roll-style, beginning from longest side. Seal seams. Cut into 12 pieces as shown below. Repeat with remaining dough and filling. In saucepan combine ⅔ cup packed *brown sugar*, ¼ cup *butter or margarine*, and 2 tablespoons *light corn syrup*; cook and stir till blended. Divide between two 9x1½-inch round baking pans. Sprinkle each pan with ¼ cup chopped *pecans*. Place rolls in prepared pans. Cover; let rise till nearly double (about 30 minutes). Bake in 375° oven 20 to 25 minutes. Invert onto serving plate.

Cinnamon Rolls: Prepare Basic Sweet Roll dough as directed above. Divide dough in half. Roll one *half* of dough into a 12x8-inch rectangle. Melt 3 tablespoons *butter or margarine*; spread *half* over dough. Combine ½ cup *granulated sugar* and 2 teaspoons *ground cinnamon*; sprinkle *half* over dough. If desired, measure ¾ cup *raisins*; sprinkle about *half* over dough. Roll up jelly roll-style, beginning from longest side. Seal. Cut into 12 pieces as shown below. Place in greased 9x1½-inch round baking pan. Repeat with remaining dough and filling. Cover; let rise till nearly double (about 30 minutes). Bake in a 375° oven for 20 to 25 minutes. Cool slightly; remove from pans. If desired, drizzle with Powdered Sugar Icing (see recipe, page 136).

To Slice Sweet Roll Dough

Use a piece of ordinary sewing-weight or heavy-duty thread to slice each roll of dough into equal pieces.

Place thread under rolled dough where you want to make the cut; pull thread up around sides. Crisscross thread over top of roll, pulling quickly as though tying knot.

Cinnamon Crisps

Another name for these deliciously spicy rolls is "elephant ears." You'll find these hard to resist!—

3½ to 4 cups all-purpose flour
  1 package active dry yeast
1¼ cups milk
  ¼ cup granulated sugar
  ¼ cup shortening
  1 teaspoon salt
  1 egg
  ½ cup granulated sugar
  ½ cup packed brown sugar
  ¼ cup butter or margarine, melted
  ½ teaspoon ground cinnamon
  ¼ cup butter or margarine, melted
  1 cup granulated sugar
  ½ cup chopped pecans
  1 teaspoon ground cinnamon

In a large mixer bowl combine *2 cups* of the flour and the yeast. Heat milk, ¼ cup granulated sugar, shortening, and salt just till warm (115° to 120°); stir constantly. Add to flour mixture; add egg. Beat at low speed of electric mixer ½ minute, scraping sides of bowl constantly. Beat 3 minutes at high speed. With a wooden spoon stir in as much of the remaining flour as you can. On a lightly floured surface, knead in enough of the remaining flour to make a moderately soft dough that is smooth and elastic (3 to 5 minutes total). Shape into a ball. Place in a lightly greased bowl; turn once to grease surface. Cover; let rise in a warm place till double (1 to 1½ hours).

Punch down; divide in half. Cover; let rest 10 minutes. Roll *half* of the dough into a 12-inch square. Combine ½ cup granulated sugar, brown sugar, ¼ cup melted butter or margarine, and ½ teaspoon ground cinnamon; spread *half* over dough. Roll up jelly roll style, beginning from longest side; seal seams. Cut into 12 rolls as shown on page 118. Place on greased baking sheets 3 to 4 inches apart. Flatten each roll to about 3 inches in diameter. Repeat with remaining dough and cinnamon-sugar mixture. Cover; let rise till nearly double (about 30 minutes). Cover with waxed paper. Use a rolling pin to flatten to ⅛-inch thickness; remove paper. Brush rolls with ¼ cup melted butter. Combine 1 cup granulated sugar, pecans, and 1 teaspoon ground cinnamon. Sprinkle over rolls. Cover with waxed paper; roll flat. Remove paper. Bake in a 400° oven 10 to 12 minutes. Remove from baking sheets immediately. Makes 24.

German Stollen

4 to 4½ cups all-purpose flour
  1 package active dry yeast
  ¼ teaspoon ground cardamom
1¼ cups milk
  ½ cup butter or margarine
  ¼ cup granulated sugar
  1 teaspoon salt
  1 egg
  1 cup raisins
  ¼ cup diced mixed candied fruits and peels, chopped
  ¼ cup dried currants
  ¼ cup chopped blanched almonds
  2 tablespoons finely shredded orange peel
  1 tablespoon finely shredded lemon peel
  1 cup sifted powdered sugar
  2 tablespoons hot water
  ½ teaspoon butter or margarine

Combine *2 cups* of the flour, the yeast, and cardamom. In a saucepan heat milk, the ½ cup butter or margarine, granulated sugar, and salt just till warm (115° to 120°) and butter is almost melted; stir constantly. Add to flour mixture; add egg. Beat at low speed of electric mixer for ½ minute; scrape sides of bowl constantly. Beat 3 minutes at high speed. With wooden spoon stir in as much of the remaining flour as you can. Stir in raisins, candied fruits and peels, currants, almonds, orange peel, and lemon peel.

Turn dough out onto a lightly floured surface. Knead in enough of the remaining flour to make a moderately soft dough that is smooth and elastic (3 to 5 minutes total). Shape into a ball. Place in a greased bowl; turn once to grease surface. Cover; let rise in a warm place till double (about 1¾ hours). Punch down; turn out onto a lightly floured surface. Divide into thirds. Cover; let rest 10 minutes.

Roll *one-third* of the dough into a 10x6-inch rectangle. Without stretching, fold the long side over to within 1 inch of the opposite side; seal. Place on greased baking sheet; repeat with remaining dough.

Cover; let rise till almost double (about 1 hour). Bake in a 375° oven for 18 to 20 minutes or till golden. Combine the powdered sugar, hot water, and ½ teaspoon butter; brush over warm bread. Makes 3.

Breads

Sour Cream-Cinnamon Loaves

    2 cups all-purpose flour
 1½ teaspoons baking powder
    1 teaspoon baking soda
 1¼ cups sugar
    ½ cup shortening
    2 eggs
    1 teaspoon vanilla
    1 cup dairy sour cream
    ¼ cup milk
    2 teaspoons ground cinnamon
 1½ teaspoons finely shredded orange peel

Stir together flour, baking powder, baking soda, and ½ teaspoon *salt*; set aside. In large mixer bowl cream together *1
cup* of the sugar and shortening till light and fluffy. Add eggs
and vanilla; beat well. Blend in sour cream and milk. Add flour
mixture to sour cream mixture; mix well. Spread *one-fourth* of
the batter in each of two greased 7½x3½x2-inch loaf pans.
Combine remaining ¼ cup sugar, the cinnamon, and shredded orange peel. Sprinkle all but *1 tablespoon* of the sugar-
cinnamon mixture over the batter in pans. Top each with *half*
of the remaining batter. Cut through batter gently with spatula,
as shown on page 138, to make swirling effect with cinnamon. Sprinkle with remaining sugar-cinnamon mixture. Bake
in 350° oven for 35 to 40 minutes. Cool in pans 10 minutes.
Remove from pans; cool thoroughly on wire racks. Makes 2.

Orange-Bran Bread

    1 cup whole bran cereal
    1 cup orange juice
    ½ cup honey
    ¼ cup sugar
    2 tablespoons shortening
    1 egg
    1 tablespoon finely shredded orange peel
 2¼ cups all-purpose flour
 2½ teaspoons baking powder
    ½ teaspoon baking soda

In small mixing bowl combine bran cereal and *½ cup* of the
orange juice; let stand several minutes. In another mixing
bowl stir together honey, sugar, and shortening. Add egg and
shredded orange peel; mix well. Stir together flour, baking
powder, baking soda, and ½ teaspoon *salt*; add to honey
mixture alternately with the remaining orange juice, beating
after each addition. Stir in bran-orange juice mixture.

Turn batter into two greased 7½x3½x2-inch loaf pans or
one 9x5x3-inch loaf pan. Bake in 325° oven for 45 to 50
minutes for small pans (55 to 60 minutes for large pans) or till
wooden pick inserted near center comes out clean. Cool
loaves in pans for 10 minutes. Remove from pans; cool thoroughly on wire racks. Makes 2 small loaves or 1 large loaf.

Pictured: **Cherry-Pecan Bread.**

Cherry-Pecan Bread

    2 cups all-purpose flour
    1 teaspoon baking soda
    ½ teaspoon salt
    ¾ cup sugar
    ½ cup butter or margarine
    2 eggs
    1 teaspoon vanilla
    1 cup buttermilk or sour milk
    1 cup chopped pecans
    1 cup chopped maraschino cherries
      Powdered Sugar Icing (see recipe, page 136)

In a mixing bowl stir together flour, baking soda, and salt; set
aside. In a large mixer bowl cream together sugar, butter,
eggs, and vanilla till fluffy. Add flour mixture and buttermilk alternately to creamed mixture. Beat just till blended after each
addition. Fold in pecans and cherries. Turn batter into
greased 9x5x3-inch loaf pan. Stud top with pecan halves and
cherries, if desired. Bake in 350° oven for 55 to 60 minutes.
Cool in pan 10 minutes. Remove from pan; cool on wire rack.
If desired, drizzle with Powdered Sugar Icing. Makes 1 loaf.

To Slice Nut Breads

Nut breads should be completely cool before slicing so the
slices don't crumble. Wrap and store the whole loaf overnight
for easier slicing. Use a gentle sawing motion with a sharp
bread/utility knife as you slice.

Breads

Basic Muffins

1¾ cups all-purpose flour
¼ cup sugar
2½ teaspoons baking powder
1 beaten egg
¾ cup milk
⅓ cup cooking oil

In large mixing bowl stir together the flour, sugar, baking powder, and ¾ teaspoon *salt*. Make a well in the center. Combine egg, milk, and oil. Add egg mixture all at once to flour mixture. Stir just till moistened; batter should be lumpy. Spoon into greased muffin cups or muffin cups lined with paper bake cups, filling each about ⅔ full. Bake in 400° oven for 20 to 25 minutes or till golden. Remove from pans; serve warm. Makes 10 to 12 muffins.

Blueberry Muffins: Prepare Basic Muffin batter as above. Combine ¾ cup fresh or frozen *blueberries*, thawed, and *2 tablespoons* additional sugar. Add 1 teaspoon finely shredded *lemon peel*, if desired. Carefully fold into batter.

Cranberry Muffins: Prepare Basic Muffin batter as above. Coarsely chop 1 cup fresh or frozen *cranberries*; combine with ¼ cup additional sugar. Fold into batter.

Apple-Raisin Muffins: Prepare Basic Muffin batter as above, *except* stir ½ teaspoon *ground cinnamon* into the flour mixture. Carefully fold 1 cup chopped, peeled *apple* and ¼ cup *raisins* into batter.

Jelly Muffins: Prepare Basic Muffin batter as above. Spoon 1 teaspoon *jelly* atop batter in *each* muffin cup before baking.

Cheese Muffins: Prepare Basic Muffin batter as above, *except* stir ½ cup shredded *Swiss or cheddar cheese* into flour mixture.

Ham 'n Cheesers: Prepare Basic Muffin batter as above, *except* stir ½ cup finely chopped, fully cooked *ham* into the egg mixture. Stir ½ cup shredded *cheese* (2 ounces) and ½ teaspoon *dry mustard* into the flour mixture.

Bacon Muffins: Prepare Basic Muffin batter as above, *except* cook 4 slices *bacon* till crisp; drain and crumble, reserving drippings. Combine bacon drippings with enough cooking oil to make ⅓ cup total mixture; use in place of the ⅓ cup cooking oil. Carefully fold bacon into batter.

Banana-Nut Muffins: Prepare Basic Muffin batter as above, *except* decrease milk to ½ cup. Stir 1 cup mashed *banana* and ½ cup chopped *nuts* into batter.

Pumpkin Muffins: Prepare Basic Muffin batter as above, *except* increase sugar to ⅓ cup. Add ½ cup canned *pumpkin* to the egg mixture. Stir ½ teaspoon *each ground cinnamon and ground nutmeg* into flour mixture. Stir ½ cup *raisins* into batter.

Apple-and-Spice Muffins: Prepare Basic Muffin Batter as above, *except* stir ½ teaspoon *ground cinnamon* into flour mixture. Add 1 cup chopped, peeled *apple* with the egg mixture; stir just till moistened. Mix 2 tablespoons *sugar* and ½ teaspoon *ground cinnamon*; sprinkle mixture over muffins before baking.

Popovers

1½ teaspoons shortening
2 beaten eggs
1 cup milk
1 tablespoon cooking oil
1 cup all-purpose flour

Grease six 6-ounce custard cups using ¼ *teaspoon* of the shortening for *each* cup. Place custard cups on a 15x10x1-inch baking pan or baking sheet and place in oven; preheat oven to 450°. Meanwhile, in a 4-cup liquid measure or mixing bowl combine eggs, milk, and oil. Add flour and ½ teaspoon *salt*. Beat with electric mixer or rotary beater till mixture is smooth. Remove pan from oven. Fill the *hot* custard cups *half* full. Return pan to oven. Bake in a 450° oven for 20 minutes. Reduce oven to 350° and bake 15 to 20 minutes more or till popovers are very firm. (If popovers brown too quickly, turn off oven and finish baking in the cooling oven till very firm.) A few minutes before removing from oven, prick each popover with a fork to let steam escape. Serve hot. Makes 6 popovers.

Cinnamon Popovers: Prepare Popover batter as above, *except* add 1 teaspoon *ground cinnamon* to egg mixture.

Whole Wheat Popovers: Prepare Popover batter as above, *except* use only ⅔ cup all-purpose flour and substitute ⅓ cup *whole wheat flour* for the remaining.

Note: If you like popovers dry and crisp, turn off the oven after popovers are completely baked. Leave them in the oven 30 minutes more with door ajar.

Homemade Biscuit Mix

10 cups all-purpose flour
⅓ cup baking powder
¼ cup sugar
2 cups shortening that does not require refrigeration

In a large mixing bowl stir together flour, baking powder, sugar, and 4 teaspoons *salt*. With pastry blender cut in shortening till mixture resembles coarse crumbs. Store in covered airtight container up to six weeks at room temperature. To use, spoon mix lightly into measuring cup; level off with a straight-edged spatula. (For longer storage, place in a sealed freezer container; store in freezer up to six months. To use, allow mix to come to room temperature). Makes 12½ cups.

Biscuits: Place *2 cups* of the Homemade Biscuit Mix in a bowl; make a well in center. Add ½ cup *milk*. Stir with fork just till dough follows fork around bowl. On lightly floured surface, knead dough 10 to 12 strokes. Roll or pat to ½-inch thickness. Cut dough with floured 2½-inch biscuit cutter. Bake on baking sheet in a 450° oven for 10 to 12 minutes or till golden. Makes 10 biscuits.

Muffins: Combine *3 cups* of the Homemade Biscuit Mix and 3 tablespoons *sugar*. Mix 1 beaten *egg* and 1 cup *milk*; add all at once to dry ingredients. Stir till moistened. Fill greased muffin cups ⅔ full. Bake in a 400° oven for 20 to 25 minutes or till golden. Makes 12 muffins.

Fruit-Filled Ladder Loaf

    1 3-ounce package cream cheese
    ¼ cup butter or margarine
    2 cups Homemade Biscuit Mix (see recipe, page 122)
    ½ cup chopped pecans
    ¼ cup milk*
    ½ of a 12-ounce can cherry or apricot cake and
         pastry filling
       Powdered Sugar Icing (see recipe, page 136)

In a mixing bowl cut cream cheese and butter or margarine into Homemade Biscuit Mix till crumbly. Add pecans and milk; mix well. Knead on a lightly floured surface for 8 to 10 strokes. Roll dough into a 12x8-inch rectangle on waxed paper. Turn onto greased baking sheet; remove paper. Spread fruit filling lengthwise down center third of dough. Make 2½-inch cuts at 1-inch intervals on both long sides. Fold strips over filling, pinching into narrow points at center. Bake in a 425° oven about 15 minutes or till golden. Drizzle with Powdered Sugar Icing while warm. Makes 1 loaf.

   *Note: You can substitute 2 cups *packaged biscuit mix* for the Homemade Biscuit Mix, *except* increase the milk to ⅓ *cup* liquid.

Applesauce Coffee Cake

    1¾ cups all-purpose flour
     ½ cup sugar
     ½ cup butter or margarine
     2 beaten eggs
     1 teaspoon vanilla
    1½ teaspoons baking powder
     ½ teaspoon baking soda
     ½ teaspoon salt
     1 cup chunk-style applesauce
     ¼ cup chopped nuts
     ½ teaspoon ground cinnamon

In mixing bowl stir together ¾ *cup* of the flour and the sugar; cut in butter or margarine till crumbly. Set aside ½ *cup* of the crumb mixture for topping. To remaining crumb mixture, add beaten eggs and vanilla; beat by hand till smooth.

Stir together remaining 1 cup flour, the baking powder, soda, and salt. Add flour mixture and applesauce alternately to creamed mixture, stirring after each addition. Turn into greased 8x8x2-inch baking pan. Stir nuts and cinnamon into reserved crumb topping; sprinkle atop coffee cake. Bake in 375° oven for 30 minutes or till done. Serve warm. Makes 1.

Rhubarb-Strawberry Coffee Cake

       Rhubarb-Strawberry Filling
    3 cups all-purpose flour
    1 cup sugar
    1 teaspoon baking soda
    1 teaspoon baking powder
    1 cup butter or margarine
    1 cup buttermilk or sour milk
    2 slightly beaten eggs
    1 teaspoon vanilla
    ¾ cup sugar
    ½ cup all-purpose flour
    ¼ cup butter or margarine

Prepare Rhubarb-Strawberry Filling; set aside to cool. In large mixing bowl stir together the 3 cups flour, the 1 cup sugar, the baking soda, baking powder, and 1 teaspoon *salt*. Cut in the 1 cup butter or margarine till mixture resembles fine crumbs. Beat together buttermilk, eggs, and vanilla; add to flour-butter mixture. Stir just till moistened. Spread *half* the batter in a greased 13x9x2-inch baking pan.

Spread *cooled* Rhubarb-Strawberry Filling over batter in baking pan. Spoon remaining batter in small mounds atop fruit filling. Combine ¾ cup sugar and ½ cup flour; cut in the ¼ cup butter or margarine till mixture resembles fine crumbs. Sprinkle crumb mixture over batter. Bake in 350° oven for 40 to 45 minutes. Makes 1 coffee cake.

Rhubarb-Strawberry Filling: In saucepan combine 3 cups fresh or frozen cut-up *rhubarb* and one 16-ounce package frozen sliced *strawberries*. Cover and cook rhubarb and strawberries about 5 minutes. Stir in 2 tablespoons *lemon juice*. Combine 1 cup *sugar* and ⅓ cup *cornstarch*; add to rhubarb mixture. Cook and stir 4 to 5 minutes more or till thickened and bubbly.

Spicy Buttermilk Coffee Cake

    2½ cups all-purpose flour
     2 cups packed brown sugar
     ⅔ cup shortening
     2 teaspoons baking powder
     ½ teaspoon baking soda
     ½ teaspoon ground cinnamon
     ½ teaspoon ground nutmeg
     1 cup buttermilk or sour milk
     2 beaten eggs
     ⅓ cup chopped nuts

Combine flour, brown sugar, and ½ teaspoon *salt*. Cut in shortening till mixture is crumbly; set aside ½ *cup* of the crumb mixture. To remaining crumb mixture add baking powder, soda, and spices; mix well. Add buttermilk or sour milk and eggs; mix well. Pour into two greased 8x1½-inch or 9x1½-inch round baking pans. Combine reserved crumbs with nuts; sprinkle atop cakes. Bake in a 375° oven for 20 to 25 minutes. Serve warm. Makes 2 coffee cakes.

Poached Pears and Chocolate in Custard Sauce

The color of the poached pear will vary depending upon the type of pear you use. Some will be light and golden; others will be a soft brown—

 2 beaten eggs
 1⅓ cups milk
 ¼ cup sugar
 Dash salt
 2 tablespoons white crème de cacao
 or coffee liqueur (optional)
 ½ teaspoon vanilla
 1 6-ounce package semisweet chocolate pieces
 2 tablespoons cooking oil
 3 large pears
 1½ cups water
 ¼ cup sugar
 2 tablespoons lemon juice
 4 inches stick cinnamon

For custard sauce, in a heavy saucepan combine eggs, milk, the first ¼ cup sugar, and the salt. Cook and stir over medium heat 10 minutes or till mixture coats a metal spoon. Remove from heat and pour sauce into a bowl; set in a larger bowl filled with ice. Stir in liqueur and vanilla. Continue stirring 1 to 2 minutes to hasten cooling. Cover surface with clear plastic wrap; chill thoroughly.

In a small saucepan combine chocolate pieces and cooking oil. Cook and stir over low heat till melted. For chocolate leaves, use a clean small paintbrush to spread melted chocolate on the underside of six small silk-cloth leaves, building up layers of chocolate to make the leaves sturdy. Place leaves on a baking sheet lined with waxed paper; refrigerate till hardened. Let remaining chocolate stand at room temperature till serving time.

Cut pears in half lengthwise; core pears. In a 12-inch skillet combine water, the second ¼ cup sugar, the lemon juice, and cinnamon. Arrange pear halves in skillet. Bring to boiling; reduce heat. Cover; simmer 20 to 30 minutes or till pears are tender. Drain pears, reserving poaching liquid. Place pears on a baking sheet. Boil the poaching liquid about 7 minutes over high heat till reduced to about ¼ *cup* liquid; spoon liquid over pears. Chill pears.

At serving time, spoon ¼ *cup* of the custard sauce in *each* of 6 shallow dessert plates or soup plates. Place a pear half, cut side down, in each dish. Spoon about *2 teaspoons* of glaze on each pear half. Drizzle melted chocolate (about 1 tablespoon per serving) into the custard sauce. Slowly draw a spatula or knife through the chocolate and the custard sauce to marble. Gently peel silk leaves away from chocolate leaves. (As much as possible, avoid touching the chocolate to keep it from melting.) Place one chocolate leaf at each pear's stem. Makes 6 servings.

Apple Dumplings

 2¼ cups all-purpose flour
 ½ teaspoon salt
 ⅔ cup shortening
 6 to 8 tablespoons cold water
 6 small cooking apples, peeled and cored
 ⅔ cup sugar
 ¼ cup light cream
 ⅛ teaspoon ground nutmeg
 ¾ cup maple-flavored syrup
 Light cream

Mix flour and salt. Cut in shortening till pieces are the size of small peas. Sprinkle *1 tablespoon* water over part of the mixture; gently toss with fork. Push to side of bowl; repeat till all is moistened. Form dough into a ball. On a lightly floured surface, roll out to an 18x12-inch rectangle; cut into six 6-inch squares.

Place an apple in center of each square. Mix sugar, the ¼ cup light cream, and nutmeg; spoon about *1½ tablespoons* into center of each apple. Moisten edges of each pastry square with a little water. Fold corners of each square to center; seal by pinching together. Place in an ungreased 11x7x1½-inch baking pa Bake in 375° oven for 35 minutes. Pour maple-flavored syrup over dumplings. Return to oven and bake 15 minutes more or till apples are done. Serve the dumplings warm with additional light cream. Makes 6.

Strawberries Brûlée

You'll receive rave reviews when you serve this winning dessert. Besides tasting fabulous, it's extra-easy to make—

 2 3-ounce packages cream cheese, softened
 1 cup dairy sour cream
 2 tablespoons brown sugar
 1 quart fresh strawberries
 ¼ cup packed brown sugar

In bowl beat cream cheese with electric mixer till fluffy. Add sour cream and the 2 tablespoons brown sugar; beat till smooth. Reserve *1 or 2 berries* for garnish; halve remaining berries and arrange evenly in bottom of a shallow 8-inch round broiler-proof dish. Spoon cream cheese mixture over berries. Sieve remaining ¼ cup brown sugar evenly over cream cheese mixture. Broil 4 to 5 inches from heat for 1 or 2 minutes or till sugar turns golden brown. Slice reserved berries; arrange atop dessert. Serve immediately. Serves 8.

Pictured: **Poached Pears and Chocolate in Custard Sauce.**

Baked Apples in Wine

4 **large cooking apples**
¼ **cup raisins**
¼ **cup packed brown sugar**
¼ **teaspoon ground nutmeg**
4 **teaspoons butter or margarine**
1 **cup rosé wine**
½ **cup dairy sour cream**
 Ground nutmeg

Core apples; peel strip from top of each as shown on page 127. Place apples in an 8x8x2-inch baking pan. Stir together raisins, brown sugar, and ¼ teaspoon nutmeg; spoon into apple centers. Top each apple with *1 teaspoon* of the butter. Pour wine into baking dish. Bake in 350° oven for 1 to 1¼ hours or till apples are tender, spooning wine over apples occasionally. Serve apples warm; top with a dollop of sour cream and a dash of additional nutmeg. Makes 4 servings.

Fresh Fruit Mixer with Watermelon Ice

1 **medium watermelon, well chilled**
1 **medium pineapple, peeled, cored, and cubed**
3 **cups seedless green grapes, halved**
3 **medium nectarines, pitted and sliced**
4 **medium plums, pitted and sliced**
2 **cups blueberries**
 Watermelon Ice

Choose a well rounded, elongated ripe melon. Try to select a watermelon which has a natural flat bottom or make a long bottom cut to prevent it from tipping.

Carve watermelon as shown at right. Carefully scoop out melon pulp and remove seeds; reserve pulp. Cover melon shell; refrigerate. Do not fill melon basket till ready to serve.

Prepare Watermelon Ice.

Cube any remaining melon pulp. In a large mixing bowl combine cubed melon, pineapple, grapes, nectarines, plums, and blueberries; turn into chilled watermelon shell. Just before serving top fruit in shell with scoops of Watermelon Ice. (Or, serve Watermelon Ice atop individual servings of the fruit mixture.) Garnish with fresh mint, if desired. Serves 12 to 14.

Watermelon Ice: In blender container place about *2 cups* of the reserved melon pulp. Cover and blend till smooth. Measure and transfer to large bowl. Repeat with enough of the remaining melon to make *3 cups* puree. Stir in ¾ cup *sugar*, 3 tablespoons *lemon juice*, and dash *salt*.

In small saucepan soften 1 teaspoon *unflavored gelatin* in ¼ cup *cold water*. Heat and stir till gelatin dissolves. Add gelatin mixture to melon mixture; blend thoroughly. Pour mixture into 9x9x2-inch pan; cover and freeze till partially frozen. Turn mixture into chilled large mixer bowl. Beat at medium speed of electric mixer till light and fluffy. Return to pan. Freeze till firm. Let stand at room temperature for 5 minutes before scooping. Makes 4 cups ice.

To Carve a Watermelon Basket

1

With a sharp bread/utility knife draw a horizontal line around the middle of the melon, dividing the melon into two equal halves. Make a handle by drawing two vertical lines, about 3 inches apart, across the center of the melon.

2

Starting anywhere on horizontal line, firmly push knife tip well into the melon, *except* between the two handle lines, using straight or zigzag cuts. Cut one side at a time; do not cut through the base of the handle. Make cuts for the handle.

3

Carefully remove both sides of melon with your hands. To hollow melon, use a grapefruit/melon knife to loosen and remove the juicy red fruit from melon cavity; cut away the fruit from the two portions removed and under handle.

To Cut Melon

1

To remove rind from a wedge of melon, first cut the melon in half lengthwise; remove the seeds. Cut each half into two wedges. Loosen fruit from the protective outer skin by running the blade of a sharp utility knife between the fruit and rind.

2

To make melon balls, cut melon in half and remove seeds. Scoop the fruit out into balls with a melon baller. Once you've scooped out as many balls as possible, cut the leftover fruit into chunks and store in the refrigerator for snacking.

To Prepare Apples for Baking

Rinse baking apples in cold water. Use a sharp paring knife to core apples. With paring knife peel off a strip around top of each apple, about ⅓ of the way down, as shown; repeat with remaining apples.

To Prepare Fresh Pineapple

1

Remove the crown from a fresh pineapple by holding the pineapple in one hand and the crown (top) in the other hand. Then twist in opposite directions to release.

Trim the top of the pineapple and cut off the base; set pineapple upright on a cutting board. Cut off wide strips of peel with a sharp chef's knife, starting at the top of the fruit and working toward the bottom, as shown.

2

To remove the eyes from the fruit, make narrow wedge-shaped grooves into the pineapple. Cut diagonally around the fruit, following the pattern of the eyes, as shown. Cut away as little of the fruit as possible.

3

To cut pineapple spears, cut the pineapple vertically into eighths or tenths. Then cut the hard center core from each spear, as shown. To make pineapple chunks, cut each spear into fourths or sixths.

Fruits & Desserts

Cherries Jubilee

- 1 16-ounce can pitted dark sweet cherries
- ¼ cup sugar
- 2 tablespoons cornstarch
- ¼ cup brandy, cherry brandy, or Kirsch
  Vanilla ice cream

Drain cherries, reserving syrup. Add cold water to syrup, if necessary, to make *1 cup* liquid.

In a medium saucepan combine sugar and cornstarch; blend in reserved syrup. Cook and stir till mixture is thickened and bubbly. Cook and stir 1 minute more. Remove from heat; stir in cherries. Turn mixture into a heat-proof bowl or into the blazer pan of a chafing dish placed over hot water. Heat brandy in a small saucepan. (If desired, pour heated brandy into a large ladle.) Ignite and pour over cherry mixture. When flames die, stir to blend brandy into sauce. Serve at once over ice cream. Makes 6 to 8 servings.

Chilled Peach Soufflé

- ½ cup sugar
- 1 envelope unflavored gelatin
- ¼ teaspoon ground nutmeg
- ⅛ teaspoon salt
- ½ cup water
- 4 beaten egg yolks
- 1 tablespoon lemon juice
- ½ teaspoon vanilla
  Few drops almond extract
- 4 large fresh peaches
- 4 stiff-beaten egg whites
- ½ cup whipping cream
  Toasted sliced almonds (optional)

Combine sugar, gelatin, nutmeg, and salt. Stir in water. Cook and stir over low heat till gelatin dissolves. Gradually stir hot mixture into beaten egg yolks. Return to saucepan; add lemon juice. Cook and stir till thickened and bubbly. Remove from heat. Stir in vanilla and almond extract. Peel, pit, and slice *two* of the peaches (about 1½ cups). Place the sliced peaches in a blender container. Cover; blend till peaches are finely chopped. Stir into gelatin mixture. Chill till partially set (consistency of unbeaten egg whites). Peel, pit, and chop remaining peaches. Fold into gelatin mixture. Fold in the stiff-beaten egg whites. Whip cream; fold into gelatin. Chill till mixture mounds when dropped from a spoon. Turn into a 1½-quart soufflé dish. Chill till firm. If desired, garnish with toasted almonds and additional sliced peaches. Makes 8 to 10 servings.

Cherry Sorbet

- 2 cups fresh or frozen pitted dark sweet cherries
- ½ cup sugar
- ½ cup light cream
- ¼ cup lemon juice
- 2 egg whites
- ¼ cup sugar

Thaw cherries, if frozen. In a saucepan combine the ½ cup sugar and 1 cup *water*. Bring to boiling; reduce heat. Simmer 5 minutes; cool. In a blender container or food processor bowl combine cherries and cream. Cover; blend till smooth (about 1 minute). Stir in cooled sugar syrup and lemon juice. Turn into a 9x9x2-inch pan; cover and freeze till firm.

Beat egg whites till soft peaks form; gradually add the ¼ cup sugar, beating till stiff peaks form. Break the frozen mixture into chunks; turn into chilled mixer bowl. Beat till smooth with electric mixer. Fold in beaten egg whites. Return to cold pan; cover and freeze till firm. Let stand at room temperature for 5 minutes before serving. Scoop to serve. Serves 6 to 8.

Peach-Orange Sorbet: Prepare Cherry Sorbet as above *except* substitute 2 or 3 *peaches*, peeled, pitted, and chopped (should have about 2 cups), for the cherries, and ¼ cup *orange juice* for the lemon juice. Stir 1 tablespoon finely shredded *orange peel* into the fruit and cream mixture in blender or food processor.

Pineapple Sorbet: Prepare Cherry Sorbet as above *except* substitute one 8-ounce can *crushed pineapple* (juice pack) for cherries, and ¼ cup *orange juice* for lemon juice.

Strawberry Sorbet: Prepare Cherry Sorbet as above *except* substitute 2 cups fresh or frozen *whole strawberries* for the cherries.

Bananas Foster

- 4 ripe medium bananas
  Lemon juice
- 6 tablespoons butter or margarine
- ⅔ cup packed brown sugar
  Ground cinnamon
- 3 tablespoons crème de bananes liqueur or light rum
- 3 tablespoons light rum
  Vanilla ice cream

Peel bananas; bias slice. Brush with lemon juice. In blazer pan of chafing dish melt butter over direct heat. Stir in sugar. Add bananas. Cook and stir for 3 to 4 minutes. Sprinkle with cinnamon. Drizzle the 3 tablespoons liqueur or rum over all. Remove from heat. Heat remaining rum in large ladle or small saucepan till it almost simmers. Ignite rum and pour over bananas. Serve immediately over ice cream. Serves 6.

Peach and Banana Flambé: Prepare as above, *except* substitute 1 cup sliced, peeled *peaches* for 1 banana. Sprinkle *each* serving with 1 tablespoon toasted *coconut*.

Vanilla Cream Pie

- 1 cup sugar
- ½ cup all-purpose flour or ¼ cup cornstarch
- 3 cups milk
- 4 egg yolks
- 3 tablespoons butter or margarine
- 1½ teaspoons vanilla
- 1 9-inch Baked Pastry Shell (see recipe below)
  Meringue for Pie (see recipe at right)

For filling, in a medium saucepan combine sugar, flour or cornstarch, and ¼ teaspoon *salt*; gradually stir in milk. Cook and stir over medium heat till thickened and bubbly. Cook and stir 2 minutes more. Beat egg yolks slightly. Gradually stir *1 cup* of the hot mixture into yolks. Return egg mixture to saucepan. Cook and stir 2 minutes more. Remove from heat. Stir in butter and vanilla. Pour hot filling into Baked Pastry Shell. Spread meringue over hot filling; seal to edge. Bake in a 350° oven for 12 to 15 minutes or till golden. Cool. Cover; chill to store. Makes 8 servings.

Coconut Cream Pie: Prepare Vanilla Cream Pie as above, *except* stir in 1 cup *flaked coconut* along with the vanilla. Sprinkle ⅓ cup *flaked coconut* over meringue; bake.

Banana Cream Pie: Prepare Vanilla Cream Pie as above, *except* slice 3 *bananas* into bottom of Baked Pastry Shell. Pour hot filing over bananas. Continue as directed.

Dark Chocolate Cream Pie: Prepare Vanilla Cream Pie as above, *except* increase sugar to 1¼ *cups*. Chop 3 squares (3 ounces) *unsweetened chocolate*; add to filling along with milk. Continue as directed.

Pastry for Single-Crust Pie

- 1¼ cups all-purpose flour
- ⅓ cup shortening or lard
- 3 to 4 tablespoons cold water

In a medium mixing bowl stir together flour and ½ teaspoon *salt*. Cut in shortening or lard till pieces are the size of small peas. Sprinkle *1 teaspoon* of the water over part of the mixture; gently toss with a fork. Push to side of bowl. Repeat till all is moistened. Form dough into a ball.

On lightly floured surface flatten dough with hands. Roll dough from center to edge, forming a circle about 12 inches in diameter. Wrap pastry around rolling pin. Unroll onto a 9-inch pie plate. Ease pastry into pie plate, being careful to avoid stretching pastry. Trim pastry to ½ inch beyond edge of pie plate. Make a fluted, rope-shaped, or scalloped edge.

For a baked pastry shell, prick bottom and sides with tines of a fork. Bake in 450° oven for 10 to 12 minutes. Or, line pastry with foil and fill with dry beans or line the pastry with double thickness heavy-duty foil. Bake in 450° oven for 5 minutes. Remove beans and foil or heavy-duty foil; bake for 5 to 7 minutes more or till golden. Makes one 9-inch pastry shell.

Note: When you use commercial frozen piecrusts, remember that one of our pie filling recipes will fill two regular frozen piecrusts or one deep-dish frozen pie crust.

Meringue for Pie

- 3 egg whites*
- ½ teaspoon vanilla
- ¼ teaspoon cream of tartar
- 6 tablespoons sugar

In mixer bowl beat egg whites, vanilla, and cream of tartar at medium speed of electric mixer 1 minute or till soft peaks form. Gradually add sugar, about 1 tablespoon at a time, beating at high speed of electric mixer about 4 minutes more or till mixture forms stiff, glossy peaks and sugar is dissolved. Immediately spread over pie, carefully sealing to edge to prevent shrinkage. Bake as directed in selected recipe.

*Note: While the 3-egg-white recipe makes an adequate amount of meringue, use the extra egg white from a 4-egg-yolk pie for a more generous meringue. Follow directions above, *except* use 4 egg whites, 1 teaspoon vanilla, ½ teaspoon cream of tarter, and ½ cup sugar. It may be necessary to beat mixture slightly longer to achieve proper consistency.

Neapolitan Snow Ball Pie

- 2 4-ounce bars German sweet chocolate
- 5 tablespoons butter or margarine
- 2 cups crisp rice cereal
- 1 pint vanilla ice cream
- 1 pint mint chocolate chip ice cream
- 1 pint strawberry ice cream

Set aside *2 ounces* of the chocolate (½ bar). In medium saucepan heat together over low heat 6 ounces (1½ bars) of chocolate and *3 tablespoons* of the butter till smooth. Remove from heat. Stir in cereal. Turn mixture into 9-inch pie plate, pressing up sides with back of a spoon to form a shell. Place in freezer 5 to 10 minutes or just till chocolate is firm.

Meanwhile, melt remaining chocolate (½ bar) and butter over low heat; stir constantly. Set aside to cool slightly. Arrange scoops of vanilla, mint chocolate chip, and strawberry ice cream in shell. Drizzle chocolate mixture over pie. Serve immediately. Makes 8 servings.

To Cut Meringue Pies

Dip a sharp chef's knife into a cup or glass filled with water. The meringue does not stick to the wet knife as it would to a dry one, ensuring neater slices. Be sure to cut completely through the crust. Remove slices with a pie/cake server.

Fruits & Desserts

Pastry for Double-Crust Pie

- 2 cups all-purpose flour
- 1 teaspoon salt
- ⅔ cup shortening or lard
- 6 to 7 tablespoons cold water
  Desired pie filling
  Milk and sugar (optional)

In medium mixing bowl stir together flour and salt. Cut in shortening or lard till pieces are the size of small peas. Sprinkle *1 tablespoon* water over part of mixture; gently toss with a fork. Push to side of bowl. Repeat till all is moistened. Form dough into 2 balls.

On lightly floured surface flatten *1 ball* of dough with hands. Roll dough from center to edge, forming a circle about 12 inches in diameter. Ease pastry into pie plate, being careful to avoid stretching pastry. Trim pastry even with rim of pie plate.

For top crust, roll out second ball of dough. Cut slits for escape of steam. Place desired pie filling in pie shell. Top with pastry for top crust. Trim top crust ½ inch beyond edge of pie plate. Fold extra pastry under bottom crust; flute edge. Using pastry brush, brush pastry with some milk; sprinkle with a little sugar, if desired. To prevent overbrowning, cover edge of pie with foil. Bake as directed in selected recipe. Remove foil after about half the baking time to allow crust to brown.

All-American Apple Pie

  Pastry for Double-Crust Pie (see recipe above)
- 6 cups thinly sliced cooking apples (2 pounds)
- 1 tablespoon lemon juice (optional)
- 1 cup sugar
- 2 tablespoons all-purpose flour
- ½ to 1 teaspoon ground cinnamon
  Dash ground nutmeg
- 1 tablespoon butter or margarine
  Sugar (optional)

Prepare and roll out pastry. Line a 9-inch pie plate with *half* of the pastry. Trim pastry to edge of pie plate.

If apples lack tartness, sprinkle with the 1 tablespoon lemon juice. In mixing bowl combine sugar, flour, cinnamon, and nutmeg. (For a very juicy pie, omit the flour.) Add sugar mixture to the sliced apples; toss to mix. Fill pastry-lined pie plates with apple mixture; dot with butter or margarine. Cut slits in top crust for escape of steam; place pastry atop filling. Seal and flute edge. Sprinkle some sugar atop, if desired. To prevent overbrowning, cover edge of pie with foil. Bake in a 375° oven for 25 minutes. Remove foil; bake for 20 to 25 minutes more or till crust is golden. Cool pie on rack. Serve with vanilla ice cream, if desired. Makes 8 servings.

Deep-Dish Peach Pie

- ¾ cup sugar
- 3 tablespoons all-purpose flour
- ¼ teaspoon ground nutmeg
- 6 cups peeled, thickly sliced fresh peaches
  (3 pounds)
- 3 tablespoons grenadine syrup
- 2 tablespoons lemon juice
- 2 tablespoons butter or margarine
  Pastry for Single-Crust Pie (see recipe, page 129)

In large bowl combine sugar, flour, and nutmeg; add peaches and toss till well-coated. Let mixture stand 5 minutes. Carefully stir in grenadine and lemon juice. Turn mixture into a 1½-quart casserole or a 10-inch round deep baking dish, spreading peaches evenly; dot with butter or margarine.

Prepare and roll out pastry to an even 9-inch or 11-inch circle (depending on dish size). Cut slits in pastry. Place over peach mixture in baking dish. Trim pastry; flute to sides of dish but not over edge. To prevent overbrowning, cover edge with foil. Place dish on baking sheet in oven. Bake in 375° oven for 25 minutes. Remove foil; bake for 30 to 35 minutes more or till crust is golden. Cool on rack before serving. Makes 8 servings.

Strawberry Glacé Pie

- 7 cups fresh medium strawberries
- 1 cup water
- ¾ cup sugar
- 3 tablespoons cornstarch
- 5 drops red food coloring (optional)
- 1 9-inch Baked Pastry Shell (see recipe, page 129)
  Whipped cream

To prepare strawberry glaze, in a small saucepan crush *1 cup* of the smaller berries; add water. Bring to boiling; simmer 2 minutes. Sieve berry mixture to remove seeds. (Place a sieve over a bowl and pour mixture through. Work the sauce through the sieve with the back of a wooden spoon).

In a saucepan combine sugar and cornstarch; stir in the sieved berry mixture. Cook over medium heat, stirring constantly, till mixture is thickened and clear. Stir in red food coloring, if desired. Spread about *¼ cup* of the strawberry glaze over bottom and sides of Baked Pastry Shell. Slice *2 cups* of the whole strawberries. Arrange in pastry shell. Carefully spoon *half* of the remaining glaze over the sliced berries. Arrange remaining whole strawberries, stem end down, atop first layer; spoon on remaining glaze, covering each berry. Chill pie at least 3 to 4 hours before serving. If desired, garnish with whipped cream. Makes 8 servings.

Pictured: **Strawberry Glacé Pie.**

Fruits & Desserts

Pumpkin Pie

    Pastry for Single-Crust Pie (see recipe, page 129)
 1 16-ounce can pumpkin
 ¾ cup sugar
 1 teaspoon ground cinnamon
 ½ teaspoon ground ginger
 ½ teaspoon ground nutmeg
 3 eggs
 1 5⅓-ounce can (⅔ cup) evaporated milk
 ½ cup milk
    Whipped cream (optional)

Prepare and roll out pastry. Line a 9-inch pie plate. Trim pastry to ½ inch beyond edge of pie plate. Flute edge high; do not prick pastry.

In large mixing bowl combine pumpkin, sugar, cinnamon, ginger, nutmeg, and ½ teaspoon *salt*. Add eggs; lightly beat eggs into pumpkin mixture with a fork. Add evaporated milk and milk; mix well. Place pie shell on oven rack; pour mixture into the pastry-lined pie plate. To prevent overbrowning, cover edge of pie with foil. Bake in a 375° oven for 25 minutes. Remove foil; bake for 25 to 30 minutes more or till knife inserted off-center comes out clean. Cool the pie thoroughly on a wire rack before serving. Garnish with dollops of unsweetened whipped cream, if desired. Cover; chill to store.

Honey-Pumpkin Pie: Omit the ¾ cup sugar and add ½ cup *honey* to pumpkin mixture.

Raisin-Pumpkin Pie: Add ⅛ teaspoon *ground cloves* and ¾ cup *light raisins* to pumpkin mixture.

Blueberry Strata Pie

 1 15-ounce can blueberries
 1 8¼-ounce can crushed pineapple
 1 8-ounce package cream cheese, softened
 3 tablespoons sugar
 1 tablespoon milk
 ½ teaspoon vanilla
 1 9-inch Baked Pastry Shell (see recipe, page 129)
 ¼ cup sugar
 2 tablespoons cornstarch
 1 teaspoon lemon juice
 ½ cup whipping cream

Drain blueberries and pineapple, reserving syrups. Combine softened cream cheese, 3 tablespoons sugar, milk, and vanilla. Reserve *2 tablespoons* crushed pineapple for top; stir remainder into cream cheese mixture. Spread cream cheese mixture over bottom of cooled Baked Pastry Shell; chill.

In saucepan combine the ¼ cup sugar, cornstarch, and ¼ teaspoon *salt*. Combine reserved syrups; measure *1¼ cups* syrup (discard remaining). Stir syrup into cornstarch mixture. Cook and stir till bubbly. Cook and stir 2 minutes more. Stir in blueberries and lemon juice; cool. Pour over cream cheese layer; chill again. Whip cream; spread over pie. Garnish with reserved pineapple. Cover; chill to store. Serves 8.

Fruit Cobbler

    Peach Filling or Rhubarb Filling
 1 cup all-purpose flour
 2 tablespoons sugar
 1½ teaspoons baking powder
 ¼ teaspoon salt
 ¼ cup butter or margarine
 1 slightly beaten egg
 ¼ cup milk

Prepare Peach or Rhubarb Filling; keep warm. For biscuit topper, in mixing bowl stir together flour, sugar, baking powder, and salt. Cut in butter or margarine till mixture resembles coarse crumbs. Combine egg and milk; add all at once to flour mixture. Stir just to moisten. Turn hot filling into a 1½-quart casserole. Immediately spoon biscuit topper in 8 mounds over hot filling. Bake in a 400° oven about 20 minutes. Serve warm. Makes 8 servings.

Peach Filling: Combine ½ cup packed *brown sugar*, 4 teaspoons *cornstarch*, and ¼ teaspoon *ground nutmeg*. Stir in ½ cup *water*. Cook and stir till thickened and bubbly. Stir in 4 cups sliced, peeled, fresh *peaches* (8 medium); 1 tablespoon *lemon juice*; and 1 tablespoon *butter or margarine*. Heat through.

Rhubarb Filling: Combine 1 cup *sugar*, 2 tablespoons *cornstarch*, and ¼ teaspoon *ground cinnamon*. Stir in 4 cups *fresh rhubarb* cut into 1-inch pieces (or one 18-ounce package *frozen rhubarb*, thawed) and ¼ cup *water*. Cook and stir till thickened and bubbly. Stir in 1 tablespoon *butter*.

Meringue Shells

 3 egg whites
 1 teaspoon vanilla
 ¼ teaspoon cream of tartar
    Dash salt
 1 cup sugar
    Ice cream or pudding
    Fruit or ice cream topping

Let egg whites stand in a small mixer bowl about 1 hour or till they come to room temperature. Meanwhile, cover baking sheets with brown paper. Draw eight 3-inch circles or one 9-inch circle; set aside. Add vanilla, cream of tartar, and salt to egg whites. Beat to soft peaks. Gradually add sugar, beating till very stiff peaks form. Spread meringue over circles on paper to make 8 individual shells or one 9-inch meringue shell; use the back of a spoon to shape into shells. Bake individual shells in a 300° oven for 1 hour (bake large shell for 50 minutes). Turn off oven and let individual shells dry in oven, with door closed, for 1 hour (large shell for 2 hours). Peel off paper. To serve, fill shells with ice cream or pudding and top with fruit or ice cream topping. If necessary to store shells before serving, place in a plastic bag or airtight container. Makes 8 servings.

Choose-a-Flavor Cheesecake

¾ cup all-purpose flour
3 tablespoons brown sugar or sugar
⅓ cup butter or margarine
1 slightly beaten egg yolk
1 teaspoon vanilla
1 8-ounce package cream cheese, softened
½ cup packed brown sugar or sugar
1 teaspoon vanilla
2 eggs
1½ cups dairy sour cream
   Strawberry or Raspberry Glaze, Orange Topper,
   Blueberry Topper, or 1 cup dairy sour cream

In a bowl combine flour and the 3 tablespoons sugar; cut in butter till crumbly. Add egg yolk and 1 teaspoon vanilla; mix well. Pat *one-third* of dough onto bottom of an 8-inch spring-form pan (or a 9-inch pie plate).

Pat remaining dough onto sides of springform pan to a height of 1¼ inches (or, pat remaining dough up sides of pie plate); set aside.

In a small mixer bowl beat softened cream cheese till fluffy. Add the ½ cup sugar and 1 teaspoon vanilla; beat well. Add eggs; beat at low speed with electric mixer just till combined. (Do not overbeat.) Stir in sour cream.

Turn into crust-lined springform pan or pie plate. Bake in a 375° oven 35 to 40 minutes for springform pan (35 minutes for pie plate) or till center appears set. Cool 15 minutes on wire rack. Loosen sides of cheesecake from springform pan with a spatula. Cool 30 minutes; remove sides of pan. Cool completely. (If you use a pie plate, cool cheesecake completely in pie plate.) Chill thoroughly. Spread desired glaze, topper, or sour cream atop cheesecake. Serves 8 to 10.

Strawberry or Raspberry Glaze: Thaw and drain one 10-ounce package frozen *sliced strawberries or red raspberries*; reserve syrup. In a saucepan combine ¼ cup *sugar* and 1 tablespoon *cornstarch*. Add *water* to syrup to make ⅔ cup liquid; add to saucepan. Cook and stir till mixture is thickened and bubbly; cook and stir 2 minutes more. Remove from heat; stir in drained strawberries or raspberries and 1 tablespoon *lemon juice*. Cover surface with clear plastic wrap. Cool.

Orange Topper: Drain and reserve liquid from one 11-ounce can *mandarin orange sections*; add enough *orange juice* to liquid to make ½ cup liquid; set aside liquid and orange sections. In saucepan combine ¼ cup *sugar* and 2 teaspoons *cornstarch*. Stir in the ½ cup liquid. Cook and stir over medium heat till thickened and bubbly. Cook and stir 2 minutes more. Gradually stir hot mixture into 1 beaten *egg yolk*; return to saucepan. Cook and stir till bubbly. Remove from heat. Stir in 1 tablespoon *butter* and ¼ teaspoon *vanilla*. Cover surface with clear plastic wrap. Cool. Spoon sauce atop cheesecake and arrange orange sections atop sauce.

Blueberry Topper: Stir in 1 to 2 tablespoons *brandy or favorite liqueur* into *half* of a 21-ounce can *blueberry pie filling*.

Red Raspberry Crepes

1 4-ounce container whipped cream cheese, softened
10 Dessert Crepes (see recipe below)
⅓ cup toasted slivered almonds
1 10-ounce package frozen red raspberries, thawed
   Cranberry juice cocktail
⅓ cup sugar
4 teaspoons cornstarch
   Dash salt
2 tablespoons butter or margarine
2 tablespoons orange liqueur (optional)
2 teaspoons lemon juice

To assemble, spread cream cheese over *unbrowned* side of crepe, leaving ¼-inch rim around edge. Sprinkle with some of the almonds. Roll up jelly roll style. Repeat with remaining crepes. Reserve remaining almonds for garnish. Cover crepes and chill.

For raspberry sauce, drain raspberries; reserve syrup. Add cranberry juice to syrup to make *1 ½ cups* liquid. In saucepan combine sugar, cornstarch, and salt. Blend in syrup mixture. Cook and stir till bubbly. Add butter, liqueur, lemon juice, and berries. Keep warm, or chill and heat before serving.

To serve: Arrange crepes in chafing dish or skillet; add hot sauce. Cover; heat through. Sprinkle with reserved almonds. Makes 5 servings.

Dessert Crepes

1 cup all-purpose flour
1½ cups milk
2 eggs
2 tablespoons sugar
1 tablespoon cooking oil
⅛ teaspoon salt

In a bowl combine flour, milk, eggs, sugar, oil, and salt; beat with a rotary beater till blended. Heat a lightly greased 6-inch skillet. Remove from heat. Spoon in *2 tablespoons* of the batter; lift and tilt skillet to spread batter evenly. Return to heat; brown on *one side* only. (Or, cook on inverted crepe pan according to manufacturers directions.) Invert pan over paper toweling; remove crepe. Repeat to make 16 to 18 crepes, greasing skillet often.

Baklava

Allowing this pastry to stand overnight gives the flavors time to blend and makes it easier to eat—

- **16 ounces frozen filo dough**
  (twenty-one 16x12-inch sheets)
- **4 cups finely chopped walnuts**
- **3 cups finely chopped pecans**
- **¾ cup sugar**
- **1 tablespoon ground cinnamon**
- **1½ cups unsalted butter, melted**
- **2 cups sugar**
- **1 cup water**
- **2 tablespoons honey**
- **2 tablespoons lemon juice**
- **4 inches stick cinnamon**

Thaw frozen filo dough at room temperature for 2 hours. Cut the 16x12-inch sheets in half crosswise. (If filo is a different size, cut to fit pan.) Cover with a slightly damp towel. Lightly butter the bottom of a 13x9x2-inch baking pan. Combine the walnuts, pecans, the ¾ cup sugar, and ground cinnamon; set nut mixture aside.

Layer *nine* of the half-sheets of filo in the pan, brushing each sheet with some of the melted butter. Sprinkle about *1 cup* of the nut mixture over the filo in the pan. Drizzle with some of the melted butter. Top with another *four* half-sheets of the filo, brushing each with more of the melted butter. Repeat the nut and 4-half-sheet filo layers *five* times more. Sprinkle with the remaining nut mixture. Drizzle with some of the melted butter. Top with the remaining *nine* half-sheets of filo, brushing each with some of the remaining melted butter. Cut into diamond-shaped pieces or squares, cutting to *but not through* the bottom layer. Bake in 325° oven for 60 minutes. Finish cutting diamonds or squares; cool thoroughly.

Meanwhile, in a saucepan combine the 2 cups sugar, the water, honey, lemon juice, and stick cinnamon. Boil gently, uncovered, for 15 minutes. Remove from heat. Remove cinnamon. Stir till blended. Pour warm syrup over cooled pastry. Cool completely. Garnish each diamond with a *whole clove*, if desired. Makes 3 to 4 dozen pieces.

Cream Puffs

Next time, fill the cream puffs with your favorite ice cream, pudding, or fresh fruit—

- **½ cup butter or margarine**
- **1 cup all-purpose flour**
- **4 eggs**
  Crème Pâtisserie
  Chocolate Icing or powdered sugar (optional)

In a medium saucepan melt butter or margarine. Add 1 cup *water*; bring to boiling. Add flour and ¼ teaspoon *salt* all at once; stir vigorously. Cook and stir till mixture forms a ball that doesn't separate. Remove from heat; cool about 10 minutes.

Add eggs, one at a time, beating with a wooden spoon about 30 seconds after each addition.

For large puffs, drop dough by heaping tablespoonfuls 3 inches apart onto a greased baking sheet. Bake in a 400° oven about 30 minutes or till golden brown and puffy. For small puffs, drop by heaping teaspoonfuls 2 inches apart onto a greased baking sheet. Bake in a 400° oven about 20 minutes. Split large and small puffs and remove any soft dough as shown below. Cool on wire racks. Fill cream puffs with Crème Pâtisserie. Glaze with Chocolate Icing or sprinkle with powdered sugar, if desired. Makes about 10 large or 60 small Cream Puffs.

Crème Pâtisserie: In a heavy saucepan combine ⅔ cup *sugar*, 2 tablespoons *cornstarch*, and ¼ teaspoon *salt*. Stir in 2 cups *milk*. Cook and stir till thickened and bubbly. Remove from heat. Stir about *half* of the hot mixture into 3 beaten *egg yolks*; return to remaining mixture. Bring to boiling; cook and stir 2 minutes longer. Stir in 1 tablespoon *butter or margarine* and 1 teaspoon *vanilla*. Cover surface with clear plastic wrap; cool.

Chocolate Icing: Melt 2 ounces *German sweet chocolate* and 2 tablespoons *butter or margarine*. Remove from heat. Stir in 1 cup sifted *powdered sugar* and enough *hot water* (2 to 3 tablespoons) to make of glazing consistency. Cool.

Éclairs: Prepare Cream Puff dough as above. Spoon dough into a pastry bag with a 1- to 1¼-inch opening. Pipe dough onto greased baking sheet. Make Éclairs about 5 inches long and 1½ to 1¾ inches wide. Bake in a 400° oven about 30 minutes or till golden. Split, cool, and fill as for Cream Puffs. Makes 8.

To Split Cream Puffs

Immediately split the cream puffs after they have been removed from the oven. Use a sharp utility knife to gently cut around the top of the cream puff, about ¼ of the way down. The puff may have a slightly soggy center. This soft membrane of dough may be removed to leave a crisp, hollow puff. Gently lift out the soft dough with a fork, as shown.

Italian Orange Flan

1½ cups all-purpose flour
3 tablespoons sugar
½ teaspoon salt
5 tablespoons butter or margarine, chilled
1 beaten egg
2 tablespoons cooking oil
4 teaspoons cold water
⅓ cup sugar
2 tablespoons cornstarch
¼ teaspoon salt
1¼ cups milk
3 beaten egg yolks
3 tablespoons brandy
2 cups fresh strawberries, halved
3 oranges, peeled and sectioned
  (see photos at right)
½ cup orange marmalade
Fresh mint leaves (optional)

For flan shell, in bowl stir together flour, 3 tablespoons sugar, and salt. Cut in butter or margarine till crumbly. Add beaten egg and oil; stir till flour mixture is moistened. Sprinkle water over mixture 1 teaspoon at a time, tossing with fork. Work mixture with hands till well blended. On lightly floured surface roll dough into a 13-inch circle. Fit dough into an 11-inch flan pan, pressing bottom and sides gently. Prick bottom; line with foil. Bake in 375° oven for 10 minutes; remove foil. Bake for 12 to 14 minutes more or till golden brown. Cool thoroughly on wire rack. Remove from pan; transfer flan shell to platter.

For custard filling, in heavy saucepan combine ⅓ cup sugar, cornstarch, and ¼ teaspoon salt; blend in milk. Cook and stir till thickened and bubbly. Cook and stir 2 minutes more. Gradually stir about *half* of the hot mixture into the beaten egg yolks; return to remaining hot mixture. Cook and stir till bubbly. Cook and stir 2 minutes more. Remove from heat. Stir in brandy. Cover surface with clear plastic wrap; cool thoroughly without stirring.

Spread the cooled custard filling in bottom of flan shell; chill. About 1 to 1½ hours before serving, place strawberry halves around outer edge of flan atop custard filling, reserving *three* strawberry halves. Arrange the orange sections spiral fashion in remaining area. Place reserved strawberry halves in center. Melt orange marmalade; spoon over fruit. Chill. Garnish with mint leaves, if desired. Makes 8 to 10 servings.

To Slice and Section Citrus Fruits

1

To slice or section oranges or grapefruit, begin by cutting off the peel and the white membrane. Work on a cutting board and cut down from the top of the fruit with a sharp paring knife, as shown.

2

To slice a peeled orange or grapefruit, use a sharp knife to cut the fruit crosswise into thin slices, as shown.

3

To section a peeled orange or grapefruit, remove the sections by cutting into the center of the fruit between one section and the membrane. Then turn the knife and slide the knife down the other side of the section next to the membrane, as shown. Remove any seeds. Allow fruit sections to fall into a bowl. Work over a bowl to catch the juice.

Dutch Apple Cake

    2 cups all-purpose flour
    1 teaspoon baking soda
    1 teaspoon salt
    1 teaspoon ground cinnamon
    4 medium cooking apples
    2 eggs
    1 teaspoon vanilla
    1 cup cooking oil
 1½ cups sugar
    1 cup finely chopped walnuts
       Powdered Sugar Icing (see recipe below)

Grease and lightly flour a 9-inch tube pan. Stir together flour, baking soda, salt, and cinnamon. Peel, core, and finely chop apples; set aside.

In a large mixer bowl stir together eggs and vanilla; beat on high speed of electric mixer for 2 minutes or till light. Gradually add oil, beating for 2 minutes or till thick. Gradually beat in sugar. Add dry ingredients, apples, and walnuts alternately to beaten mixture, beating well after each addition. Beat at medium speed for 3 minutes. Turn batter into prepared pan. Bake in a 350° oven for 55 to 60 minutes or till cake tests done. Place cake on wire rack; cool for 10 to 15 minutes. Remove from pan; cool thoroughly on rack. Drizzle with Powdered Sugar Icing. Makes 12 servings.

Powdered Sugar Icing

    1 cup sifted powdered sugar
  ¼ teaspoon vanilla
       Milk

In mixing bowl combine powdered sugar, vanilla, and enough milk (about 1½ tablespoons) to make of pouring consistency. Glaze or drizzle over top of tube cake, bar cookies, cookies, nutbreads, or sweet rolls.

Cream Cheese Icing: Beat together one 3-ounce package softened *cream cheese* and the powdered sugar till fluffy. Beat in vanilla. If necessary, beat in enough milk (about 1 teaspoon) to make of pouring consistency. Cover; store in refrigerator.

Chocolate Mousse Torte

    2 eggs
    1 cup sugar
    1 cup all-purpose flour
    1 teaspoon baking powder
  ½ cup milk
    2 tablespoons butter or margarine
  ¼ cup sugar
    4 teaspoons cornstarch
    2 teaspoons unflavored gelatin
 1⅓ cups milk
 1½ squares (1½ ounces) unsweetened chocolate, chopped
    2 slightly beaten egg yolks
    2 egg whites
  ½ teaspoon vanilla
  ¼ cup sugar
 1⅓ cups whipping cream
    2 tablepoons sugar
  ½ cup toasted sliced almonds
       Chocolate curls and sifted powdered sugar

To prepare sponge cake, grease and flour two 8x1½-inch round baking pans. In a small mixer bowl beat the 2 whole eggs at high speed of electric mixer 4 minutes or till thick and lemon colored. Gradually add the 1 cup sugar, beating at medium speed 4 to 5 minutes or till sugar is nearly dissolved. Mix flour, baking powder, and ¼ teaspoon *salt*. Add to egg mixture; stir just till blended. In a small saucepan heat the ½ cup milk and 2 tablespoons butter till butter melts; stir into batter. Beat at low speed till well mixed. Turn batter into prepared pans. Bake in a 350° oven for 20 to 25 minutes or till done. Cool 10 minutes. Remove from pans; cool thoroughly.

To prepare chocolate mousse filling, in saucepan stir together the ¼ cup sugar, cornstarch, gelatin, and ⅛ teaspoon *salt*. Stir in 1⅓ cups milk; add chocolate squares. Cook and stir over medium heat till bubbly; cook and stir 2 minutes more. Remove from heat. Stir about *half* the thickened milk mixture into the 2 beaten egg yolks; return all to saucepan. Return to gentle boil. Cook and stir 2 minutes more. Transfer to bowl; cover with clear plastic wrap. Cool 20 minutes.

In large mixer bowl beat the egg whites and vanilla till soft peaks form. Gradually add the ¼ cup sugar; beat till stiff peaks form. Gently fold in the chocolate mixture. Turn into an 8x1½-inch round baking pan or round baking dish that has been lined with clear plastic wrap. Spread evenly; chill till firm.

To assemble, unmold chocolate filling and place on one cake layer. Top with second layer. In large mixer bowl beat whipping cream and the 2 tablespoons sugar till soft peaks form. Frost top and sides of cake with *2 cups* whipped cream. Pipe remaining whipped cream through rosette pastry tube to form a lattice top. Pipe around edge of cake. Garnish sides of torte with almonds. Top cake with chocolate curls. Sift powdered sugar over. Chill till serving time. Serves 10 to 12.

Pictured: **Chocolate Mousse Torte.**

Orange-Cherry Cake

    8 egg yolks
    ⅔ cup sugar
    1 teaspoon finely shredded orange peel
    ¼ cup orange juice
    1 cup all-purpose flour
    8 egg whites (1 cup)
    1 teaspoon cream of tartar
    ½ teaspoon salt
    ⅔ cup sugar
    4 cups fresh dark sweet cherries, pitted
    2 cups whipping cream
    2 tablespoons sugar
    2 tablespoons brandy (optional)

In a mixer bowl beat egg yolks at high speed of electric mixer till thick and lemon colored. Gradually add ⅔ cup sugar, beating till sugar dissolves. Combine orange peel and orange juice. Beat juice mixture and flour alternately into yolk mixture.

In a large mixer bowl beat egg whites, cream of tartar, and salt till soft peaks form. Gradually add ⅔ cup sugar, beating till stiff peaks form. Stir *1 cup* of the whites into yolk mixture. By hand fold yolk mixture into remaining whites. Turn batter into an *ungreased* 10-inch tube pan. Bake in a 325° oven for 50 to 60 minutes. Invert cake in pan; cool. Remove cake from pan; split into 3 layers as shown on page 139.

Quarter the cherries. Whip the cream and the 2 tablespoons sugar till stiff peaks form. If desired, fold in brandy. Assemble cake by alternating layers of cake, whipping cream, and cherries. Makes 12 servings.

Chocolate Pudding Cake

Serve with vanilla ice cream or whipped cream—

    1 cup all-purpose flour
    ½ cup sugar
    2 tablespoons unsweetened cocoa powder
    2 teaspoons baking powder
    ½ teaspoon salt
    ½ cup milk
    2 tablespoons cooking oil
    1 teaspoon vanilla
    ½ cup chopped walnuts
    ¾ cup sugar
    ¼ cup unsweetened cocoa powder
    1½ cups boiling water

In a large mixing bowl stir together flour, ½ cup sugar, the 2 tablespoons cocoa powder, baking powder, and salt. Add milk, oil, and vanilla; stir till smooth. Stir in nuts. Turn into an ungreased 8x8x2-inch baking pan. Combine ¾ cup sugar and ¼ cup cocoa powder; gradually stir in boiling water. Pour liquid mixture evenly over batter in pan. Bake in a 350° oven about 30 minutes or till cake tests done. Serve warm or chilled in individual dessert dishes. Makes 8 servings.

Marble Pound Cake

    ¾ cup butter or margarine
    3 eggs
    ½ cup milk
    2 cups all-purpose flour
    1 teaspoon baking powder
    ¼ teaspoon salt
    1¼ cups sugar
    1 teaspoon finely shredded lemon peel
    1 tablespoon lemon juice
    1 square (1 ounce) unsweetened chocolate,
       melted and cooled
    2 tablespoons boiling water
    1 tablespoon sugar
    ¼ teaspoon ground cinnamon
       Powdered sugar (optional)

Bring butter, eggs, and milk to room temperature. Grease a 9x5x3-inch loaf pan. Stir together flour, baking powder, and salt. In mixer bowl beat butter on medium speed of electric mixer till fluffy. Gradually add 1¼ cups sugar, beating till fluffy. Add eggs, one at a time, beating 1 minute after each; scrape bowl often. Add milk, lemon peel, and juice; beat on low speed till blended. Gradually add dry ingredients to beaten mixture, beating on low speed just till smooth.

Divide batter in half. Combine chocolate, boiling water, 1 tablespoon sugar, and cinnamon; stir into *half* of the batter. In pan alternate spoonfuls of light and dark batters. Using a narrow spatula, stir gently through batter to marble as shown below. Bake in a 325° oven about 70 minutes or till done. Cool 10 minutes on wire rack. Remove from pan; cool. Sift powdered sugar over cake, if desired. Makes 12 servings.

To Marble Batter

Achieve a marbled appearance in baked products by using a frosting spatula to gently swirl through light and dark batters. Don't swirl too vigorously or you'll lose the marble effect.

Party Cherry Torte

3 egg whites
1 teaspoon vanilla
1 cup sugar
¾ cup finely chopped walnuts
½ cup crushed saltine crackers (about 14)
½ teaspoon baking powder
1 16½-ounce can pitted dark sweet cherries
1 tablespoon sugar
4 teaspoons cornstarch
1 tablespoon cherry or orange liqueur
1 cup whipping cream

In a mixer bowl beat egg whites and vanilla till foamy. Gradually add the 1 cup sugar, beating till stiff peaks form. Stir together chopped nuts, crushed crackers, and baking powder; fold into beaten egg whites. Spread about *one-third* (1 cup) of the mixture on bottom of a well-greased 9-inch pie plate. Dollop remaining mixture around edge of dish forming high sides. Bake in a 300° oven about 40 minutes or till meringue is dry to the touch and very lightly browned. Cool.

Meanwhile drain cherries, reserving *⅓ cup* of the syrup. Halve cherries; set aside. In a saucepan combine the reserved syrup, the 1 tablespoon sugar, and cornstarch. Add cherries; cook and stir till thickened and bubbly. Cook and stir 2 minutes more. Remove from heat. Stir in cherry or orange liqueur. Cool. Whip *½ cup* of the whipping cream to soft peaks. Spread whipped cream in meringue shell. Fill shell with cooled cherry mixture. Chill several hours or overnight. At serving time, whip remaining cream and dollop around the inside edge of the meringue shell. Makes 6 to 8 servings.

Boston Cream Pie

2 eggs
1 cup sugar
1 cup all-purpose flour
1 teaspoon baking powder
¼ teaspoon salt
½ cup milk
2 tablespoons butter or margarine
Vanilla Cream Filling (see recipe at right)
Chocolate Glaze (see recipe at right)

Grease and flour a 9x1½-inch round baking pan. In a small mixer bowl beat whole eggs at high speed of electric mixer 4 minutes or till thick and lemon colored. Gradually add sugar, beating at medium speed 4 to 5 minutes or till sugar is nearly dissolved. Mix flour, baking powder, and salt. Add to egg mixture; stir just till blended.

In a small saucepan heat milk and butter till butter melts; stir into batter. Beat at low speed till well mixed. Turn into pan. Bake in a 350° oven for 25 to 30 minutes or till done. Cool 10 minutes on wire rack. Remove from pan; cool thoroughly. Split cake horizontally into 2 layers as shown at right. Fill with Vanilla Cream Filling. Spread Chocolate Glaze over top of cake, drizzling down sides. Makes 8 servings.

Chocolate Glaze

¼ cup sugar
2 teaspoons cornstarch
Dash salt
⅓ cup water
½ square (½ ounce) unsweetened chocolate, cut up
½ teaspoon vanilla

In small saucepan combine sugar, cornstarch, and salt. Stir in water; add chocolate. Cook and stir till chocolate is melted and mixture is thickened and bubbly. Cook and stir 2 minutes more. Remove from heat; stir in vanilla.

Vanilla Cream Filling

⅓ cup sugar
2 tablespoons all-purpose flour
1 tablespoon cornstarch
¼ teaspoon salt
1¼ cups milk
1 tablespoon butter or margarine
2 slightly beaten eggs
1 tablespoon brandy or desired liqueur (optional)
1 teaspoon vanilla

In a saucepan thoroughly combine sugar, flour, cornstarch, and salt. Stir in milk; add butter or margarine. Cook and stir over medium heat till thickened and bubbly. Cook and stir 2 minutes more. Gradually stir about *half* of the hot mixture into eggs; return to remaining hot mixture. Cook and stir 2 minutes more. Remove from heat; stir in brandy and vanilla. Cover surface with waxed paper; cool without stirring, then chill. Makes enough filling to spread between 3 cake layers.

To Split a Cake Layer

Make a plain cake fancy by splitting the layers and spreading your favorite filling or frosting between the halves.

As a cutting guide, insert wooden picks halfway up the side of each cake layer, as shown. Then use a serrated bread knife to slice through the layer.

Lemon Cheesecake Squares

2 cups crushed graham crackers (28 squares)
6 tablespoons butter or margarine, melted
1 3-ounce package lemon-flavored gelatin
¾ cup boiling water
¾ cup sugar
1 8-ounce package cream cheese, softened
½ teaspoon finely shredded lemon peel
2 tablespoons lemon juice
1 teaspoon vanilla
1 13-ounce can (1⅔ cups) evaporated milk, chilled icy cold

Stir together crushed crackers and melted butter or margarine; reserve ⅓ cup of the mixture. Press remaining into the bottom of a 13x9x2-inch baking pan. If desired, bake crust in a 375° oven for 6 to 9 minutes. Cool.

Dissolve gelatin in boiling water. Chill till syrupy. Meanwhile, in a small mixer bowl gradually beat sugar into cream cheese. Add lemon peel, lemon juice, and vanilla; beat till fluffy. Beat in gelatin mixture.

In a large mixer bowl beat evaporated milk till soft peaks form. Fold cream cheese mixture into whipped milk. Turn mixture into prepared crust. Sprinkle reserved cracker mixture atop. Chill at least 4 hours or overnight before serving. Makes 12 to 16 servings.

Whole Wheat-Mocha Bars

2 cups all-purpose flour
1 cup whole wheat flour
1 teaspoon baking soda
1 teaspoon salt
2 eggs
2 cups packed brown sugar
1 cup cooking oil
2 teaspoons vanilla
2 teaspoons instant coffee crystals
1 cup cold water
1 cup semisweet chocolate pieces
1 cup chopped walnuts

Stir together flours, soda, and salt. In large mixer bowl beat eggs till light and fluffy. Gradually add brown sugar, oil, and vanilla; beat well. Dissolve coffee crystals in cold water; gradually stir into egg mixture. Add dry ingredients; beat till well combined. Pour batter into a greased 15x10x1-inch baking pan. Sprinkle chocolate pieces and nuts evenly atop. Bake in a 350° oven for 25 to 30 minutes. Cool slightly. Drizzle with Coffee Glaze. Cut into squares to serve. Makes 36 bars.

Coffee Glaze: Dissolve ½ teaspoon *instant coffee crystals* in 4 teaspoons *water*. Combine 1 cup sifted *powdered sugar*, 1 tablespoon softened *butter or margarine*, and the coffee mixture till smooth. (If necessary, add more water for drizzling consistency.)

Peanut Butter Ice Cream Squares

The tasty, nutty filling can be made with either salted or unsalted peanuts—

1¼ cups graham cracker crumbs
¼ cup sugar
6 tablespoons butter or margarine, melted
1 cup dry-roasted peanuts, chopped
½ cup light corn syrup
⅓ cup chunky peanut butter
1 quart vanilla ice cream

In mixing bowl combine crumbs, sugar, and melted butter or margarine. Press onto bottom of a 9x9x2-inch baking pan. Place in freezer 30 minutes.

Meanwhile, stir together ⅔ cup of the peanuts, the corn syrup, and peanut butter. Stir ice cream to soften. Spoon *half* of the softened ice cream evenly over chilled crust. Spread peanut mixture atop. Carefully spread remaining ice cream over all. Sprinkle with the remaining ⅓ cup chopped peanuts. Cover and freeze till firm. Let stand at room temperature for 10 to 15 minutes before serving. Makes 9 servings.

Chocolate-Covered Cherry Cookies

1½ cups all-purpose flour
½ cup unsweetened cocoa powder
¼ teaspoon salt
¼ teaspoon baking powder
¼ teaspoon baking soda
½ cup butter or margarine, softened
1 cup sugar
1 egg
1½ teaspoons vanilla
1 10-ounce jar maraschino cherries (about 48)
1 6-ounce package semisweet chocolate pieces (not imitation)
½ cup Eagle Brand sweetened condensed milk

In large bowl stir together flour, cocoa powder, salt, baking powder, and soda. In mixer bowl beat together butter or margarine and sugar on low speed of electric mixer till fluffy. Add egg and vanilla; beat well. Gradually add dry ingredients to creamed mixture; beat till well blended. Shape dough into 1-inch balls; place on ungreased cookie sheet. Press down center of dough with thumb. Drain maraschino cherries, reserving juice. Place a cherry in the center of each cookie.

In a small saucepan combine chocolate pieces and sweetened condensed milk; heat till chocolate is melted. Stir in *4 teaspoons* of the reserved cherry juice. Spoon about *1 teaspoon* frosting over each cherry, spreading to cover cherry. (Frosting may be thinned with additional cherry juice, if necessary.) Bake in a 350° oven about 10 minutes or till done. Remove to wire rack; cool. Makes 48 cookies.

Mocha Logs

2¼ cups all-purpose flour
½ teaspoon salt
¼ teaspoon baking powder
2 tablespoons instant coffee crystals
1 teaspoon water
1 cup butter or margarine
¾ cup sugar
1 egg
1 teaspoon vanilla
4 squares (4 ounces) semisweet chocolate, melted
⅔ cup finely chopped pecans

Stir together flour, salt, and baking powder. In mixer bowl combine coffee crystals and water, stirring till dissolved. Add butter or margarine; beat on medium speed of electric mixer for 30 seconds. Add sugar and beat till fluffy. Add egg and vanilla; beat well. Add dry ingredients to beaten mixture and beat till well blended.

Pack dough, half at a time, into cookie press with star plate inserted. Force through press onto ungreased cookie sheet into 3-inch-long strips. Bake in 375° oven for 8 to 10 minutes or till done. Remove; cool on wire rack. Dip top of one end of each cookie in melted chocolate; coat with the finely chopped nuts. Place cookies in refrigerator for a few minutes till chocolate becomes firm. Makes about 80.

Pecan Tassies

½ cup butter or margarine
1 3-ounce package cream cheese
1 cup all-purpose flour
1 egg
¾ cup packed brown sugar
1 tablespoon butter or margarine, softened
1 teaspoon vanilla
Dash salt
½ cup coarsely chopped pecans

For pastry, in a mixer bowl beat the ½ cup butter or margarine and the cream cheese. Add flour; beat well. If dough is too soft, cover and chill for 1 hour. In mixing bowl stir together egg, brown sugar, the 1 tablespoon butter, the vanilla, and salt just till smooth; set aside.

Shape chilled pastry into 2 dozen 1-inch balls; place each ball in an ungreased 1¾-inch muffin cup. Press dough into bottom and sides of cups. Spoon about *1 teaspoon* of the chopped pecans into each pastry-lined muffin cup; fill each with egg mixture. Bake in a 325° oven about 25 minutes or till filling is set. Cool; remove from pans. Store, covered in refrigerator. Makes 24.

Dessert Coffees

Complete a meal with a steaming cup of flavored coffee. Try the liqueur variations we've suggested, then experiment with your favorite liqueurs. Cappuccino, Turkish Coffee, and Coffee Milano are specialties you're sure to enjoy—

To ½ cup double-strength hot *coffee*, stir in the ingredients for the desired flavored coffee. Top with a dollop of sweetened *whipped cream*. Makes 1 serving.

Orange Coffee: Stir in 2 tablespoons *chocolate-flavored syrup* and 2 tablespoons *orange liqueur*. Garnish with an orange twist shown on page 21.

Coffee Benedictine: Stir in 2 tablespoons *Benedictine* and 2 tablespoons *light cream*. Sprinkle *ground nutmeg* over the whipped cream.

Café Mocha: Stir in 2 tablespoons *coffee liqueur* and 1 tablespoon *chocolate-flavored syrup*.

Chocolate-Mint Coffee: Stir in 2 tablespoons *chocolate-mint liqueur*. Garnish with chocolate curls.

Irish Coffee: Stir in 1 tablespoon *Irish whiskey* and 2 tablespoons *sugar*.

Cappuccino: In a mixer bowl combine ½ cup *whipping cream* and 1 tablespoon *powdered sugar*; beat till stiff peaks form. Pour 2 cups hot *espresso coffee** into 6 small cups, filling cups only *half* full. Add a large spoonful of whipped cream to each cup. Sprinkle each serving with finely shredded *orange peel*. If desired, sprinkle with *ground cinnamon* and *ground nutmeg*. Gently stir whipped cream into espresso coffee till melted. Makes 6 servings.

Turkish Coffee: In large saucepan combine 6 cups *water* and ½ cup *sugar;* bring to boiling. Remove from heat; stir in ¾ cup ground *Turkish coffee*. Return to heat immediately. Bring to boiling again. As soon as the liquid foams, lift pan from heat and stir till foaming subsides. Repeat boiling and removing from heat 2 more times. Strain and serve *immediately* in demitasse cups. Makes 6 cups.

Coffee Milano: Place ½ cup *regular-grind coffee* in basket of coffee maker; sprinkle ¼ teaspoon *ground cinnamon* over top. Using 4 cups *water*, prepare coffee according to manufacturer's directions. Dip rims of 6 small brandy snifters in 1 slightly beaten *egg white*, then in *sugar*. Add 1 tablespoon *Galliano* and 2 teaspoons *coffee liqueur* to *each* snifter. Pour in *½ cup* of the hot coffee. Top each with *whipped cream*. Makes 6 servings.

*Note: For espresso coffee, use finely ground espresso roast coffee and brew in an espresso coffee machine or an ordinary coffeepot, or prepare instant espresso coffee powder according to package directions to make 2 cups.

Index

144

QUILT COUN 3

Lesa Cline-Ransome

paintings by James E. Ransome

QUILTING

SeaStar Books · New York

Stitched in a swatch of countryside
beneath a patch of blue
sits a family homestead
one farmhouse, proud and true

2

The wind treads lightly up the stairs
and stops to peek inside
then softly knocks a quiet greeting
two doors open wide

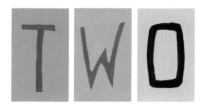

Inside a family gathers
three generations stand
to piece a family history
by joining heart and hand

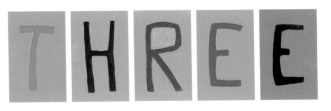

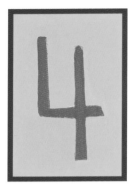

Four scissors make fast work
of snipping cloth and thread
creating patch and pattern
sharp edges cut and shred

Five thimbles standing guard
against each prick and pin
shining shields of armor
protectors of soft skin

Adding up each design
six tape measures prepare
to calculate and measure
each inch, seam, and square

A cluster of **seven cushions**
makes a cozy nest
upon which pins and needles
can stop and take a rest

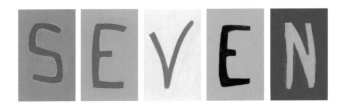

8

Eight baskets of cloth
nearly overflow
with fabrics in every pattern
from gingham to calico

Nine spools dressed in finest threads
standing short and round
with just a tug they spin and twirl
and quickly come unwound

NINE

10

All pieces join together
as hands begin to sew
a pathway paved with thread
ten stitches in a row . . .

TEN

The woven fabric of the land
is stitched with seed to sow
before the season's harvest
nine fields will bloom and grow

Eight sheep dot a landscape
blanketed in green
drifting clouds of creamy wool
graze in a tranquil scene

On wings embroidered with rainbows
seven butterflies alight
a sampler of sweet nectar
awaits in blossoms bright

6

A golden tasseled crop
tucked in silken threads
six ears of corn
gently stirring in their beds

SIX

5

Plumes of red perched on their heads
feathers primped and neat
five chickens cluck on a barnyard stroll
greetings to all they meet

FIVE

4

Keepers of the garden
wearing crowns of gold
four noble sunflowers
reigning tall and bold

FOUR

A chorus of **three little pigs**
tickled pink from tail to snout
squealing, rooting, snorting
in a pen they wallow about

On the porch, a welcome mat
perched where **two dogs** lie
while one drifts quietly off to sleep
one keeps a watchful eye

The last stitches are sewn
fine handiwork shines through
a legacy handcrafted
one quilt lies proud and true

A NOTE ABOUT QUILTS

The quilting tradition found its way to America from across the sea, traveling in the hearts and minds of European women seeking a new life in a New World. While there are many styles of quilting, one of the more popular forms, the block or patchwork quilt, is a purely American variation on a traditional European style, the *broderie perse* or "whole cloth" style. Yet another popular form is the appliqué quilt, in which stencils for cutting out shapes of fabric to sew onto cloth are used. It is this type of quilt that is being created by the characters in this book.

Appliqué quilting gained popularity beginning in 1775. The roots of appliqué quilting were both practical and artistic. With scarcity of cloth a factor in colonial America, reusing fabric scraps was a frugal solution to recycling clothing. The designs varied from purely decorative, depicting everyday images and objects such as flowers and animals, to, as in the case of many quilts made by African Americans, elaborate scenes telling stories and ideas, thereby passing down legends and lessons from one generation to the next.

Across the seas, from generation to generation, the art of quilt-making has endured. With needle, cloth, and thread, and for all kinds of people, quilts are the fabric onto which their lives, their loves, and their passions are stitched.

For my children,
Jaime, Maya, Malcolm, and Leila
—L. C. R.

In loving memory,
my nephew Brian Sean Cameron, Jr.
August 22, 2001–November 8, 2001
—J. E. R.

SeaStar Books
A division of North-South Books Inc.

First published in the United States in 2002 by SeaStar Books, a division of North-South Books Inc., New York.
Published simultaneously in Canada by North-South Books, an imprint of Nord-Süd Verlag AG, Gossau Zürich, Switzerland.

Library of Congress Cataloging-in-Publication Data is available.
The artwork for this book was prepared by using acrylics.
Book design by Nicole de las Heras

ISBN 1-58717-177-5 (trade edition)
1 3 5 7 9 HC 10 8 6 4 2
ISBN 1-58717-178-3 (library edition)
1 3 5 7 9 LE 10 8 6 4 2

Printed in Hong Kong

For more information about our books, and the authors and artists who create them, visit our web site: www.northsouth.com

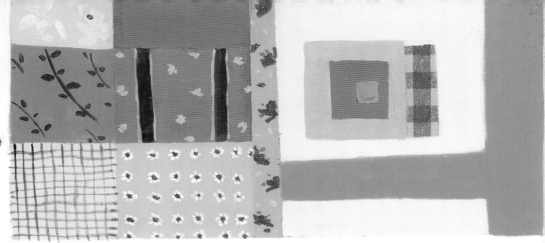